HEARING THE VOICE OF GOD

HEARING THE VOICE OF GOD

In Search of Prophecy

Mordecai Schreiber

JASON ARONSON
Lanham • Boulder • New York • Toronto • Plymouth, UK

Published by Jason Aronson
A wholly owned subsidiary of The Rowman & Littlefield Publishing Group,
Inc.
4501 Forbes Boulevard, Suite 200, Lanham, Maryland 20706
www.rowman.com

10 Thornbury Road, Plymouth PL6 7PP, United Kingdom

British Library Cataloguing in Publication Information Available

Library of Congress Cataloging-in-Publication Data

Schreiber, Mordecai.
Hearing the voice of God : in search of prophecy / Mordecai Schreiber.
p. cm.
Includes bibliographical references and index.
ISBN 978-0-7657-0971-4 (cloth : alk. paper) — ISBN 978-0-7657-0972-1 (electronic)
1. Prophecy—Judaism. 2. Bible. O.T. Prophets—Criticism, interpretation, etc. 3. Prophecy. 4.
Messiah—Judaism. I. Title.
BM645.P67S37 2012
296.3'1155—dc23
2012051558

♾™ The paper used in this publication meets the minimum requirements of
American National Standard for Information Sciences Permanence of Paper
for Printed Library Materials, ANSI/NISO Z39.48-1992.

Printed in the United States of America

"Blessed is he who puts his brother before himself."
—*Baha'i*

"Hurt not others with that which pains yourself."
—**Buddhism**

"Do to others as you would have them do to you."
—**Christianity**

"What you do not want done to yourself, do not do to others."
—**Confucianism**

"One should always treat others as they themselves wish to be treated."
—**Hinduism**

"Hurt no one so that no one may hurt you."
—**Islam**

"Love your neighbor as yourself."
—**Judaism**

"Whatever is disagreeable to you, do not do to others."
—**Zoroastrianism**

CONTENTS

IN THE BEGINNING

A rare breed of people, unlike any the world has ever known, appeared in a small corner of the ancient Near East three thousand years ago and transformed history. They taught their people and the rest of the world that man was created for a purpose; that there is a creator who transcends human understanding; that this creator is the only God of the universe; that this God spoke to them and through them to all people; that this God had made a covenant with their people and with all people, whereby life as we know it will not perish from the earth. We call these people prophets, and we find their words in a book we call the Bible. We wonder what they meant when they said God spoke to them, and we wonder whether their words still speak to us today.

Throughout time, people have followed many prophets. Adherents of different creeds believe their prophet is the one closest to God, or to the truth, and find it difficult to understand why members of other creeds do not see it the same way. More than a few go so far as to assert that those who do not believe the way they do are misguided or, worse yet, are either infidels or heretics. These are offensive words that are not often used in polite society. But this stance still persists. It stands in the way of bringing people of different faiths closer together. Worse yet, it continues to create conflicts around the globe, which result in bloodshed and in widespread human misery.

So the purpose of this book is to find the common voice that unites rather than divides the prophets of history and to point to a common ground that would enable people of all the many different creeds and cultures to come together in peace for the common good of all. The voice of the Hebrew prophets resonates in the teachings of many of those creeds and cultures around the world, East and West. That the world today is still beset by hatred and prejudice, by poverty and hunger, by war and strife is not because of those teachings. It is because people, especially people in positions of power, continue to ignore them. What we call civilization is still a thin layer underneath that lurk all those evil drives that have been with us since the dawn of time.

This author agrees with Pope Benedict XVI who wrote in his recent book *Jesus of Nazareth*,

> What did Jesus actually bring, if not world peace, universal prosperity, and a better world? What has he brought? The answer is very simple: God. He has brought the God that formerly unveiled his countenance gradually, first to Abraham, then to Moses and the prophets. (44)

In other words, the prophets of ancient Israel, who may not have brought us world peace, universal prosperity, and a better world, nevertheless brought us a faith and a hope that still sustains millions of people around the world who continue to believe that someday war will end, people will work together so that all may prosper, and the world will be a better place.

To find out who these prophets were, and why their words continue to have such an impact, we need to turn to the pages of the Bible.

The Hebrew Bible is a prophetic book, the composite work of individuals known as prophets. What is particularly significant about it is that during a period of some two hundred years, from about 750 to 540 BCE, several such individuals envisioned a utopian world, a world that pursues peace instead of war, a world where people put the common good above self-interest. They started with one small nation in the belief that eventually that nation would bring about world peace and goodwill toward all people. Now, three thousand years later, their vision is yet to be fulfilled. But they did succeed in making that small nation a witness to the world; and through that nation the belief in the one God of the universe, a God who cares about the world, was carried to all the corners of the earth by the monotheistic faiths that were born out of that prophetic vision.

Is their vision still valid? Is a world without war possible?

All the major religions share a belief in a messianic age when human conflict no longer exists. None, however, can tell us with any certitude when and how such a world will come about. Since we have never known a world without war, it is very hard for us to envision such a world. But there is a common human yearning for a world at peace, without conflict, when all living beings, man and beast alike, live in harmony and work together for the common good. This yearning was addressed by the prophets Isaiah and Micah when they predicted an "end of days" when nations would learn war no more and none should make them afraid.

At the center of every religion there is a golden rule. The golden rule is imparted to mortals by a prophetic voice. The prophet is someone who receives a divine message and relays it to others. In Judaism, the golden rule, "Love your neighbor as yourself," is delivered by God to Moses, who conveys it to the Israelites who are wandering through the desert after the liberation from Egypt. We know all of this by reading chapter 19 in the book of Leviticus, the third of the five books of the Torah.

One may wonder: If this rule has been enunciated and promulgated by great prophetic voices like those of Moses, Jesus, Buddha, and others for thousands of years, and if countless millions of human beings have revered those teachers throughout time and have sought to follow their teachings, why has war been a constant in human affairs throughout time, and still is? What good is a golden rule that is routinely ignored? This is one of the questions we will attempt to answer in the ensuing chapters as we look to rediscover those prophets of old and try to understand their relevance to our own time.

The above-mentioned chapter in Leviticus opens with a lofty statement made by God to Moses and, through him, to the Israelites: "You shall be holy, for I, Adonai your God, am holy." Here the prophetic message introduces a new dimension into human life. Human life is not a free-for-all. It is not about the rule of might, but the rule of right. A life ruled by might is pagan and profane. A life ruled by right is godly. What follows in this chapter are some of the noblest concepts ever articulated by the human species: you must share your harvest with the poor; you must never delay payment to a day laborer; you must never distort justice; you must never hate your brother in your heart; and finally, you must "love your neighbor as yourself."

Prophetic Judaism is the foundation of all monotheism and of monotheistic morality. All enlightened societies in the world today are guided by its teachings. When the ruler of a country is indicted by an international court for ethnic cleansing, the moral basis for such an indictment is found in the prophetic teaching of the Ten Commandments. The great prophets of the Bible, from Moses to Amos, Isaiah, and Jeremiah, loom as giants of the human spirit in every church, synagogue, and mosque in the world. And yet despite centuries of study and scholarship, we know very little about them, and we still struggle to understand who they were, how they came by those timeless verities they were able to articulate so early in human history, and how we are to understand them now, centuries later. It is my purpose in these pages to take a new look at these ancient words spoken so long ago and find out if they have truly withstood the test of time. Have we found something better? Are we to consign them to the dustbin of history? For most of the twentieth century, major social and political ideologies occupied center stage, and the stature of the prophets of old was diminished. Most of those ideologies are now gone. The world today is facing an ideological vacuum, and much of what goes by the notion of faith is two-dimensional, devoid of real depth and meaning. Now is the time to launch a quest for those prophetic voices and find out whether they can still guide us as they sought to guide our ancestors so many generations before us.

Let us begin with this question: Did God actually speak to the prophets?

GOD SPEAKS TO MAN

In the Hebrew Bible, God begins to speak even before there are any human beings around. In other words, speech precedes man. Speech, then, can be looked upon as pre-human, or even as a divine gift. We are told in the New Testament, "In the beginning was the word" (John 1:1). Here the Hebrew and the Christian Bibles agree that the material universe was preceded by and created by a spoken word (see *Pirke Avot* [Sayings of the Fathers], V:1, "The world was created in ten utterances"). A scientist may argue that the material world follows laws that can be put into words, hence those words existed and might have even been articulated before the appearance of matter. Without going too far afield with such speculations, suffice it to say that speech is regarded by the major religions as the link between the human and the divine. Speech is what makes us human, and yet it makes us more than human. Speech is used not only to communicate with others, but also to speak to God, most commonly through prayer. Even people who rarely if ever attend a house of prayer do find themselves on occasions—especially at times of emotional stress—speaking to God or to some unknown cosmic power in the hope of being heard and having their wish granted.

There are many things that speak to us. Nature speaks to us in many voices—through the song of birds, through thunder and lightning, through a rumbling ocean, a wind whispering in the forest. Babies speak to us through innocent eyes and a wide smile. The past speaks to us through the written words of previous generations and through visual images from the past. Voices within us speak to us and guide us, warn us, lift our spirits. Speech exists on many more levels than the spoken word. We hear words in our own mind before we begin to utter a sound. Speech is something that can also be expressed by the written word—in a letter, a note, or any of the new forms of communication, such as e-mail, texting, messaging. And speech can even be expressed through nonverbal communication—a touch, a smile, a nod. In short, the entire phenomenon known as speech is far more complicated than what we normally understand as the act of uttering words. Among Eastern religions, Zen has much to say (or rather express) about nonverbal communication.

The Hebrew Bible unfolds around the central concept of divine speech. As was mentioned before, the story of creation, which describes the gradual formation of the physical world, is driven by divine utterances, beginning with "And God said, Let there be light; and there was light." (Here again light precedes the creation of the sun, as speech precedes the creation of man.) In other words, God tells the light to come into being, and subsequently God tells the day and the night, the heaven and the earth, the sun, the moon and the stars, and the plants and the animals to come into being. And so the reality of speech is not limited to God and man. It is shared by all of creation that is capable of hearing God's words. Finally, God creates the human race, beginning with Adam and Eve, who are created "in God's image," which includes speech, and as soon as they are created God speaks to them, saying, "Be fruitful and multiply, and fill the earth." God then proceeds to explain to them how they are expected to have dominion over both the plant and the animal kingdoms, enabling them to find food and sustenance. As God presents the animals to Adam, the first human starts to give them names, which enables him to incorporate them in his human speech.

The next time God speaks to the blissful couple marks the beginning of the human conflict with the divine. The conflict results from God's admonition to Adam and Eve not to eat from the fruit of the tree of the knowledge of good and evil. God expects man to live a life of innocent bliss. But the first human couple disobeys God, and tastes of the fruit of the tree. By doing so, the two acquire a sense of self-awareness. The awareness of their nakedness leads to shame, and subsequently to all the other human emotions such as fear, guilt, and so on. The couple is banished from the Garden of Eden, and human life as we know it, with all its toil and trouble, begins.

As with all folk stories of creation throughout the world and throughout time, the biblical stories of creation seek to provide a seemingly simple narrative that explains the origins of life on earth. The idea of God as the creator and of speech as the force that makes creation possible can be understood on several levels. The literal level is quite simple. One can take the stories of creation at face value, conceptualizing God as a supreme, all-powerful person who speaks the way people speak and as depicted by Michelangelo in the painting describing the creation of man on the ceiling of the Sistine Chapel in Rome. This depiction of God shows a very attractive and muscular old man with flowing hair and a flowing white beard floating in space and reaching out his hand as his finger creates man. This kind of literal depiction has few questions to ask. All you need to do is read the text and believe every word in its most literal sense.

But this is not the only way to understand Genesis. The Talmudic sages back in the early centuries of our common era understood that the Scriptures are not one-dimensional. Their approach to the stories of creation and all subsequent biblical stories was highly sophisticated and multilayered. God to them was certainly not a Hollywood-type, an attractive old man, and God's voice was not a magnified human voice. They were well versed in the concept of "as if." They found explicit references in the biblical text itself to the nonliteral meaning of the text.

For example: "The hidden things belong to Adonai our God, and the revealed things belong to us and to our children forever to do all that this Torah commands" (Deut. 29:28); or "My thoughts are not your thoughts, and your ways are not my ways" (Isa. 55:8). They did not pretend to have a clear picture of God, or to hear divine voices. Yet to them the biblical stories were more than folk tales or mythologies or literary works, although they knew that such elements did exist in the narrative. They understood that the text was meant to instruct and to illuminate. In other words, it carried a moral message, and it contained layers of meaning that are not readily discernible by a casual reader. We use words like "allegorical" and "mystical" to refer to such layers of meaning, and only a few people are privileged enough to decode them.

One way to understand the biblical concept of creation and a creator, and of the role speech plays in the process of creation and in the interaction between the creator and the world, is by considering those inspired individuals whom we call prophets. At a certain point in time, most likely in the eighth or seventh century BCE, these prophets took it upon themselves to gather old oral traditions and perhaps some written texts as well and write them down from a prophetic perspective, thus creating the text known to us as the Holy Scriptures. This perspective can be characterized by the following basic tenets: the unity of an all-powerful divinity; the moral purpose of creation; and the destiny of the Jewish people as a moral agent of the divinity. Thus, for example, each day in the biblical stories of creation concludes with the statement "And God saw and it was good." To my knowledge, this is the only story of creation among the countless ones found around the world that offers a moral judgment about the nature of creation. Most such stories are devoid of moral judgment, and some are even downright whimsical. This prophetic perspective also explains the centrality of the divine voice in the biblical narrative. To a prophet writing down this text, the divine voice is critical for understanding the relationship between the human and the divine. Hence God speaks to Adam and Eve and to their biblical descendants, whereby the element of prophecy is present even among those who are not, strictly speaking, prophets. What comes to mind at this point is Moses's words to his restive and doubting people in the desert "Would that all God's people were prophets" (Num. 11:29).

Perhaps the most important event in the Bible is the giving of the law at Mount Sinai. Here, all the Israelites are gathered at the foot of the mountain, as Moses ascends the mountain. When he comes back forty days later, we hear,

> So it came about on the third day, when it was morning, that there were thunder and lightning flashes and a thick cloud upon the mountain and a very loud trumpet sound, so that all the people who were in the camp trembled. (Exod. 19:16)

What follows is the divine voice pronouncing the Ten Commandments and all the subsequent laws and statutes. The people, we are told, are afraid to hear the voice of God, which they believe will result in their death (Exod. 20:16). They ask Moses to act on their behalf and bring the divine message to them. Moses assures them that nothing will happen to them, and that God wishes to test them so that they may obey the divine message and not sin. What is not clear is what they actually do hear, since this is believed to be the only time ever that the entire community of Israel heard a divine voice. According to the Talmudic sages, the only one who actually heard the words of God was Moses, while the rest of the Israelites only heard a deafening sound, which they recognized to be the voice of God. There is, however, a rabbinic opinion that maintains that the first two commandments, about the unity of God and prohibitions on worshipping other gods, were actually heard by all present. In short, it is not clear what people did or did not hear, but this remains the most central event in the Bible regarding humans hearing God speak.

While later prophetic retelling of these events may explain the prominence of the divine voice in the biblical narrative, it does not answer the question Did God actually speak to the prophets? This question will continue to unfold in this book. What should begin to become clear at this point and in the following chapters, however, is that the phenomenon of God speaking to man is by no means a simple form of verbal communication.

DID THE PROPHET HEAR HIS OWN VOICE?

At this point some readers may be saying to themselves that God has never spoken to anyone, and that the prophet's claiming to hear God's voice is an illusion. The voice the prophet reports hearing is his own.

This view stands at the extreme opposite end to the view that every word in the Bible is literally true. It dismisses the Bible's central idea of a divine voice, and it renders the Scriptures meaningless. There is nothing different about the prophet. The claims made by an Amos or an Isaiah are false and are hence not worthy of the term "prophecy." In other words, the words that have influenced the human race more than any other words in human history are merely words articulated by the human mind. If this view is correct, then monotheism is meaningless. The contact between the human and the divine is nonexistent. God may as well be nonexistent. All discussion ends here.

The idea of a divine voice and of a special kind of person who hears that voice goes beyond the grasp of human reason, and therefore it is easy to dismiss. Moreover, why did God speak to a few people centuries ago and not to anyone since? There seems to be no ready explanation to this question. So we may as well abandon this enterprise and resign ourselves to the idea that there is no answer. This would be the easy way out. The purpose of the following pages is not to take the easy way out but rather to continue our search in the hope of finding at least a partial answer. The question before us is too important to simply dismiss without any attempt at an answer. Let us, therefore, persevere rather than abandon the whole enterprise by concluding that the prophet simply spoke to himself.

WHO IS A PROPHET?

Who is a prophet? I have plowed the entire Bible in search of an answer to this question, checking every mention of a prophet or a prophetic activity. Instead of gaining a new understanding, I became more confused than I was before I started. And so here I am, embarking on my search for the prophet.

The first time the word "prophet" appears in the Bible is in the story of Abraham and Abimelech.

Now Abraham moved on from there into the region of the Negev and lived between Kadesh and Shur. For a while he stayed in Gerar, and there Abraham said of his wife Sarah, 'She is my sister.' Then Abimelech king of Gerar sent for Sarah and took her.

But God came to Abimelech in a dream one night and said to him, "You are as good as dead because of the woman you have taken; she is a married woman."

Now Abimelech had not gone near her, so he said, 'Lord, will you destroy an innocent nation? Did he not say to me, 'She is my sister,' and didn't she also say, 'He is my brother?' I have done this with a clear conscience and clean hands.'

Then God said to him in the dream, 'Yes, I know you did this with a clear conscience, and so I have kept you from sinning against me. That is why I did not let you touch her. Now return the man's wife, for he is a *prophet*, and he will pray for you and you will live. But if you do not return her, you may be sure that you and all yours will die.' (Gen. 20:1–7)

In Jewish tradition, the first official prophet is Moses, who is called the "Father of the Prophets." Abraham is known as the first Jew, or rather Hebrew, the first patriarch of the tribes of Israel. In reading the classical commentaries on this passage, it is clear that they differ in their understanding of the word "prophet" in this context. Rashi, the greatest medieval biblical commentator, explains it as Abraham having the ability to know what is happening to his wife, Sarah, at Abimelech's palace. In other words, he does not take it to mean that Abraham is actually a prophet; he is rather a person with special mental powers. The Rashbam, Rashi's grandson and a great commentator in his own right, takes it to mean that the word "prophet" in this case refers to "one who speaks," whereby God is letting Abimelech know that Abraham is someone who converses with God and receives God's favor. It is quite clear that here the word "prophet" is not used in its formal sense.

The first time the official title of "Prophet" is used in the Bible is not in reference to Moses, but rather to his sister, Miriam, who is called Miriam the Prophet at the time when she sings and dances after the crossing of the Red Sea (Exod. 15:20). Here again, Rashi and the Rashbam puzzle over this title, trying to find reasons why Miriam should be called a prophet. They impute to her prophetic qualities, such as foreseeing the future preeminence of Moses (Rashi) and pronouncing oracles (Rashbam). But here again, the prophetic role of Miriam is quite different from the career of a prophet, as will become clear when we reach the classical period of biblical prophecy.

Even more puzzling is the use of the word "prophet" in regard to Moses's brother, Aaron. When God sends Moses to speak to the pharaoh and tell him to "let my people go," Moses replies that he has difficulties speaking. God tells Moses that Aaron, his brother, will speak for him and will be "his prophet" (Exod. 7:1). Here again, the classical commentators struggle with the usage of the word "prophet" in this particular context. Rashi explains that "prophet" here means "interpreter." The Rashbam takes it to mean "substitute speaker." What becomes clear in this instance is that the term "prophet" in the early stages of the history of the Hebrew tribes did not have a well-defined meaning and was used to describe such functions as clairvoyance, eloquence, interpretation, and so on. This leaves us with the original question, "Who is a prophet?"

If the short answer to this question is "Someone God speaks to," then people in the Bible who have absolutely nothing to do with prophecy have to be included in the venerable company of the prophets. Indeed, there are several different versions within and outside Judaism as to who the biblical prophets are. In both Islam and Judaism, there are traditions about Adam being a prophet, even though the Bible gives no indication of any prophetic activity on Adam's part. Abraham and Sarah, the biblical progenitors of the Hebrew and Arab people, are considered prophets by those two faiths as well as by Christianity. Here again, the Bible gives no indication of any prophetic activity attributable to either one of them. Within Christianity, denominations like Mormonism, Jehovah Witnesses, and Seven Day Adventists have their own prophets or, in the case of Jehovah Witnesses, their own take on what prophecy is. In short, the seemingly simple question "Who is a prophet?" is by no means so simple. It is a question that has been asked for millennia, many times within the pages of the Bible itself, and was never given a conclusive answer. The biblical Israelites questioned the authority of all the prophets, from Moses to Jeremiah, and never seemed to reach a consensus. Kings like Saul and others tried to wear the mantle of prophecy, only to be scorned by their subjects ("Is Saul also a prophet?" people ask mockingly when they see Saul prophesying). A commoner like Samson's mother saw and heard God's angel, letting her know about the birth of her powerful son who would save his people from the Philistines, but she remained a common woman. It is left to us to struggle with the answer to the question "Who is a prophet?" Clearly, there is more to being a prophet than hearing a divine voice.

IS A PROPHET SOMEONE WHO PREDICTS THE FUTURE?

A common meaning of the word "prophet" is "someone who predicts the future." Throughout history there have always been special individuals to whom their followers imputed special powers that enabled them to foretell future events. The kings of antiquity were surrounded by future-tellers, soothsayers, diviners—the list goes on and on. They consulted them on nearly every matter, large or small, particularly on affairs of state, and most importantly when the king prepared to go to war. At the same time, self-styled future-tellers existed in every village and in every culture throughout the world and were accessible to even the lowliest member of society, from a girl who wanted to know her marriage prospects to a farmer who wanted to find out how his crops would fare. For most of us, those future-tellers have long been replaced by pundits and talking-heads who speak endlessly on radio and television and purport to know how the stock market will perform, how national and world leaders should act, and many other such matters for which there is no clear answer.

The Hebrew word for "prophet," *navi*, does not mean one who foresees the future, but rather one who speaks to the people. Other names for a prophet in the Bible are *hozeh* and *roeh*, a visionary and a seer, respectively, and also *ish elohim*, or "man of god." The visionary sees divine visions, as does the seer. They do not see the future. In fact, the Bible on several occasions issues a stern warning against consulting future-tellers. And yet, in spite of these warnings, the Hebrews of biblical times, like people everywhere, had a great need to know the future. King Saul, the first Hebrew king, about to be defeated by the Philistines, goes to the woman of En Dor and asks her to conjure up the spirit of the dead prophet Samuel to find out the outcome of the coming battle. King Zedekiah, the last king of Judah, asks the prophet Jeremiah to tell him about his fate at the hands of the Babylonians who are about to overrun Jerusalem. All the kings of Israel and Judah surrounded themselves with court prophets who were diviners, but who were denounced by prophets like Jeremiah as false prophets.

What is perhaps most difficult to understand about the biblical prophets is that despite the fact that they received divine messages, they did not always havè a clear idea about the future. The messages they received invariably had to do with the correct way their people were expected to act. This behavior had consequences that impacted future events, and yet the future seemed to remain open and not always predictable. In other words, God could have a change of heart due to all sorts of circumstances. Or, for that matter, God might choose not to disclose everything to the prophet but rather to hold something back. The prophet then could not give a full account of events about to happen, but only an indication, and sometimes could even make a mistake.

In short, future-telling may be considered a by-product of the prophetic profession but not its main purpose. The Hebrew prophets stand apart from all the future-tellers, wise men, philosophers, counselors and all those who possess special knowledge or special powers who have ever graced (or disgraced) the stage of history. They stand apart because of the simple fact that it was never their task to bring people any form of knowledge people craved, about either present or future events, or, as in the case of the philosophers, to deal with ideas for their own sake. Their task was to act on what might be described as a moral compulsion and deliver a message that people for the most part were not too eager to receive, a message that in the long run was ineluctable.

THE PROPHET'S MORAL COMPULSION

When we listen to the words of biblical prophets such as Amos or Jeremiah, it becomes clear that what animates them is not a carefully thought-out decision to become teachers of ethics and morality, but rather a compulsion to speak out on what seems to enter their heart as a divine message.

> A lion roars, who will not shudder?
> Adonai spoke, who will not prophesy? (Amos 3:8)

The message overwhelms them and leaves them no choice but to bring it to the attention of their people. This can be referred to as the prophetic *moral compulsion*. It is a total compulsion that does not stop at anything, regardless of the consequences. There is no attempt whatsoever to sugar-coat the message, make it more palatable, or revise it in any way. The words of the prophet come down on their listeners' heads like blows of a sledgehammer. The message is vivid and unequivocal, harsh and uncompromising. It is like a sentence pronounced by a judge. The trial is over. All the testimonies have been heard. The lawyers have spoken their piece. The decision is being handed down by the court. A transgression was committed. There is no way back. A prophet, in other words, is someone who shows up at a critical moment in the midst of a crisis. Only after the transgression has been duly punished and atoned for may the prophet proceed to speak words of comfort and consolation, and offer new hope. When Jews began to return to Jerusalem from the Babylonian Exile, the anonymous prophet whom we call the Second Isaiah said,

> Be comforted, be comforted My people, says your God.
> Speak tenderly to Jerusalem, and proclaim to her
> That her hard service has been completed,
> That her sin has been paid for,
> That she has received from God's hands
> Double for all her sins. (Isa. 40:1–2)

This is the prophetic drama as it is enacted and reenacted in the biblical narrative over a period of several centuries. And this is the yardstick by which we can take the measure of a biblical prophet. Any other scenario may produce a prophetlike person, but only the moral compulsion scenario qualifies one as a prophet.

The classical dichotomy in the Bible is one that differentiates the role and the character of the prophet from that of the priest, or *kohen*. It was best articulated a century ago in a celebrated essay by the Hebrew thinker Ahad Ha'am. While the prophet is uncompromising and unyielding, the priest is a peacemaker eager to accommodate. The archetypal prophet, Moses, smashes the tablets of the law when he comes down from Mount Sinai and discovers that the Israelites have erected a golden calf during his absence. His brother, Aaron, the archetypal priest, is the one who accedes to the wishes of the people to fashion a golden calf in the first place. From that moment on this becomes the pattern for prophetic and priestly behavior.

And here is where we begin to detect a pattern in the composite character of the prophets. Whether the prophet is Elijah, or Amos, or Jeremiah, or Ezekiel, or Huldah, he or she always possesses the same moral compulsion. The manner and the method may vary, but the character is very similar. One is inclined to ask whether the prophets' mission makes them behave the way they do, or whether it takes a certain personality to be a prophet. Either way, what we begin to see here, as we will find out more specifically when we examine each of the prophets, is one of several patterns that will make it clear that the prophets are not a random collection of individuals, but rather voices with a common mission and message. We will begin by looking at the best known of the Hebrew prophets, namely, Moses.

IS MOSES THE FIRST PROPHET?

Moses is known in Jewish tradition as the father of the prophets. "There has never arisen a prophet in Israel like Moses, whom God knew face to face" (Deut. 34:10). According to Moses ben Maimon, or Maimonides, Judaism's greatest philosopher and author of the thirteen principles of Judaism, there never was and there never will be another prophet like Moses. Thus, according to Maimonides, Jews are to accept the preeminence of Moses as an article of faith. As we have seen before, there are those in and out of Judaism who consider Adam the first prophet, and Abraham the first Hebrew prophet. This is a very broad application of the concept of a prophet since we never hear of Adam having any moral compulsion (quite the opposite), and since Abraham, great and virtuous person that he was, was more of a peacemaker (as in the case of the quarrel with Lot or in defending the evil cities of Sodom and Gomorrah) than an uncompromising oracle, hence closer to an Aaron than a Moses.

This brings us back to Moses. To follow Maimonides' thinking, Moses stands apart as a prophet. In fact, the designation of "prophet" seems too limiting when it comes to Moses. As the one who liberates his people from Egyptian bondage and takes them to the mountain where he brings down the divine law, it would be quite fitting to consider Moses a liberator and a lawgiver. As such, he is the founder of the Israelite polity and the formulator of the faith of his people. One has to wonder whether the role of prophet might have been bestowed on him posthumously by prophetic writers who inserted the words "There has never arisen a prophet in Israel like Moses" into the closing chapter of Deuteronomy. For even if Moses did write the Torah, he could not have made such a statement, especially since the previous verses describe his demise, and since the Torah tells us that Moses was the humblest of men.

I would propose that the three major, so-called Abrahamic religions (I prefer the term "Jeremiac religions," as I shall later explain), which look upon their founder as a prophet, should leave this title to lesser luminaries, so to speak. Moses is the Hebrew liberator and lawgiver. Jesus is the Christian messiah. Muhammad is *rasul allah*, the messenger of God to the Muslims. For their followers they stand apart from persons like Isaiah, or John the Baptist, or Isma'il (Ishmael), whom these religions, respectively, consider prophets. In other words, the story of Moses is not a story of moral compulsion. It is a story of liberation and legislation. The first five books of the Bible, known as the "Torah of Moses," presage the age of moral compulsion, which begins to take shape gradually after the tribes of Israel enter the Promised Land. It is a process that will last some five hundred years, from about 1000 BCE to 600 BCE.

Who, then, might be considered the first biblical prophet?

This question may have to remain unanswered for now. It is not clear who was the first one to meet the criterion of moral compulsion and set the whole process of biblical prophecy in motion. Let us instead look at the genesis of the prophetic vocation in the period following the time of Moses and see how it all evolved.

FALSE PROPHETS

Throughout the biblical period we encounter what the Bible calls "false prophets." The criteria for recognizing false prophets are enunciated by Moses during the Exodus from Egypt, as the Israelites are warned against following someone who proclaims himself a prophet yet lacks the legitimacy of a prophet.

> If a prophet or a dreamer of dreams arises among you and gives you a sign or a wonder, and the sign or wonder that he tells you comes to pass, and if he says, 'Let us go after other gods,' which you have not known, 'and let us serve them,' you shall not listen to the words of that prophet or that dreamer of dreams. For Adonai your God is testing you, to know whether you love Adonai your God with all your heart and with all your soul. You shall walk after Adonai your God and fear him and keep his commandments and obey his voice, and you shall serve him and hold fast to him. But that prophet or that dreamer of dreams shall be put to death, because he has taught rebellion against Adonai your God, who brought you out of the land of Egypt and redeemed you out of the house of slavery, to make you leave the way in which Adonai your God commanded you to walk. So you shall purge the evil from your midst. (Deut. 13:1–6)

For every legitimate prophet there are countless would-be prophets who fail to pass the test of moral compulsion and who lack the uncompromising integrity of the "prophet of God." As the above passage indicates, the way the would-be prophet sought to establish his legitimacy was through "signs and wonders," reminiscent of the scene of Moses and Aaron appearing before the pharaoh and performing the magic of turning a stick into a snake, or of Elijah bringing fire from heaven to consume the offering on the altar while the four hundred so-called prophets of Baal fail to follow suit. Another common approach for proving one's prophetic powers was claiming to be able to receive divine messages in a dream. Moses warns his people that "signs and wonders" and so-called prophetic dreams in and of themselves do not imply true prophecy. The only touchstone of authentic prophecy is the law they have received at Sinai, written on the two tablets of the law by the hand of God.

As was mentioned before, the ancient world was teeming with people who took on the title of "prophet" and operated on all levels of society, from the court of the king to the most remote village. Sometimes the Hebrew prophets would find themselves being challenged by those counterparts—as in the case of Moses before the pharaoh and Elijah before the prophets of Baal—and would have to prove themselves by using the method of "signs and wonders." But unlike all the other practitioners of prophecy, the mission of the Hebrew prophets was not to satisfy the need of the king or the common person to interpret the future, but to uphold the simple truth that "the righteous lives by his faith." In looking at post-biblical history, we shall see that the dichotomy of true and false prophets continues, in all of its many permutations, throughout time to this day.

PROPHECY AFTER MOSES

The history of the Jews in their land begins after the death of Moses. Moses himself is not permitted to enter the Promised Land. The reason given is that he doubted God during the trek in the desert when God told him to strike a rock so that water might come gushing out (Num. 20:10–12). It will take three hundred years from the time of the death of Moses to the time when the first major prophet, namely, Samuel, appears in the Land of Israel. Moses himself is succeeded by a warrior named Joshua, the son of Nun. Joshua is able to conquer the Land of Canaan and is succeeded by a series of warrior-leaders known as judges, only one of whom is referred to as a prophet, namely, Deborah, and, as we shall see, this title does not seem to be supported by the biblical narrative. It is not clear why Moses is not succeeded by a prophet, who could continue the prophetic tradition of keeping the people close to their God. The Israelites in their land go through a very difficult settlement process. They are besieged on all sides by bitter enemies, and their existence becomes precarious. They have no central authority, no central place of worship, and each of the twelve tribes has to fend for itself, often under very dire conditions. The absence of prophets during those three long centuries, when the Hebrew tribes were in great need of spiritual guidance, cannot be easily explained. The answer may possibly be found in the following verse from the first book of Samuel: "The boy Samuel ministered before Adonai under Eli. In those days the word of Adonai was rare; there were not many visions " (1 Sam. 3:1).

In other words, there are times in biblical history and perhaps in all of history when the word of God or perhaps the presence of God is more common than in other times. One could also point to the four-hundred-year period between the time of the patriarchs to the time of Moses, during which time the Israelites were enslaved in Egypt and there were no prophets who could hear the voice of God, until we are finally told that God heard the crying of the Israelites and saw their suffering and decided to send Moses to redeem them. In our time, this question of the presence or absence of God will become one of the most critical points of discussion among scholars and theologians in the aftermath of the Holocaust.

Samuel will pick up where Moses left off. He will succeed in uniting the tribes under one leader, and he will launch the prophetic tradition that will continue for the next five centuries and will leave its stamp on Judaism and on the world to this day.

I

THE EARLY PROPHETS

PROPHETIC BEGINNINGS: SAMUEL

Once the Hebrew tribes settle in the Land of Canaan, they become a rural (and later urban) people like all their many neighbors. They start out as a loose confederacy of tribes with a common ancestry, historical memory, and language, but otherwise each tribe keeps to itself until they finally crown a king over all of Israel. They are all committed to obeying the God of Israel who took them out of Egyptian bondage and gave them the law. But they do not have a central house of worship, and their holiest object, the Ark of the Covenant, is moved around and even falls into the hands of their archenemy, namely, the Philistines. This period is known as the time of the judges. Those so-called judges are tribal chieftains and self-styled tribal leaders who take action against local enemies. The period is marked by constant battles, large and small, and ongoing lawlessness, when "each person does what he or she considers right" (Judg. 21:25).

As was previously mentioned, the time of the judges was marked by the absence of prophets. The only person in the book of Judges who receives the designation of prophet is, once again, a woman, namely, Deborah, who is also a judge. Her claim to fame is rallying the tribes of Israel against the common Canaanite enemy and winning a spectacular victory by fighting iron chariots with foot soldiers. This has little to do with moral compulsion, which again leaves us wondering why Deborah deserves the title of prophet.

At the end of the period of the judges, a young man appears at the temple in Shiloh—in the land of the tribe of Benjamin—who is destined to become what may well be the first official prophet of his people. His name is Samuel. His first encounter with God's voice may be the model for all future encounters between the prophet and the divinity.

> And the boy Samuel ministered to Adonai before Eli. And the word of the Almighty was rare in those days. There was no frequent vision. On that day Eli was lying in bed and his eyes dimmed, and could not see. The light of God had not yet gone out. And Samuel was lying in the temple of Adonai where the Ark of God was. And God called out to Samuel, and Samuel said, Here I am. And he ran to Eli and said to him, Here I am, for you have called me. And he said, I did not call, go lie down. And he went and he lay down. And Adonai called out again and said, Samuel. And Samuel stood up and went to Eli and said, Here I am, for you have called me. And he said, I did not call you, my son, go lie down. And Samuel had not yet known God, and the word of God had not yet been revealed to him. And God called Samuel for the third time, and he stood up and went to see Eli and said, Here I am, for you have called me. And Eli understood that God was addressing the boy. And Eli told Samuel, Go lie down, and if you are addressed again you will say, Speak, O God, for your servant is listening. (1 Sam. 3:1–10)

No other passage in the Bible provides more detailed information about this key phenomenon of prophecy, namely, hearing the divine voice. What is clear from this passage is that the boy Samuel did not actually hear a nonhuman voice, but rather the divine was made audible to him through the voice of his master, the priest Eli. What this passage also reveals is that at the time there was an official formula of invoking the divine voice, as we hear Eli telling the boy Samuel to say "Speak, O God, for your servant is listening."

Samuel hears the voice as he falls asleep, and it may have come to him in a dream. Whether or not he was actually hearing the voice of God is something we will continue to explore. What we do know is that Samuel, who lived three centuries after the time of Moses, played a critical role in the history of his people, which puts him only second to Moses as a pivotal prophet who brought his people to their God, to the divine law, and to their coalescing as a people. Samuel was the first to unify the tribes of Israel, and the one who gave them their greatest king ever, namely, King David.

Samuel is the last of the tribal judges and the first of the prophets of the united tribes. He is also a priest, which rounds out his authority and makes him the undisputed spiritual leader of his time. He is charged with a monumental task, second only to the task of freeing the Hebrews from Egypt and giving them the law. Samuel's task is to turn history's first monotheistic people from a loose association of tribes, who more often than not fail to live by the law of the one God and are easy prey for their marauding neighbors, into a unified nation with a central authority and a strong faith. As such, he is more of a political figure than a spiritual voice. Indeed, he understands from the very beginning that for a spiritual leader to step into the political arena is to diminish his or her spiritual or prophetic stature. The idea of finding a human authority known as a king to rule over the unified tribes who are expected to live by the laws of God is very difficult for him to come to terms with. He tries to talk the leaders of the tribes out of crowning a king, but to no avail. They need a strong central authority to be able to cope with hostile neighbors who are stronger than any one tribe, and there are no viable alternatives to a king.

Here the stage is set for the next five centuries, during which time the monarchy will remain unified during the first century, and then divide into two thereafter. During that entire time prophets will play an important role as advisors to the king and as king-makers. The advisors, or court prophets, will for the most part be yes-men who will tell the king what he wants to hear, and therefore they will be decried as false prophets. The king-makers, who for the most part will be self-employed outsiders, will be cast in the mold of Samuel, men with a moral compulsion who will always remind the king that there is a higher authority a king or queen must submit to in order to prosper and be triumphant, or else face dire consequences for the court and for the people. Few kings during those five centuries will feel at ease with those gadflies known as prophets.

Samuel proceeds to look for a king who will not only provide political and military leadership but will also operate as a spiritual authority. He believes he finds the answer in a tall and handsome young man from the tribe of Benjamin named Saul the son of Kish. Saul is a brave warrior and he has an interest in prophesying. Here we come across a phenomenon that is common among the Hebrews during Samuel's lifetime and for perhaps a century thereafter, but which seems to disappear during the late eighth century when the literary prophets begin to make their mark. Suddenly, without forewarning, around the time when Samuel meets Saul, we are told about "schools of prophets," which seem to resemble the monastic orders of other religions, consisting of men who are interested in pursuing the craft of prophecy. The biblical text does not provide a clear idea of what exactly these men accomplish, and we never hear of anyone "graduating" from such a school and becoming an honest-to-goodness prophet. For the most part they seem to roam the countryside, often with portable musical instruments, Hare Krishna–style, dancing or perhaps twirling like dervishes and going into ecstasy, at which point they "prophesy." What exactly they prophesy is never made clear. And yet, the biblical text does not criticize them or mock them. Neither Samuel nor other prophets such as Elijah or Elisha cast any aspersion on them. They seem to be accepted by their contemporaries as a legitimate manifestation of the craft of prophecy, in whatever way it was understood and accepted in those days. And, unfortunately, they do not help us better understand the nature and evolution of prophecy during the early years of the monarchy, from the time of Saul to approximately the time of King Ahab of the Northern Kingdom.

What we do learn is that Saul makes several attempts to join such a school of prophets, and apparently he does not get too far. People who know Saul are taken aback by his interest in prophecy, perhaps because he is a warrior rather than a reflective or pious type. We are told twice that people would say to each other, "Is Saul to be counted among the prophets?" But Samuel seems to take this as an indication that Saul has a spiritual side to him, and he crowns him king. Here one may wonder why Samuel, who is accepted by everyone as the leading prophet of Israel, is so wrong about Saul. Here, at the very outset of what might be considered the beginning of the formal era of Hebrew prophecy, we begin to realize that prophets are not infallible. They may have some great insights. They are exemplars of moral compulsion, but they are not all-knowing or omniscient. By implication, the only one who is all-knowing is God. But even God, as we shall see, does not always act infallibly, perhaps because God, as the Kabbalists have taught us, chose to limit the godly powers in creating the world (*tzimtzum*), since the encounter between the finite and the infinite (*ein sof*) is only possible through self-limitation on the part of the infinite.

Saul turns out to be an ineffectual king and, indeed, a tragic figure. He is put to the test by his mentor when he is ordered by divine decree to exterminate the Amalekites, who have been long-standing, ruthless enemies of the Israelites dating back to the time of the Exodus, during which time they followed the Israelites in the desert and attacked and killed the stragglers. Saul captures Agag, the king of the Amalekites, but spares his life. By doing so he defies divine authority and acts as the supreme arbiter. This results in the first of many showdowns between king and prophet. The prophet, we learn, is not a compromiser. He is letting the king know in no uncertain terms that divine authority cannot be questioned. The prophet proceeds to execute Agag with his own hands. It now becomes clear to Samuel that he has made the wrong choice in selecting Saul to be the king. Saul, who seems to be a sensitive soul and who is mentally and emotionally unstable, is overtaken by an "evil spirit" that turns him into a moody and paranoiac monarch, and it becomes clear that his days as king are numbered.

What are we to conclude about prophecy from the stories of Samuel, Saul, and the schools of prophets?

As was mentioned at the outset, the Bible makes it very clear that the issue of prophets and prophecies is by no means easy to understand. The author or authors of the stories in the books of Samuel and the books of Kings (who, again, are either prophets themselves or scribes with prophetic connections) seem to find it very hard to understand the phenomenon known as prophecy, despite the fact that they themselves live at the height of the prophetic era. They don't seem to have any cogent explanation for the phenomenon known as "schools of prophets." There is no indication that in their time, the time of the literary prophets, a Micah or a Jeremiah had anything to do with such a school. What is being made amply clear when we get to those later prophets is that they are suddenly called upon to be prophets, sometimes at a very young age, and that the gift (or burden) of prophecy is bestowed on them spontaneously, without formal schooling. This is also true of Samuel himself. The narrative gives no indication that he might be a product of a school of prophets. As was shown before, one evening he hears the voice of God and he is instantly transformed into a prophet. Saul, on the other hand, is a different matter altogether. He wishes to be a prophet, and he pursues the schools of prophets, but instead of becoming a prophet he becomes eventually possessed by "an evil spirit from God" (1 Sam. 16:14). Moreover, we never hear of Samuel practicing any of the rituals of the schools of prophets, such as music, dance, or going into ecstasy. He is a man with a mission who is consumed by the momentous tasks God charges him with, and who seems to have no direct involvement with those schools. He knows about them, and he does not disapprove of them, but they remain outside his own sphere of political and prophetic activities.

THE PROPHET, DIVINE AUTHORITY, AND EVIL

There are stories in the Bible that make both God and the prophet appear extremely cruel. The story of Agag, the Amalekite king, is one of them (some of the best known are the stories of the sacrifice of Isaac and the sacrifice of Jephthah's daughter, which prompted the Danish philosopher Soren Kierkegaard to speak of "the suspension of the ethical"). Saul shows mercy to the captured king, while Samuel insists on killing him, and executes him with his own hands. Samuel remains a righteous biblical character, while Saul is seen as a failed, tragic monarch. Where does the truth lie?

Stories of this kind have given fuel throughout the ages to detractors of Judaism who have referred to the God of the Old Testament as an angry and vengeful Jehovah, radically different from the loving God of the New Testament. This argument cuts to the heart of the question of the nature of the prophetic character. The prophet does God's bidding without deviating one iota. Who, then, is cruel in this instance, God or Samuel, or both?

Generations of Jewish scholars have been hard-pressed to answer their detractors in a way that made sense to the audiences on either side of the argument. In the post-Holocaust world, however, it is much easier to counter this allegation. In his book *This People Israel* (written clandestinely on toilet paper while he was imprisoned at the Theresienstadt concentration camp), Leo Baeck, the revered Jewish philosopher and leader of German Jewry at the time of the Nazis' rise to power, writes as he tries to understand the need to eradicate Nazism from the face of the earth,

> For only if the punishing Judgment of God would fall on all these masters and servants of blasphemy, only then would those lands once again become pure and free and wide, so that humanity would be able to live there. It is anger, often fiery anger, which speaks here, but humanity's yearning and conscience seek expression in it. It contains more true humanness than is found in many a sweet song of man. (11)

In Jewish history, the Amalekites became the prototype of all those throughout the ages who sought to annihilate the Jews. Haman was called "the Agagite," or descendant of the Amalekite king Agag (Esther 3:1). More than a few have since vied for the title, most notoriously Adolf Hitler, and most recently Mahmoud Ahmadinejad who, like Haman, is a Persian. Had Hitler been captured by the Allies, they would have done to him exactly what Samuel did to Agag, and no decent person would have objected. It is indeed in this context that the story of Samuel and the Amalekite king should be understood .

FOLK RELIGION AND THE PROPHET

Another type of quasi-prophetic activity that existed during the time of Samuel (and, for that matter, throughout biblical times) can be seen within the realm of what might be referred to as folk religion. By folk religion we mean practices, customs, and beliefs that do not form part of the official or high religion. Those include superstitions, beliefs in powers other than God (such as spirits and demons), rituals borrowed from pagan religions and practiced at home rather than publicly, and so on. The best example of this is to be found in the story of Saul who, at the end of his royal career, is about to go into battle against the Philistines while knowing that his prospects are very slim. Wearing a disguise, he rides his horse in the middle of the night to visit a woman in En Dor who is presumably adept at using necromancy, or consulting with the spirits of the dead, to predict the future. She conjures up the spirit of the prophet Samuel who has since died, and Saul consults his old mentor about the outcome of the battle, only to find out that his own fate is sealed. It is clear from reading this story that Samuel strongly disapproved of this practice.

What is interesting, however, is that the woman of En Dor, clearly a folk religion figure and not an official religious functionary, is able to conjure up the spirit of the dead prophet, who was the leading prophet of his time. This leads us to two conclusions: first, the practice of necromancy was common in those days and it yielded results. And second, the line of demarcation between the official religion and the folk religion was not clear. This is true of folk religion throughout the Bible and throughout time, to this day. Religious faith and practice cover much ground and are not confined to an official set of laws and statutes. Much of religious practice is the result of individual, familial, and communal activities that become ritualized and institutionalized over time. The problem prophetic religion in the Bible seems to have with folk religion, however, is that much of folk religion is rooted in the pagan religions of Israel's neighbors, which to the prophets are the main enemy of monotheism. An early example of pagan folk religion is reported in the story of Rachel who on her journey with Jacob to the Land of Canaan takes along small figurines known as *terafim*, which represent home deities to which she, as a young woman, is apparently attached. A similar story will be told centuries later about Michal, King Saul's daughter. Then, at the end of the monarchic period, at the time of the prophet Jeremiah, we hear that the women of Jerusalem worship a female home deity known as the "Queen of Heaven," a worship which they take with them to Egypt after the destruction of Jerusalem. Such stories make it abundantly clear that folk religion was widely practiced among the Hebrew tribes, and that the prophets who represented the one and only God of Israel and of the universe dedicated their lives to the seemingly impossible task of weaning their people away from such practices and elevating them to a higher spiritual level.

WAS KING DAVID A PROPHET?

Having lost faith in Saul, the prophet Samuel crowns the young David as the second king of Israel. David is in a class by himself in the Bible and also in world history. It is surprising that despite his preeminence as the greatest king Israel ever had, the only physical evidence of his existence we have to date is the inscription "the House of David," found in an archeological excavation in Israel in 1994, which refers to his descendants rather than to himself as a king. Be that as it may, unlike Saul who always seemed to be at the mercy of Samuel, David establishes a direct and intimate relationship with God. In the popular mind of Israel and the world, David, as his name indicates, is God's beloved. This is how he is perceived by Jews, Christians, and Muslims alike. The New Testament makes him the ancestor of Jesus. To the Muslims he is a prophet. The Jews have gone a step further and made him the progenitor of the future messiah or perhaps even the very messiah himself who would redeem the world. And the biblical prophets keep reminding us that the House of David will rule forever. David is second only to Moses in the prominence he is given in the Bible. Moses's story runs through four books (Exodus to Deuteronomy), while David's story runs through three books (1 Samuel to 1 Kings). David is also credited as the main author of the book of Psalms, which is the main source of both Jewish and Christian prayer.

Unlike the other two religions, Judaism does not look upon David as a prophet. The official prophet of his time was Nathan, while David spent his life mainly as a warrior who shed much blood in consolidating the Hebrew kingdom. The Bible portrays David as having many human failings, most blatantly the seduction of Bathsheba and the dispatching of her husband, Uriah the Hittite, to die in battle. God seems to forgive David more than once, but not before punishing him for his sins. And God speaks to him on a rather regular basis; that is, unless the text was rewritten to sound that way. Moreover, David seems to be quite adept at folk religion, acting as one of his subjects, while paying profuse homage to the one and only God. In short, the stories about David are full of contradictions, none of which stopped people from embracing him as possibly the most beloved personality in world history.

I propose that David, like Moses, is in a class by himself. While Moses is the liberator and the lawgiver who stands apart from all subsequent prophets, David is Israel's greatest king who has a unique relationship with God and stands apart from all the other kings and prophets. In our search for the meaning of prophecy, we do not look to either Moses or David for answers. The answer seems to lie elsewhere.

SOLOMON AND THE BREAKUP OF THE KINGDOM:
A PROPHETIC VIEW

While the prophets without an exception accepted the special relationship between God and David and the permanence of the House of David, how did they feel about his illustrious son and successor, Solomon?

Before we attempt to answer this question, we should ask another equally compelling question: Why is it important to know what the prophets thought about a particular king?

As was mentioned at the outset, the prophets envisioned a utopian world of peace and harmony, which would begin with the small nation of Israel. This will become clearer when we turn to the era of the literary prophets in the latter part of the history of the Hebrew monarchy. The key player in this vision was the king, who was anointed as the one who enforced God's will on earth. In Hebrew, the noun "messiah" (*mashiah*), the emissary of God who brings redemption, is derived from the verb "to anoint" (*mashah*). The first king fails to implement God's will, while the second, David, becomes in time the one on which the prophets peg their hopes. Solomon, the third king of Israel, is the one who builds the Holy Temple in Jerusalem. Surely he should have had a great impact on the prophets. And yet, the prophets who live after his time seem to ignore him altogether. The Bible pays great tribute to him as "the wisest of all people." Later generations believe him to be the author of the Song of Songs, Proverbs, and Ecclesiastes. In his time the kingdom reaches its apex. And yet he is not associated with anything messianic and does not play any part in the utopian vision of the prophets. What went wrong?

A careful analysis of the Solomonic career may explain this prophetic snub. Solomon might have been the most magnificent of all the kings of Israel, and he did build the house which, people believed, was the place where God's presence dwelled. But at the same time he set back the utopian vision of the prophets in an irreversible way. He did so because he got carried away with his own wisdom and his great good fortune. (Here again, ironically, we have found no written or artefactual evidence of the grandeur of Solomon's reign; in the mid-twentieth century some archeologists thought they had found his mines and stables, only to be proven wrong by later tests and explorations.) As a result, he married many foreign women who brought their pagan practices to Jerusalem and set monotheism back; he pressed his subjects into service to work on his grandiose projects, and at the same time he exacted high taxes from them, which resulted in the northern tribes of Israel breaking away from the kingdom; and he vitiated the great promise the prophets envisioned for their people. One could argue that Solomon had a golden opportunity to help realize the utopian vision of the prophets, but he forfeited it, and it was downhill from then on for the remaining four centuries of the period of the kings. One is reminded of the words of the prophet Jeremiah:

> Let not the wise glory in his wisdom,
> And let not the mighty glory in his might,
> And let not the rich glory in his wealth.
> But let him glory who knows me,
> Who knows that I am Adonai,
> Who does mercy and justice and
> Righteousness in the land,
> For this is what I want, says Adonai. (Jer. 9:22–23)

The biblical text and later on rabbinic tradition give Solomon full credit for his knowledge and wisdom, which made him "the wisest of men" and one who could even speak the language of the animals and the plants. But his wisdom was the wisdom of the natural world, not the wisdom of piety. Unlike his father David, with whom God communicated freely and spontaneously, Solomon only saw God in a dream, and in the end God let Solomon know that he had failed to live up to his anointed mission and that because of his failing, the kingdom would be split in two.

Once the kingdom split, the utopian vision of the prophets had to be deferred. Its target date became the elusive and mysterious "end of days" rather than any time during the reign of the House of David.

THE AGE OF ELIJAH

The most dominant prophetic personality during the first century of the divided kingdom is Elijah. This prophet lives in the Northern Kingdom during the reign of King Ahab and his Phoenician wife, Jezebel, about a century after the time of King Solomon. The seeds Solomon had sown by marrying foreign wives and letting their pagan gods take root in his kingdom have now resulted in an existential threat to Israel's God posed by Jezebel's extermination campaign against God's prophets, whom she seeks to replace with the prophets of her own god, Baal.

The prophets on both sides of the conflict number in the hundreds. Who exactly are the prophets of Baal is not very clear. Most likely, they are court functionaries in charge of divination, whose task it is to advise the king on important matters of state, particularly whether or not to go to war. The prophets of Adonai fulfill a similar function, except that they seek the answer in the word of the God of Israel, and are expected to live according to the laws of the Torah. Jezebel engages in a ruthless campaign to eliminate the Israelite prophets and nearly succeeds in driving them away from the center of power, namely, the capital city of Samaria.

Along comes Elijah to save the day. A strange, hairy loner who hails from Gilead, a remote province of the kingdom on the other side of the Jordan, Elijah proves to be a formidable foe to the queen. He is a miracle worker who can bring about drought or rain, and a healer who can revive a dead child. He challenges the prophets of Baal to the supreme test of bringing fire down from heaven to consume an animal offering upon a stone altar to prove the power of their god. They fail, and in turn Elijah performs the miracle and inspires the crowd to support him in slaughtering 450 prophets of Baal. When Jezebel hears about the massacre of her prophets, she issues a decree to kill Elijah. The prophet escapes to the place in the desert where God gave the Torah to Moses, and there he has a magnificent revelation when he hears the voice of God speak to him after a storm in a "still small voice." Unlike Moses, who brings down the tablets of the law in the midst of a deafening thunderstorm and what seems to be an earthquake, Elijah has a private, low-key interview with God. He is not sent on a mission to renew the covenant between God and Israel, but rather to intensify the campaign to root out idolatry among the people of the Northern Kingdom of Israel. God tells Elijah,

> Go back the way you came, to the wilderness of Damascus, and when you get there anoint Hazael as king of Aram. Also anoint Jehu son of Nimshi as king of Israel. And anoint Elisha son of Shaphat of Abel-Meholah to succeed you as a prophet. Whoever escapes the sword of Hazael shall be slain by Jehu, and whoever escapes the sword of Jehu

shall be slain by Elisha. I will leave in Israel only seven thousand, every knee that has not knelt to the Baal and every mouth that has not kissed him. (1 Kings 19:15–18)

This short passage encapsulates the life mission of Elijah and his successor, Elisha. Unlike the later prophets, they do not preach and teach. Rather, they are soldiers in the service of their God. They will go to any length to physically destroy the prophets of Baal and reinstate the faith of their God. In short, like David who is a mighty warrior with much blood on his hands, Elijah is God's warrior. He has God's ear, and he becomes the dominant prophet of his time.

Next to King David, Elijah may be the most beloved biblical personality in Jewish history. Little children love him because he is an invisible guest at the Passover Seder, when he is supposed to slip into the house to taste of the wine from a special ceremonial cup set aside for him, known as Elijah's cup. A special chair called Elijah's chair is set up for him at the circumcision ceremony. At the end of the Sabbath he is invoked with a special song. And, most importantly, he is believed to be the one who will arrive on earth to announce the coming of the Messiah, the son of David. This belief is derived from the closing verse of the last prophetic book of the Bible, the book of Malachi: "Behold, I will send the prophet Elijah to you before the coming of the awesome, fearful day of Adonai" (Mal. 3:23). Thus, two biblical personalities, a king and a prophet, are joined together in the collective messianic vision of the Jewish people. This raises a question: Is Elijah the pivotal prophet in the history of biblical prophecy?

In the Talmud, the vast collection of rabbinic disputations known as the Oral Law (which complements the Torah, or the Written Law), many discussions end up unresolved. The rabbis of the Talmud refer to this situation by using the acronym *teku*, which means Elijah, when he arrives on the eve of the messianic age, will solve all unsolved questions. In other words, in Judaism Elijah is the official prophet who has all the answers. Thus, perhaps in an eschatological sense, Elijah is the one who has the answers to our questions. But not here, not now, and rather at "the end of days." This does make sense when we begin to realize that Elijah, as well as his disciple and successor, Elisha, and their particular prophetic age, belong more to the realm of folk religion than to the context of moral compulsion where our search for the meaning of prophecy is taking place. Like Moses and his successor, Joshua, Elijah and Elisha are miracle workers. If we discount their miracle working as legends, and if we go past their struggle with the prophets of Baal, not much else is left. The only example of moral compulsion on the part of Elijah is the story of Naboth the Jezreelite whom Jezebel puts to death so that her husband, Ahab, may take over Naboth's field that abuts on the grounds of the king's palace, whereupon Elijah addresses the king and pronounces the famous words "You murder and then you inherit?" (1 Kings 21:19).

Elijah is both a folk hero and a messianic figure who, along with his disciple Elisha, stands apart from other prophets. The Bible makes them more creatures of legend than credible historical personalities. In the end, they do not succeed in rooting out paganism, nor, with all their political machinations, are they able to change the character of the monarchy in the Northern Kingdom. All the kings who follow Ahab are described by the biblical author as failed leaders who lead their people astray. Finally, a century after the time of Elisha, the kingdom of the north is destroyed by Assyria (722 BCE) and the ten tribes of the north are lost, leaving only one sovereign tribe in the southern kingdom of Judah. This opens the door to the classical period of the prophets known as the literary prophets, the ones who have left us written records of their prophecies.

WHAT HAVE WE LEARNED THUS FAR ABOUT PROPHECY?

By now we have covered a period of four centuries in the biblical annals. During this period three prophetic personalities stand out— Moses, Samuel, and Elijah. Each one of them has a very distinctive mission. Moses's dual task is the liberation of the Hebrew slaves from Egyptian bondage, and the delivery of the Torah at Mount Sinai. Samuel's dual task is the unification of the Hebrew tribes, and the crowning of a king over them. Elijah's dual task is the destruction of the cult of Baal and its so-called prophets, and the restoration of the worship of the God of Israel. All three are spiritual leaders who are acting primarily as political activists. Each one of them is a distinctive personality created, so to speak, by the circumstances of his time. They all rise to the challenge of their time, and they all fulfill their mission as best they can. They are accorded a special place in the pantheon of the biblical prophets, but they are sui generis rather than prototypical. During this entire time span the role of the prophet is not clearly defined, and it undergoes various permutations. At the heart of that role is the interaction between the human and the divine, which is never fully clear.

One important thing that should be pointed out is the frequency of war and violent conflict at all levels—internal, across borders, regional, and between empires during this entire time. We do not hear of a single year of peace during all those centuries. In fact, there is an expression in the Bible which refers to springtime as "the time of the coming out of the kings" (1 Chron. 20:1). In other words, as soon as the weather is warm enough for outdoor activities, the kings come out with their armies to start a war, year in and year out. This sad reality, which has not changed too much since those days, impacts on the activities of the prophets and further complicates the problem of understanding the purpose of prophecy.

It would seem that the period we have covered thus far is a pre-prophetic period, setting the stage for what we might call the time of the prophets of the word, or the literary prophets, namely, the ones who have left us a written record—a rather short period in history of a little over two centuries, yet of incalculable significance in world history. We will now turn to those prophets, who are the focus of our search for the meaning and purpose of prophecy.

HOW "HISTORICAL" IS PROPHETIC HISTORY?

The process of writing down the Bible begins in the seventh century BCE, around the time of the prophet Jeremiah, centuries after the time of Abraham, Moses, David, Solomon, Samuel, and Elijah. To what extent these major biblical personalities are historical figures or how much of what the Bible tells us about them is historical fact is yet to be determined. But this also applies to all of ancient history until that time. Historiography, or the systematic study of history as we know it today, begins in Greece in the fifth century BCE, near the end of the Hebrew prophetic period, when biblical history also becomes more grounded in historical fact, as evidenced by archeological discoveries of recent

times. Prior to that time, people relied for the most part on oral traditions that were passed on from generation to generation and were often
embellished or exaggerated to suit the purposes of the person or the
people telling the story. Official records of major events such as armed
conflicts were kept by the ruling class, and as we can tell from ancient
inscriptions and records from places like Egypt and Mesopotamia,
these records served more for propaganda than for keeping an accurate
account. Accounts of such statistics as enemy casualties or a king's lon-
gevity were magnified to a point of bearing little resemblance to reality.
The key events mentioned in the Bible from the time of Abraham to the
time of Moses and the first kings of Israel were not recorded at the time
of their occurrence. They reflect the life of a nomadic people, and they
were written down centuries later. They became a mixture of distant
historical memory laced with literary elements added by fervent believers and enthusiastic writers.

The problem of accurate and reliable historiography is still with us
today. In recent years we have seen a major trend among historians to
cast doubt on historical records and methodologies, which are often
regarded as tendentious and self-serving, and efforts are being made to
reexamine such records or devise new methodologies (such as visual
history, for example) to arrive at a more objective understanding of
history. A good example of this trend are the so-called new historians in
Israel, who have undertaken to rewrite the history of the birth of the
State of Israel and the events and outcome of the 1948 War between
the Jews and the Arabs. Having experienced those events firsthand, it is
clear to me that in their zeal to be objective or to be fair to the other
side, some of those historians have missed the mark, and rather than
improve on the official Israeli record, they have muddied the waters of
their own history.

Furthermore, since the Enlightenment and the French Revolution
several major schools of thought have held sway concerning the nature
and driving forces of human history. Some philosophers of history lean
heavily on the role of the leader, such as a Napoleon or a Frederick the
Great, in shaping history. Others look at class struggle, such as the
assault on the Old Regime in Europe, as the moving force in history.
Some believe history to be guided by divine providence, while others
think in purely materialistic terms. Some contemporary historians, notably Arnold Toynbee in his book *A Study of History*, offer a theory of

the rise and fall of civilizations, which postulates that civilizations follow an inevitable path of rise and fall. Since Jewish civilization, which continues to reemerge throughout history, does not fit into his theory, Toynbee has concluded that this civilization is actually a "fossil," which only has the appearance of a living civilization. What becomes clear is that man is yet to arrive at a truly objective and a universally accepted understanding of history.

How does the prophetic view of history fare in the light of the various theories and methodologies of historians of the last twenty-six centuries, from Herodotus to Toynbee?

While history for the prophets, especially what to them was ancient rather than more recent history, often bordered on mythology, they had a very strong sense of the flow and direction of history. They were extremely sensitive to the events of their time and of the past. They were constantly examining those events through the prism of their prophetic vision. They looked for signs in those events to determine the shape of things to come, and they examined their people's behavior in the context of contemporary events. A perfect example of this attitude is found in the opening prophecies of Amos concerning the actions of Israel and Judah and their neighboring nations (Amos 1:3–2:9), in which the prophet sees cause and effect in the way all these nations went astray and the way they brought upon themselves divine retribution. While one could argue Amos's teleological view or his theodicy, there is little reason to doubt the accuracy of his reporting of those events. They were deeply engraved in the collective memory of his contemporaries, and they became part of the lore of the people of the region.

One could view the prophets' understanding of history as a composite of the various theories that have evolved over time. Let us examine some of those theories.

The Theory of the Great Leader

While the prophets did not see great leaders as determining the course of history, they placed great importance on the role of good political and spiritual leaders in guiding the people and the role of the bad ones in leading them astray. Jeremiah sees Moses and Samuel as great spiritual leaders who had the power to intercede with God on behalf of their erring people (Jer. 15:1), while he treats harshly the false prophets who mislead the people. The kings of the prophetic era are always under scrutiny by the prophets, and only a handful of them seem to measure up to the prophets' high expectations. For the prophets, the idea of the righteous king becomes embodied in a future descendant of the House of David who will do God's bidding and bring redemption to his people.

To the prophets, great leaders are instruments of God's will that guides human history. Both the evil they do, as in the case of Nebuchadnezzar who destroys Jerusalem and exiles its people, and the good they do, as in the case of King Cyrus of Persia who lets the Judeans return to their city and rebuild their temple, reflect the divine will.

The Theory of Class Struggle

The prophets are deeply aware of the plight of the weak classes of society, and they put great emphasis on social justice as a way to preserve the physical and spiritual health of society. Social decay, which they closely associate with paganism, leads to the fall of societies. No one has put it better than Amos who predicts the fall of Samaria for selling the poor for a pair of shoes. What determines the course of history is not great leaders leading great armies and making great conquests. It is the social behavior of those who have the power and the wealth and are willing to help those less fortunate than they and to exercise justice and compassion. Jeremiah inveighs against the evil king Jehoiakim who robs and oppresses his people and lives in luxury, and reminds him of his righteous father, King Josiah, who enjoyed a time of peace and prosperity because he ruled with justice.

> Woe to him who builds his house by unrighteousness,
> And his upper rooms by injustice;
> Who makes his neighbors work for nothing,
> And does not give them their wages;
> Who says, "I will build myself a spacious house
> With large upper rooms,"
> And who cuts out windows for it,
> Paneling it with cedar,
> And painting it with vermilion.
> Are you a king
> Because you compete in cedar?

Did not your father eat and drink
And do justice and righteousness?
Then it was well with him.
He judged the cause of the poor and needy;
Then it was well.
Is not this to know me?
Says Adonai. (Jer. 22:13–16)

The Theory of the Rise and Fall of Civilizations

The literary prophets witnessed the rise and fall of civilizations all around them. They lived during the time of the fall of two major empires, Assyria and Babylon, which were so powerful they seemed to be destined to last for centuries. They understood that those empires carried within themselves the seeds of their own destruction because of moral corruption and because of the worship of false gods. What was true in their time is still true today. In our time empires have disappeared, most notably the Soviet Union, which pursued social justice in theory but not in practice, and which was militarily so powerful that few people expected it to disintegrate when it did.

The prophets understood that this cycle of rise and fall would continue well into the future, but at the same time they envisioned a time when, to quote Isaiah, "Nation shall not lift up sword against nation, neither shall they learn war anymore" (Isa. 2:4).

The Cyclical Nature of Jewish History

Perhaps the greatest historical insight the prophets possessed was the difference between the rise and fall of civilizations and the cyclical nature of Jewish civilization. The literary prophets lived during a very precarious time in their people's history. Yet they all knew that the People of the Covenant traveled a different route than other people. The covenant had no time limit. It was timeless. Their people could bring upon themselves destruction and exile, but there would always be a return. The Babylonian destruction and exile was not the end. Nor was the Roman destruction of the Second Temple. The ten tribes were lost. The Jews of Spain were expelled. The Jews in the Soviet Union seemed about to disappear. And the Holocaust perpetrated by the Germans seemed to deal the Jews a mortal blow. But Jewish life as of this writing is flourishing once again in Israel and around the world. One can only marvel how people who lived at a time when it was hard to tell history from mythology could have had such an insight.

In asking the question "How historical is 'prophetic history'?" the answer seems to be best expressed not in examining it in the light of any particular theory of history, of which we have many, but in considering the fact that the Jewish people and their prophetic legacy are still here today despite all those who rose and still rise to destroy them. As we saw in the above analysis of some key theories of history that emerged in the past two hundred years, the prophets' instincts about the nature and direction of history were sound.

2

THE EARLY PROPHETS OF THE WORD

WHY DID THEY START WRITING IT DOWN?

There have been several profound, revolutionary transformations in Jewish history. They seem to happen quite suddenly, within a period of a few years, and are difficult to explain according to the laws of history, sociology, psychology, and so on. During Moses's lifetime, Hebrew slaves became a free people who embraced a new faith. During Samuel's lifetime, the Hebrew tribes became a unified people who went on to become a powerful nation. After the time of Elijah and Elisha, prophets in Israel completely changed from militant prophets who were healers and miracle workers, and who fought their pagan counterparts, to a new breed of prophet who did not focus on healing or miracle working but who brought along a new vision, and whose words, at least in some instances, were written down and preserved for all time. This phenomenon of sudden change continues in Jewish history to this day. A recent example is the transformation of the Jewish people after World War II from a nonmilitaristic ethnic group scattered around the world into a people who for the third time in their history returned to their ancestral land and were able within a few short years to develop a strong, highly advanced nation with one of the most formidable military forces in the world.

The phenomenon of literary prophets, who flourished from the eighth to the sixth century BCE, is not easy to explain. Before we start looking for an answer, let us introduce in chronological order the sixteen prophets who left us written records.

Eighth century

Amos
Hosea
Jonah
Isaiah
Micah

Seventh century

Jeremiah
Zephaniah
Habakkuk
Nahum
Obadiah

Sixth century

Ezekiel
Second Isaiah
Joel
Hagai
Zechariah
Malachi

It should be emphasized at the outset that these men were not professional writers. The professional writers of their time were the scribes. The scribes played a central role in the ancient Middle East as record keepers and transcribers of legal, military, royal, and sacred texts, and they performed other official duties of an administrative nature. Famous among the Judean scribes of the period was Baruch ben Neriah, who faithfully served the prophet Jeremiah, copying his prophecies and acting as his private secretary. Typically, the prophet would appear in public and speak out, most likely repeating his message over and over again over a period of time to different audiences. It is hard to believe that everything was recorded when, in fact, what we have from all but three of the prophets are fragments, sometimes only a page or two. But clearly prophecies that either made a great impression or had an impact were recorded, or perhaps even committed to memory at first. When Jeremiah is put on trial for his life for prophesying that the Temple will be destroyed, someone in the audience quotes in his defense a verse from the prophet Micah, who lived over a century earlier, making the case that Micah had made the same prediction but was not punished. The same Micah is quoted as saying, word for word, what is perhaps Isaiah's most famous prophecy, the vision of the end of days, when universal peace will prevail.

Still, why did society during the period of the literary prophets make it a point to have those prophecies written down? Why were not the words of a Samuel or an Elijah collected in a book bearing their name, as happened with their successors, instead of being only alluded to in the context of the stories of the monarchy? After all, there were scribes in those days as well, and various kinds of records were kept, including the annals of the kings and various sacred texts.

One can only speculate. One explanation might be that the practice of collecting the utterances of a prophet and putting them in a book bearing the prophet's name came into vogue after the destruction of the Northern Kingdom in 722 BCE. Up until that time, prophecy dealt mainly with the here and now. Prophets like Samuel and Elijah were concerned with the events of their time. Moreover, the prevailing belief among the people was that God would protect the People of the Covenant no matter what. The prospect of national destruction and exile was not taken seriously. All this changed with the fall of Samaria and the exile of the ten tribes of the north. While many in the remaining small kingdom of Judah continued to believe that Judah, the home of the Holy Temple of Jerusalem where God's presence dwelled, would endure, prophets like Isaiah and Micah and, later on, Jeremiah knew better. A profound change took place. Prophets began to set their sights on the future. It was no longer a Samuel reprimanding Saul or an Elijah excoriating Ahab. Now the prophecies were directed as much at generations yet to come as at one's contemporaries. To do so, it was necessary to put things down in writing to ensure that those words would help those not yet born, who would use them when the time came for guidance and inspiration.

In this author's opinion, we are now entering the most critical period in biblical history. If Jewish history had ended in 722 BCE with the fall of the Northern Kingdom of Israel, monotheistic civilizations might not have come into being. When we speak of prophetic Judaism, we are alluding to the above list of sixteen prophets, of whom some are by necessity more important than others. Here we find the vision of man transcending the common evils of greed, war, injustice, arrogance, and untruthfulness. Here is where we begin to look for answers to the problems that still beset us today. Here is where the prophets of Israel cease to be tribal and territorial, and become universal. Here is where they begin to provide, to use the words of the Second Isaiah, a "light to the nations."

AMOS AND THE PAIR OF SHOES

A few decades before the fall of the Northern Kingdom of Israel, a farmer from a town on the edge of the Judean desert near Jerusalem appears before the people of the north and pronounces dire prophecies not only about them, but also about their neighboring nations and about his own native Kingdom of Judah. His message is simple, but its implications are profound. The evil committed by nations and by individual people does not go unpunished. Amos lists historical events related to Damascus, Gaza, Tyre, Edom, Ammon, and Moab in which these cities and nations showed cruelty and treachery for which they would be punished with destruction and exile. He then turns to his own Judean people and accuses them of forsaking the laws of their God, for which they will be punished by seeing destruction in Jerusalem. Finally he turns to his listeners in Samaria and says,

> For these three sins of Israel,
> For the four, I will not reverse it:
> For they sold the righteous for money,
> And the poor for a pair of shoes. (Amos 2:6)

At first blush there seems to be a great discrepancy between the crimes imputed to the nations, who have committed heinous acts against entire populations, and the social sins of the local audience, who behave unethically toward the weaker members of society. But here lies the great social message of Amos and his successors, which echoes earlier messages of prophets such as Nathan accusing King David of stealing the "poor man's ewe lamb," namely, taking Bathsheba away from her husband, Uriah; or Elijah accusing King Ahab of stealing the vineyard of Naboth the Jezreelite. An act of callousness against a weak member of society, such as selling the poor for a pair of shoes, is no less distasteful to God than committing murder. One is reminded of the rabbinical dictum "He who insults his friend in public is like one who sheds blood" (Baba Metziah 58b).

One could argue that this attitude is unrealistic. People sometime say things or do things they do not mean, or which they may not have carefully thought out. The common wisdom is "One is only human," which means we all have our human failings and limitations. And this may be true in an isolated case. But if it becomes the rule rather than the exception, then people are not behaving ethically, and the unethical becomes the norm. In this case society becomes unjust and corrupt, which is how Amos sees the situation in Samaria. The transition of Israelite society from rural life to city life has created a class system where the rich have it all, and the poor are oppressed and have no one to protect them. Amos says to the rich women of Samaria,

> Hear this word, you cows of Bashan
> On the hill of Samaria,
> Who defraud the poor,
> Who rob the needy,
> Who say to your husbands:
> Bring forth and let's carouse. (Amos 4:1)

Needless to say, those women must have taken offense at Amos's words, and complained to their priest, who told Amos to pack up and go back to his land and bother his own people. After all, they were rich and they were entitled to do as they pleased. Not so, Amos replied. He might have quoted to them chapter 19 from the book of Leviticus regarding leaving part of the harvest for the poor. He goes on to say,

> Only you have I known

> Of all the families of the earth,
> Therefore I will call you to account
> For all your iniquities. (Amos 3:1)

In other words, God expects more from the People of the Covenant, not less. To use an old Jewish expression, Jews are expected to be "merciful people, children of merciful people," *rahamanim bnei rahamanim*. Nothing less will do.

What is remarkable about the teachings of Amos is that the more we delve into them the more we realize how timeless his words are. Clearly, he does not speak only to his own generation; he speaks to all generations. His message is as timely today as it was twenty-eight centuries ago. It is in the book of Amos that the full impact of the prophetic message appears for the first time. It is important to note that Amos is a simple farmer from the Judean countryside. He does not belong to the educated classes of Jerusalem or any other major center of learning. His is the voice of the common man who can no longer bear the injustice, hypocrisy, and waywardness all around him. He is overtaken by moral compulsion, and he lashes out, unafraid, his voice full of pain. He puts his life on the line, and when Amaziah, the priest of Bethel, tells him, "Seer, go back to the land of Judah, earn your living there and prophesy there," Amos responds, "I am not a prophet or the son of a prophet [actually, a prophet's disciple]. I am a cattle breeder and a tender of sycamore trees" (Amos 7:10–14).

Amos did not go to a prophet school. Nor did he prepare to be a prophet. One day he heard the lion roar in the wilderness of Judah, and he cried out,

> When a lion roars,
> Who is not afraid?
> Adonai Elohim speaks,
> Who will not prophesy? (Amos 3:8)

He left his work and his home and went north to Samaria. Did God tell him that the Northern Kingdom of Israel was about to fall? Did he understand the geopolitics of his time and know that Assyria was preparing to overrun that kingdom? Did he grasp intuitively that a corrupt society was courting its own doom? We have to keep in mind that Amos was a simple farmer. But like the other literary prophets, he saw beyond what other people saw, and he had a great poetic gift. His words continue to thunder through the ages. In nine short chapters, he says it all. He paints a picture of the corruption and decadence in Samaria that makes one shudder. He mocks his fellow Hebrews for having replaced the one God of the universe with worthless idols. He lets them know that God is the master of all humanity, and that the covenant does not make them better than the people of Ethiopia. God does not discriminate, and God does not have favorites. Punishment is at hand, sooner than anyone realizes.

It appears that people during that time believed in a future event which they called the "day of Adonai" (the old English term is the "day of the Lord"), when God would avenge them of all their enemies. Such a day is indeed coming, Amos tells them. But it is exactly the opposite of what you are expecting. God will come to punish you for your sins, which have now exceeded all boundaries. The day of Adonai is going to be your judgment day.

Amos does not perform any miracles. His mission is to let the people know how God is disappointed in them. It is clear to him that the fate of the Northern Kingdom is sealed. There is no turning back. He manages, however, to conclude his oracles with a prophecy of consolation.

> A time is coming, Adonai declares,
> When the plowman will meet the reaper,
> And the treader of grapes the sower,
> And the mountains will drip with wine,
> And all the hills shall melt.
> I will restore my people Israel
> And they shall build the desolate cities
> And live in them.
> And they shall plant vineyards
> And drink their wine
> And plant gardens
> And eat their fruit.
> And I will plant them on their land
> And they shall no longer be uprooted,
> From the earth which I have given them,
> Says Adonai your God. (Amos 9:13–15)

One could argue that what saved the Jewish people from extinction was their ability to preserve prophecies such as these that put them in a very bad light. The ability to take criticism and to learn from one's mistakes makes for human survival and growth. On Yom Kippur the Jew says, "Because of our sins we were exiled from our land." Following the time of the prophets, the fall of Jerusalem, and the Babylonian Exile, the Jews took responsibility for their wrongdoing, and internalized their national disaster. They brought back with them to their land three generations later the words of the prophets, and they committed them to memory. They attached them to the words of the Torah in the form of a prophetic reading known as *Haftarah*. It became a lesson for all time. "Zion will be redeemed with justice, her penitent ones with righteousness" (Isa. 1:27).

Amos's Understanding of Prophecy

The Bible provides a few glimpses into the mind of the prophet that shed some light on each prophet's understanding of his own role and mission. In the short book of Amos the term "prophet" is used four times.

> And I caused *prophets* to arise from among your sons
> And nazirites from among your young men. (Amos 2:11)

> And you made the nazirites drink wine
> And ordered the *prophets* not to prophesy. (Amos 2:12)

> For Adonai Elohim will not do a thing
> Without having revealed the secret
> To the *prophets*, to God's servants. (Amos 3:7)

> And Amos responded and said to Amaziah:
> I am not a *prophet* or a *prophet's* disciple. (Amos 7:14)

The last statement is perhaps the most famous one. It has been taken to mean that one does not choose to be a prophet, but is rather forced into this role by a power he cannot resist. What can be added here is that Amos is reacting to the general misunderstanding of the role of the prophet. The term "prophet's disciple" or "son of a prophet" may refer to the schools of prophets we encountered earlier during the time of Elijah and Elisha. The term "prophet" itself may refer to a court prophet, who does the bidding of the king (Amaziah tells Amos that he has come to a place where the king's court is, implying that in order to prophesy he must have the permission of the king). Amos, however, receives his authority directly from God, and he cannot be bound by any human authority.

The first and second statements about prophets and nazirites flow from the same argument about the misunderstanding of the role of the prophet. Amos, as do other prophets who follow him, is accusing his people of telling prophets when to speak and when not to speak. The people completely ignore the fact that the prophets are not bound by any human authority and cannot be told what to say or what not to say. He uses the example of the nazirite, a person in biblical times who dedicates his life to God and makes certain vows, such as abstaining from drinking wine. By forcing him to drink wine, people are mocking his vow and compelling him to commit blasphemy. Thus, abusing the nazirite is similar to abusing the prophet, both of which were a common practice during the time of the prophets.

The most difficult of the four statements is the third one, in which Amos tells us that God does not make a move without first disclosing it to a prophet. This seems to limit the authority of God, on the one hand, and to make the prophet privy to all of God's actions, on the other. This view does not hold when seen in the light of other prophetic views on the subject and the experience of other prophets. The traditional commentators as well as rabbinic literature do not shed much light on this puzzling statement, nor do Christian commentaries. It could be that Amos is trying here to stress the role of the prophet as the conduit for God's word when he addresses an audience that is not receptive to his admonitions and exhortations. Indeed, he uses here an esoteric term, *sod*, which in Hebrew simply means "secret," used here in the sense of the secret of the divine word that is shared with the prophets. This is a mystical term used by the Kabbalists to denote knowledge not readily available to the ordinary person. Here we reach the limit of our human knowledge and stand before the locked gates of prophecy.

Not Only Israel

The lessons the Jewish people learned from Amos and his colleagues are not limited to this one people and one faith. They are universal lessons. If Israel is called a "witness to the nations," it is because it has a universal prophetic message that applies to all humankind. Before there can be an end to war, there must be universal justice. In our time an international body founded in San Francisco in 1945 and known as the United Nations has been hard at work seeking to implement universal justice. Such efforts are still faltering, and when one crisis area, such as the Balkans, is brought under control, another crisis area, such as the Sudan, comes to the fore. There are many crisis areas in today's world. But there is also hope. The world has come together in recent years during times of regional crisis, particularly during natural disasters such as the tsunami in Southeast Asia, the earthquake in Haiti, and the mine disaster in Chile. The United Nations has taken a stand against genocide. There is still much to do, but the words of Amos and his colleagues continue to resonate in today's world. No nation, Amos reminded us, has a license to ignore the rule of law and the rights of the least fortunate of its people. Jesus said, "Whatever you do to the least of my brothers you do to me" (Matt. 25:40). If only the world could learn how to live by these words!

THE RAGE OF HOSEA

Hosea lived and prophesied right before the fall of Samaria. He was a very angry man. He was so angry at his people in the Northern Kingdom that he did something no other prophet had ever done. He married a prostitute named Gomer, daughter of Diblaim, who bore him a son whom he named Jezreel, after the Valley of Jezreel that runs between Samaria and the Galilee where, according to Hosea, evil was committed by the king of Israel. Gomer then bore him a daughter whom he named Lo-Ruhamah, or "one who is not pitied," to let the people know that God would no longer have mercy on them. Finally she bore him a son whom he named Lo-Ami, or "not my people," to let everyone know that God no longer saw Israel as God's people. In other words, he turned his private life into a living metaphor of the waywardness of his people and their king. The evil they committed was both moral and spiritual. The moral evil was the same Amos had inveighed against—absence of justice and widespread corruption. The spiritual evil was the worship of foreign idols, mainly the Canaanite and Phoenician Baal. In other words, the war Elijah and Elisha had waged against Baal worship a century earlier did not yield the expected results. The

people, the prophet argued, were doomed. Hosea was beside himself
with pain and indignation. His actions elicited the following response
from his people: "The prophet is a fool; the man of the spirit is mad"
(Hosea 9:7).

Hosea is all heart. Like Amos, he is a very sensitive poet. He does
not take the covenant of marriage between a man and a woman lightly.
Quite to the contrary, he considers marriage the most sacred of covenants. He tells us that God makes him marry a prostitute to shock his
own people into recognizing the great evil they have committed. Their
evil consists of a betrayal of the covenant between God and Israel, a
covenant Hosea compares to a marriage. God, the husband, gave Israel,
the bride, a marriage contract. The wife violated the contract by whor-
ing after foreign gods. The whole book of Hosea, all of its fourteen
short, angry chapters, is infused with the image of the unfaithful wife. It
is a *cri de coeur*, a cry from a broken heart, which will continue to
reverberate in the prophecies of later prophets such as Jeremiah and
Ezekiel, both of whom will continue to develop the theme of the
treacherous woman who exposes herself on every hill and under every
green tree, symbols of Near East paganism. The covenant between God
and Israel—the God who took Israel out of the house of bondage, out
of Egyptian slavery, and gave Israel laws to live by and a land flowing
with milk and honey—was broken and had been violated by each suc-
cessive generation in Israel and in Judah. And so the end is near.

The book of Hosea concludes with the words

> Return, O Israel, to Adonai your God,
> For you have stumbled in your iniquity.
> Take words with you and return to God.
> Say to Him: Forgive all guilt,
> And accept that which is good,
> Instead of bullocks we will pay with
> The offering of our lips. (Hosea 14:2–3)

The concept of a return to God, or *teshuvah*, is a prophetic concept
promoted by prophets like Hosea that became a central concept of
Jewish faith. God is a God of forgiveness, always waiting for the sinner
to repent and make amends, so as to have a fresh start. We saw it at the
end of the book of Amos, and we see it here. It becomes even more
prominent with later prophets like Jeremiah who says, "Return, mis-
chievous children, And I will heal your mischief" (Jer. 3:22).

Man, endowed with free will, is always prone to sin. But redemption always awaits him. Far gone as the people are in the time of Hosea, God, like a loving parent, is always waiting for their return. The prophets will reiterate this point over and over again.

Hosea's Understanding of Prophecy

There are six uses in the book of Hosea of the word "prophet."

And the *prophet* shall stumble with you in the night. (Hosea 4:5)
Therefore I have hewed down the *prophets*,
I have slain them with the words of my mouth. (Hosea 6:5)
The *prophet* is a fool; the man of the spirit is mad. (Hosea 9:7)
There are snares wherever the *prophet* goes. (Hosea 9:8)
And I spoke to the *prophets* and granted them many visions. (Hosea 12:11)
God brought Israel from Egypt through a *prophet*,
And through a *prophet* they were guarded. (Hosea 12:14)

Of the above six statements, the only two that are clear are the one in which the people call the prophet a fool and a madman, and the one which refers to Moses who brought Israel out of Egypt as a prophet. The other four are quite obscure, and all the commentators have had to guess at their meaning. The most puzzling of all is the second one, in which God hews down the prophets and kills them. This is quite a harsh statement, and it can be interpreted in various ways. Is Hosea saying that the prophet puts himself in harm's way when he delivers an unpopular message? We have no record of Hosea being attacked or hurt by his people despite the harshness of his words. On the other hand, we do know of several prophets who were put to death.

Hosea is a highly emotional prophet, and his words are often obscure. One could argue that he saw the role of the prophet as that of one who goes to extremes to awaken his contemporaries from their complacency. One wonders if his language was properly understood in his own time, since the problem is not so much with his use of esoteric words, which in his lifetime might have been more readily understood, but rather with his sentence structure and his verbal images, which are often unclear and very hard to decipher. Be that as it may, the text of the book of Hosea can be quite puzzling.

The Problem of Faith

One may ask, Why was it so hard for the people of Israel, six centuries after the Exodus from Egypt and the giving of the Torah at Mount Sinai, to keep the faith in the one God? Why was it so hard to live by the laws of the Torah, which taught justice, faithfulness, loving kindness, and so on?

We could frame the question differently: to judge from the words of prophets like Amos and Hosea, paganism and immorality were widespread among the people of their time. The question is, how widespread? Among the priestly class and the upper class and also among the common people there must have been those who were loyal to God and to the commandments. But we hardly ever hear of such people. The general impression we get from reading the words of the prophets is that there were hardly any such people. How can we account for that?

There is no simple answer to this question, but a few suggestions can be made. First, the problem starts at the top, with the king and his court. Even as great a king as Solomon fails to live by the laws of the Torah, by marrying foreign wives, by indulging in acquiring many horses and operating a vast army, and by oppressing his own people. Lesser kings come under the influence of their pagan neighbors and introduce idolatry into their kingdom. Second, the Hebrews are a relatively small nation surrounded by pagan nations who are bigger and stronger. The belief in one invisible God is more than most of them can grasp, and the power of the folk religion around them is too strong for most of them to resist. The process of weaning them away from paganism and winning them over to monotheism takes centuries. It will take the catastrophe of the fall of the Kingdom of Judah, the destruction of Jerusalem and the Holy Temple, and the exiling of the Judeans to Babylon to give the necessary push for their belief system to finally take hold of their hearts and souls. It is the sad fate of the biblical prophets to live in what is in effect the pre-monotheistic era, and therefore people like Amos and Hosea and their successors are weighed down by the heavy burden of the waywardness of their people, who must first go through the crucible of destruction and exile before they finally find faith.

THE STORY OF JONAH

The book of Jonah is different from all the other books of the prophets in that it is not a collection of prophecies but rather a short story in prose about a prophet who runs away from delivering a prophecy God charges him with. God asks Jonah to travel north to the great Assyrian city of Nineveh and let its inhabitants know that unless they repent God will punish them for their evil deeds. Jonah decides to run away from God, boards a ship in the seaport of Joppa (Jaffa), and sails for Tarshish at the far western end of the Mediterranean Sea, possibly in today's southwestern Spain. God causes a great storm to rock the ship and nearly sink it, and the sailors decide to draw lots to see who among them had committed an evil that caused the storm. Jonah turns out to be the one. He tells the sailors to toss him overboard since he is guilty of disobeying God. They do, and Jonah is swallowed by a great fish. He prays to God from the bowels of the fish, and his life is spared when the fish swims ashore and releases him. Jonah learns his lesson: no one can escape from God.

The story has captured the imagination of people everywhere, and for most people it remains a memorable work of literature. But it goes without saying that it was not included among the books of the prophets for purely literary purposes. The compilers of the books of the prophets must have identified an important prophetic message that convinced them that the story of Jonah belonged among the likes of an Amos or a Hosea. What is that message?

There may be more than one answer, but at least three things seem to jump off the page. The first is the universality of God. When the young David runs away from the ill-tempered King Saul who wants to kill him, he takes refuge among the Philistines, and he asks God how will he be able to worship God in a foreign land. The idea of the territoriality of God in prevalent in the Bible, and apparently Jonah believed that if he went far away, literally to the end of the world of that time, God would not be able to reach him. The lesson here is that there is only one God, and that God is everywhere. The value of this simple story might have been that it could be understood by everyone, includ- ing young children, and it dramatized a belief that is common today but was not common in those days.

The second point that is dramatized in this story is that the one God is the God of all people, and God cares about all people equally. Jonah might have found it unacceptable to save the souls of those who were the enemies of his people, and who did invade his land shortly after his time and exile his people. The lesson here is that God cares about all people, including Israel's enemies, and that the prophet is not tribal or territorial but is called upon to be a prophet for all of God's children, regardless of who they are.

The third is the nature of the prophetic calling. As we were told by Amos, if God speaks, who will not prophesy? A prophet has no choice but to do God's bidding. There is no escaping the prophet's mission.

These three lessons—the universality of God, the equality of all people in the eyes of God, and the ineluctable fate of the prophet—are at the heart of the prophetic teachings. While they may be self-evident to us today, in the time of the prophets they were revolutionary ideas.

ISAIAH AND THE VISION OF WORLD PEACE

Isaiah is widely considered the greatest of all the literary prophets. His poetry, his prophecies, and his visions are unsurpassed. He towers above the prophetic landscape as the highest mountain. One could argue that here is where prophecy reaches its zenith. To Christianity, Isaiah is of vital importance because of passages that have been used as proof text for the veracity of the life story and mission of the Christian savior. To all of humanity, Isaiah is the voice that enunciates the vision of world peace at the end of days. His words deserve careful attention and close scrutiny.

Along with the books of Jeremiah and Ezekiel, the book of Isaiah is one of the three "long" prophetic books. It consists of sixty-six chapters, but only the first thirty-five contain the prophecies of the original Isaiah. The next four chapters are a historical narrative of the interaction between Isaiah and King Hezekiah, which also appears in the second book of Kings. Chapters 40 to 66 take us to another era, namely, two centuries after the time of the first Isaiah, and they are attributed to an anonymous prophet known as the Second Isaiah, or Deutero-Isaiah (some add a third Isaiah as the author of chapters 56 to 66). But details about the life of the actual Isaiah are scant and do not exceed by much the few particulars of the lives of Amos and Hosea. We can assess him mainly by his prophecies, not by his person. And because the book as a whole is such a composite of different authors and different times, we need to focus on what appear to be his main prophecies, teachings, and visions.

Isaiah stands at a turning point in biblical history. He witnesses the fall of the Northern Kingdom, and he is fearful for the fate of his own people in the small kingdom of Judah. He has no doubt that the people of Israel were punished for their sins. His prophecies begin with words that strike like a thunderclap.

> Hear, O heavens, and listen, O earth;
> For God has spoken:
> I reared children and brought them up,
> And they have rebelled against me.
> The ox knows its owner,
> And the donkey its master's crib;
> But Israel does not know,
> My people do not observe.
> Ah, sinful nation,
> People laden with iniquity,
> Offspring who do evil, children who deal corruptly,
> Who have forsaken Adonai,
> Who have despised the Holy One of Israel,
> Who are utterly estranged!
> Your country lies desolate,
> Your cities are burned by fire;
> In your very presence aliens devour your land;
> It is desolate, overthrown by strangers.
> And the daughter of Zion is left
> Like a booth in a vineyard, like a shelter in a cucumber field,
> Like a besieged city.
> If the Lord of hosts had not left us a few survivors,
> We would have been like Sodom,
> And become like Gomorrah. (Isa. 1:1–9)

Did anyone in the history of the world ever speak to his own people similar words? And if anyone did, have any people ever preserved such words?

As was mentioned before, people who have the courage and the humility to make such words sacred and keep them for all time are people who can survive anything. Isaiah could have pointed an accusing finger at God and chastised God for allowing the Northern Kingdom to be destroyed. But he does exactly the opposite. He takes responsibility for the destruction in the name of his own people. We the people are guilty. We have brought it upon ourselves, as did the people of Sodom and Gomorrah.

One can feel Isaiah's pain. Now Zion, that is, the Southern Kingdom, is all alone, all by itself—"the daughter of Zion is left / Like a booth in a vineyard"—a small remnant of its former Davidic and Solomonic glory. How will it survive in an ocean of enemies? Isaiah replies, "Zion will be redeemed with justice, her penitent ones with righteousness" (Isa. 1:27).

Here again we encounter the ideas of repentance, or *teshuvah*, as a return to and reconciliation with God, and of the saving remnant. Isaiah, as other prophets of the literary era, grasps the nature of his people's history. He sees the destruction of the Northern Kingdom, and he sees how the people of Judah are constantly set upon by neighbors such as Edom, Moab, and Ammon, and by the empires of the north and the south, and he understands that destruction awaits Judah as well. It is only a question of time. Yet at the same time he knows that there will always be those among his people who will continue to carry the belief in the one God of the universe, and in the laws of justice and mercy God expects people to live by. Because of those few people of faith, a "remnant" of his people will always survive and will always come back. Here Isaiah is in step with his predecessors, Amos and Hosea, and with those who follow him.

Each Had Six Wings

Isaiah, a member of the upper class in Jerusalem and a respected prophet who has the ear of the king, approaches the Holy Temple one day and has a vision of the divine presence.

In the year that King Uzziah died, I saw Adonai sitting on a throne, high and lofty; and the hem of His robe filled the temple. Seraphs were in attendance above Him; each had six wings: with two they covered their faces, and with two they covered their feet, and with two they flew. And one called to another and said:

Holy, holy, holy is the Lord of hosts;
The whole earth is full of His glory.

The pivots of the thresholds shook at the voices of those who called, and the house filled with smoke. And I said: "Woe is me! I am lost, for I am a man of unclean lips, and I live among a people of unclean lips; yet my eyes have seen the King, Adonai of hosts!" Then one of the seraphs flew to me, holding a live coal that had been taken from the altar with a pair of tongs. The seraph touched my mouth with it and said: "Now that this has touched your lips, your guilt has departed and your sin is blotted out." Then I heard the voice of Adonai saying, "Whom shall I send, and who will go for us?" And I said, "Here am I, send me!" (Isa. 6:1–8)

This is how Isaiah explains his initiation as a prophet. Here, as in the story of the giving of the Torah at Mount Sinai, the contact between the human and the divine produces great fear. Once Isaiah's lips are purified with the live coal, he overcomes his fear and accepts his mission. Unlike a Jonah, who runs away from God's word, or a Moses who is reluctant to accept the charge, Isaiah welcomes it.

Isaiah's predecessor, Amos, has told us that God will not do a thing without first sharing the divine secret with the prophet. Here Isaiah shares what may be the greatest divine secret with the rest of the world. He offers a graphic description of the heavenly court, in which the divine presence is surrounded by the seraphim, the six-winged fiery angels. And here is where human knowledge ends and faith begins. What is interesting to note is that at first God does not speak directly to Isaiah. The ones who speak are the angels, who constantly reaffirm the holiness of God by repeating the triple sanctification "Holy holy holy." And when it is time for Isaiah's consecration, the angel who puts the live coal to his lips is the one who speaks to him and tells him that his sins have been expiated. It is only then that the purged Isaiah hears God speak, saying, "Whom shall I send?" And Isaiah responds, "Here am I, send me!" God proceeds to tell Isaiah to become God's mouthpiece and messenger to the people.

No one else in the Bible, except for Moses, has such a sendoff. It is as if the author of this book is letting us know that Isaiah is being groomed for a supreme prophetic mission that may provide the clue to our search for the meaning of prophecy. What does Isaiah have to say about the human condition? What does man need to redeem himself? How can man overcome the greatest obstacles and find an answer to his prayers? Isaiah, more than any other prophet, provides answers to these existential questions. He is as relentless and as brutally honest as any of the other prophets. But as he chastises his people and the nations of the world, he lets us know where we go wrong and what needs to be done.

Man's Pride

Isaiah lets us know at the outset what it is that holds man back and causes his downfall. In one word, it is pride. It is man's inability to recognize how small he is in the scheme of things, and how little he knows. Isaiah says,

> For Adonai of hosts has a day
> Against all that is proud and lofty,
> Against all that is lifted up and high;
> Against all the cedars of Lebanon,
> Lofty and lifted up;
> And against all the oaks of Bashan;
> Against all the high mountains,
> And against all the lofty hills;
> Against every high tower,
> And against every fortified wall;
> Against all the ships of Tarshish,
> And against all the beautiful craft.
> The haughtiness of people shall be humbled,
> And the pride of everyone shall be brought low;
> And Adonai alone will be exalted on that day. (Isa. 2:12–17)

The message here is clear. Whatever is lofty and beautiful in the universe reflects the work of the creator. Man did not create the mountains or the cedars of Lebanon or the oaks of Bashan. Yet man behaves as though he is God. Man looks at the high mountains and the high trees and instead of seeing the handiwork of God, man sees himself as all-powerful and all-knowing. This refers to the kings and emperors who consider themselves divine, and it refers to all those in power, in high office, or those who possess great wealth. They fail to pay homage to the real source of power and plenty, and they fail to live by the law of justice and mercy.

Human possessions and material success lead to pride. Prophets like Amos and Isaiah expected their people to establish a just and humane society. They expected the teachings of the Torah to result in a social order in which the community took care of the weak, the poor, the elderly, the orphan and the widow, as well as the stranger "who lives in your midst" (Exod. 12:49). This did not happen in either of the two kingdoms. Social justice was nowhere to be found. The rich and the powerful kept indulging themselves, and the rest of the people lived in poverty and had no one to champion their cause. True, things were not much better among Israel's neighbors, or among the subjects of the great empires of the day. But those people did not enter into a covenant to live by the laws of God. They were forced to accept the law of rulers who had little regard for human life. This reality, the prophets realized, could only lead to disaster. Other nations had military superiority. The People of the Covenant were expected to have moral superiority. Without it, they were lost.

Isaiah is equally concerned with the arrogance of his own people and of the rest of the nations, particularly the ruthless Assyrian emperor who terrorizes all the nations he keeps gobbling up. Isaiah sees the Assyrian emperor as a tool in the hands of God to punish Israel, but at the same time he is enraged by his behavior.

> When Adonai has finished all his work on Mount Zion
> And on Jerusalem, he will punish the arrogant boasting
> Of the king of Assyria and his haughty pride.
> For he says: "By the strength of my hand I have done it,
> And by my wisdom, for I have understanding;
> I have removed the boundaries of peoples,
> And have plundered their treasures;
> Like a bull I have brought down those who sat on thrones.
> My hand has found, like a nest,
> The wealth of the peoples;
> And as one gathers eggs that have been forsaken,
> So I have gathered all the earth;
> And there was none that moved a wing
> Or opened its mouth, or chirped."

> Shall the axe vaunt itself over the one who wields it,
> Or the saw magnify itself against the one who handles it?
> As if a rod should raise the one who lifts it up,
> Or as if a staff should lift the one who is not wood! (Isa. 10:12–15)

What we have here is the prophet's universalistic view of God's anger over the arrogance of the pagan world, which also applies to Israel. It is similar to what the ancient Greeks referred to as hubris. The Greeks recognized that hubris leads to man's downfall. Isaiah sees pride as man's undoing. Another prophet, Micah, who lives around Isaiah's time, will tell us in one sentence what God expects of us.

> It has been told you, O man, what is good,
> And what Adonai asks of you,
> But to do justice, and love mercy,
> And walk humbly with your God. (Mic. 6:8)

Walking humbly with God and practicing justice and mercy are the keys to human redemption.

What Does "Walk Humbly" Mean?

Isaiah considers pride the worst pitfall in human affairs. Here his colleague Micah provides the other side of the coin, namely, humility. But what Micah is specifically talking about is walking humbly with God. Here he agrees with Isaiah that man must recognize his insignificance in a universe he did not create, but which does have a creator. Treating God's creation and God's creatures with respect is showing humility. Another way of showing humility is accepting the limits of human knowledge, and accepting the things one does not know and does not understand. When we ask the question whether the prophets heard the voice of God, we can only go so far in our understanding of this phenomenon, but beyond a certain point we run into the unknown. We may or may not choose to believe it, but we need to "walk humbly."

The Utopian World

All throughout time people have been engaged in war. But during the time of Isaiah things were even worse than most other times. The dominant power in the ancient world during the eighth century BCE was

Assyria, centered in upper Mesopotamia, in today's northern Iraq. It was one of the most vicious empires in history. The atrocities the Assyrians committed against people throughout the ancient world rivaled those committed by the Nazis and their allies. They might have been the ones who invented what today we call "ethnic cleansing." To eliminate the national, cultural, and religious identity of smaller nations, the Assyrians brutalized entire populations and exiled them from their land to remote corners of their empire, as they did with the people of the Northern Kingdom of Israel. Isaiah lived at a time of great suffering and dislocation. It was against this backdrop that this remarkable prophet began to have visions of a future, utopian world, which eventually would be sublimated by the monotheistic religions and become a supernatural messianic age. Isaiah, however, does not speak of anything supernatural. He speaks of an age here on earth that will dawn at an unspecified time that he calls the "end of days."

> In the end of days the mountain of Adonai's house
> Shall be established as the highest of mountains,
> And it shall be raised above the hills;
> And all the nations shall flock to it.
> Many people will come and say,
> "Come, let us go up to the mountain of Adonai,
> To the house of the God of Jacob;
> That God may teach us his ways
> And that we may walk in God's paths."
> For out of Zion shall go forth the law,
> And the word of Adonai from Jerusalem.
> God shall judge between the nations,
> And shall arbitrate for many people;
> They shall beat their swords into ploughshares,
> And their spears into pruning-hooks;
> Nation shall not lift up sword against nation,
> Neither shall they learn war anymore. (Isa. 2:2–4)

Elsewhere, Isaiah adds,

> The wolf shall live with the lamb,
> The leopard shall lie down with the kid,
> The calf and the lion and the fatling together,
> And a little child shall lead them.
> The cow and the bear shall graze,
> Their young shall lie down together;

And the lion shall eat straw like the ox.
The nursing child shall play
Over the hole of the asp,
And the weaned child shall
Put its hand on the adder's den.
For the earth will be full
They will not hurt or destroy
On all of My holy mountain;
Of the knowledge of the God
As the waters cover the sea. (Isa. 11:6–9)

These two related visions represent a total departure from Hebrew prophecy in previous centuries. Here we arrive at a new pinnacle where the air is rarified and we have to pause and take a deep breath to take it all in. The first question is, When is this "end of days" to take place? Here we can follow one of two paths: either we can look for the biblical meaning of this term, or we can go along with later interpretations that have sublimated this concept and defined it as either the messianic age (Judaism), the second coming (Christianity), or judgment day (Islam).

In biblical Hebrew the term "end of days," or *aharit ha'yamim*, does not mean finality, or the end of time, but rather a later time, or later in life, or "in generations to come." The first use of the term "end of days" appears in Genesis 49:1, when Jacob, on his deathbed, assembles his sons and tells them what their destiny will be "at the end of days," which means when they each will have given rise to a tribe. In other words, Isaiah is referring to a new era here on earth, when the present era of strife and trouble will come to an end and a new era of world peace and harmony will dawn. When might that age start?

For that age to become a reality, human behavior will have to be modified. Pride, aggression, and self-interest will have to be replaced by humility, tolerance, and fair treatment of others. It is important to point out that Isaiah does not talk about each and every person on earth changing his or her behavior. Rather, he talks about the nations of the world coming together for the purpose of making peace and for learning the divine law that emanates from Jerusalem, when teachings of justice and mercy become universal. We can consider this vision in the light of today's global reality. In order to establish and maintain peace in strife-torn regions of the world, the leading nations who have economic and political influence have to work together and use their combined influence to effect change. Thus, for example, the ethnic cleansing in the Balkans was stopped when the combined forces of NATO and the United States intervened and brought the warring sides together for peace talks. The next step is the establishment of a world order in which principles of human conduct such as the ones enunciated by the prophets are agreed upon and implemented globally. In our time, the human folly of war as mass destruction has led to the invention and use of nuclear weapons. A major effort has been undertaken to do away once and for all with any weapons of mass destruction. This would be a giant step in the direction of Isaiah's vision.

While the "end of days" vision appears sound and plausible, albeit hard to attain, the second vision concerning a peaceable animal kingdom is more problematic since it alters the laws of nature. It has been variably interpreted as a fable, an allegory, or an otherworldly vision. But somehow it seems to be a corollary of the first vision. Impossible as it may sound, I do recall a moment in my recent travels around the world when I felt I was in the peaceable kingdom. It was on the island of Bora Bora in French Polynesia. I went snorkeling with a local guide off a boat in the pristine blue water near the beach. Seagulls kept flying by, and the guide was able to snatch one from the air and pat it and then release it. When we went snorkeling we saw small sharks and stingrays swimming around us with no sign of danger. Well, while on a safari in South Africa three years later I did not see lions eating straw like an ox. But we did drive by a lion family and see a lion cub on the road about to die of starvation. We were told that over seventy percent of those cubs never reach maturity, even in a protected nature preserve like Kruger National Park. There is more to nature than meets the eye.

However one may feel about Isaiah's visions, one thing cannot be denied. Isaiah, as well as his colleagues, deals with three issues that are as central to our existence today as they were twenty-eight centuries ago, namely, poverty, war, and ecology. All three are interrelated. All three confront us today with great urgency. All three require joint action by the nations of the world.

If any of the Hebrew prophets is a prophet for the ages, Isaiah certainly is.

Isaiah: The Turning Point in Biblical Prophecy

Isaiah marks the critical turning point in biblical prophecy. He elevates biblical prophecy from the narrow domain of a small people surrounded by vast nations and empires to a universal vision of the present and the future of the entire human race. This makes him the first truly universal biblical prophet, and it is little wonder that his prophecies played such a crucial role in giving rise to the world's largest religion, namely, Christianity. Isaiah prophesies on a global scale. He begins with his own people, but he quickly shifts his attention to the rest of the world when he says, "And the idols will totally disappear" (Isa. 2:18). It is hard to imagine anyone making a bolder statement than this during Isaiah's lifetime. The idols of Assyria and Babylon and Egypt reigned supreme. The kingdom of the Hebrew tribes or what was left of it was shrinking in size and power. The God of Israel was unknown and incomprehensible to the rest of the world. If anyone was about to disappear, it was the God of Israel. The pagan gods were safe and secure. One may wonder what gave an ecstatic oracle from the hills of Judea the incredible audacity to predict the total demise of the world's gods, while arrogating such powers to his own.

But predict he did, and most likely he expected them to disappear before long, but this did not happen. It would take about a thousand years from the time of Isaiah for the last great idol-worshipping empire, namely, Rome, to disappear. But it did fall, and with it fell all the glorious Greco-Roman gods. The God of Israel, as Pope Benedict points out in his book from which I quoted at the outset, triumphed over the idols through the ministry of a Jew from Galilee named Jesus. The idols of Persia and the Arabian Peninsula, heirs to the gods of the ancient empires of Isaiah's time, also fell when Islam emerged thirteen centuries ago and introduced the God of Israel to this part of the world. No doubt, the sweeping visions and the fervent faith of Isaiah greatly contributed to this course of historical events. It only took a little longer for his predictions to come to pass.

In his remarkable and massive work on the Hebrew biblical faith, partially translated into English as *The Religion of Israel*, the great biblical scholar Yehezkel Kaufmann writes,

The pagan kingdom did not fall. It defeated Jerusalem and destroyed it. But in the fullness of time the faith of Israel put an end to idolatry among many nations and vast populations. This was Jerusalem's victory. . . . The man who would come to represent the faith of Israel to the nations, who would become their redeemer and messiah, died an ignominious death by the hands of the Romans. Roman soldiers wrote on his cross "King of the Jews," showing contempt to the Jews and their "kingdom." A long road of suffering, contempt, hatred and war, from Tiglath Pileser to Pontius Pilate and Nero and Titus. And yet Jerusalem won. In the entire world, wherever Jews were scattered, idolatry came to an end. (*The Religion of Israel*, vol. 3, bk. 1, 259)

In both his prophecies to his own people and to the world Isaiah operates on a grand scale. He looks at his people and at the world he lives in, and he realizes that the God he believes in did not create this world to be run by the likes of the Assyrians and the Babylonians and the rest of the pagan nations of his time. He realizes that God did not mean for Israel to become a declining small nation, a passing episode on the stage of history. For his people, Isaiah envisions a time when the House of David will give rise to a new leader who will surpass all others.

> A shoot shall come out from the stock of Jesse,
> And a branch shall grow out of his roots.
> The spirit of Adonai shall rest on him,
> The spirit of wisdom and understanding,
> The spirit of counsel and might,
> The spirit of knowledge and the fear of Adonai.
> His delight shall be in the fear of Adonai.
> He shall not judge by what his eyes see,
> Or decide by what his ears hear;
> But with righteousness he shall judge the poor,
> And decide with equity for the meek of the earth;
> He shall strike the earth with the rod of his mouth,
> And with the breath of his lips he shall kill the wicked.
> Righteousness shall be the belt around his waist,
> And faithfulness the belt around his loins. (Isa. 11:1–5)

It is interesting to note that Isaiah does not envision a great conqueror or a military hero who will rule over many nations. He describes a world that has moved beyond the rule of power. It is a world where every

human being, no matter how weak or disadvantaged, is given due respect and consideration. It is a world where the true king is not a
human ruler, but the creator of the universe. The verse "with the breath
of his lips he shall kill the wicked" is somewhat obscure, but to judge
from the spirit of this chapter, which culminates with the vision of the
peaceable kingdom ("The wolf shall live with the lamb . . . And a little
child shall lead them" [Isa. 11:6]), the intent here is that evil will be
eliminated by the will of the wise ruler, and "the earth will be full / Of
the knowledge of God / As the waters cover the sea" (Isa. 11:9).

Here again, Isaiah is thinking of a time in the not far-off future, and
of an actual descendant from the royal house of David. Here again, a
major prophecy was not fulfilled as originally intended. It remained a
fond dream, and therefore became open to various interpretations. To
Jews it means something different from what it means to Christians.
The shoot from the stock of Jesse is to Christianity the messiah who
came and will come a second time. To some Jews it is a future messiah
who is yet to come to redeem the world. To others it is a belief in an age
of peace and harmony. But whatever one chooses to believe, the impact
of this prophecy on humanity, like most of Isaiah's prophecies, has been
enormous.

Israel as a Prophetic Nation

In the opening verses of the book of Isaiah, the prophet begins with a
complaint. He says,

> The ox knows its owner,
> And the donkey its master's crib;
> But Israel does not know,
> My people do not observe. (Isa. 1:3)

Here God refers to Israel as "My people." Isaiah, more than any other
prophet, impresses upon his people that they have a mission in this
world, namely, to bring the knowledge of the one God to the rest of the
world. In speaking about the righteous ruler from the stock of David,
the son of Jesse, and the peaceable kingdom he will establish, Isaiah
concludes with the words

> On that day the root of Jesse
> Shall stand as a banner to the nations,

And they will come to him for counsel
And his eternal rest will be honored. (Isa. 11:10)

The so-called Second Isaiah, that unnamed major prophet who lived two centuries after the time of Isaiah, will refer to his people as a "light to the nations." This concept has its roots here, in the prophecies of the original Isaiah. Here we find the turning point in biblical prophecy. No other prophet is more universal than Isaiah who lived in Jerusalem during the time of the fall of the Northern Kingdom of Israel and the exile of the ten tribes, which left Judah in the south "Like a booth in a vineyard, / Like a shelter in a cucumber field" (Isa. 1:8). It was one of the lowest points in the history of his people, but it did not plunge our prophet into despair. He understood that it was all for a purpose. God wanted to teach his people a lesson. God was preparing them for their difficult mission of becoming a prophetic people who could safeguard the word of God and bequeath it to the rest of the world. Here perhaps we have the greatest lesson of biblical prophecy: Changing the world by defeating evil and making the world a place where justice prevails takes people who are animated by the prophetic spirit, who are imbued with the teachings of the prophets, and who are able to overcome the hardships of their national and individual existence. This message will be repeated by the other prophets and will become the rock upon which the Hebrew faith will be established. The God of Isaiah will sustain the Jews through centuries of exile and great suffering until the day when they eventually return to their land. And Isaiah's vision of the end of days will continue to inspire them and the rest of the world.

MICAH'S ECSTATIC OUTBURST

Like Amos, Micah came from the countryside, or the periphery of the Kingdom of Judah, from a town called Moresheth-gath, on the coast near the Philistine border. This is an important biographical detail because at the heart of the prophetic message of the time is the corruption of city life both in Samaria and in Jerusalem and the effect it has on the entire nation. Micah was a younger contemporary of Hosea and Isaiah, and his prophecies echo both. Together with Amos, those four prophets represent the first generation of prophetic giants who try to save their people from themselves, yet who are painfully aware of the impending doom, and as a result lift their eyes to a better future when their people will become reconciled to their faith and will be redeemed. They are also the first to fully grasp the universality of their God, the common fate of the human race, and the total dependence of human well-being on moral conduct. None of them rejects the Temple cult of animal sacrifices, which is mandated by the Torah of Moses. But they are all keenly aware of the futility of ritual without moral rectitude. As we shall see, with Micah this critical belief will reach its peak.

Having said all this, I should forewarn the reader that the short book of Micah (seven brief chapters) is one of the most difficult to understand in the entire Bible, and it has given biblical scholars many headaches. The entire text sounds like one shrill ecstatic outburst, as if coming out of the mouth of someone who was greatly provoked, lost his composure, and became irrational. Toward the end of his tirade Micah says, "I bear God's deep rage" (Mic. 7:9). It is as if God can no longer bear to see the people's conduct and is overcome with rage, and this rage is coming out of Micah's mouth. The problem is that much of what Micah has to say is incoherent, hence the difficulty of following much of his train of thought. What is also very hard to comprehend is how such an outburst was committed to writing, and by whom. Did a scribe follow Micah and write it down? Did the prophet repeat the same oracles until they became engraved in people's memory? How could such an emotional outburst be repeated more than once? There does not seem to be any clear answer. We do know, however, from reading the book of Jeremiah, which describes events about a century after the time of Micah, that people in Jeremiah's time were able to quote Micah, and that his words were taken with utmost seriousness.

What makes all of this even more remarkable is that in the midst of all the raving, Micah manages to utter some words that have had a singular impact on the Jewish people and on humankind, most notably, "It has been told you, O man, what is good . . . But to do justice, and to love mercy, / And to walk humbly with your God" (Mic. 6:8). Indeed, most people identify Micah by these words, which make him sound perfectly rational and a master of the perfect phrase. Throughout his brief book the paradox of eloquence peeking out of what is otherwise a confused discourse is in evidence throughout.

Micah and Isaiah

Like all the other prophets, Micah has his own unique voice, which is evident in his temper and his use of language. But there is an almost uncanny connection between his prophecies and those of his formidable contemporary, Isaiah. If we read his words with Isaiah's book in mind, this becomes evident from the very beginning of chapter 1. Micah begins by summoning the world to listen to God's word. He tells us how God rises from the divine throne in God's Temple in Jerusalem, and what follows is an apocalyptic vision of divine punishment, which begins with Samaria. Here we are reminded of Isaiah's Temple Vision, in which the divine presence is seated upon the throne in the Holy Temple. It is as if Micah is out to reinforce Isaiah's message with greater force and urgency. It is possible that the lad from the coast came to Jerusalem and heard Isaiah prophesy. The prophet of Jerusalem made a great impression on him, and he proceeded to carry his message further and with greater fervor.

Then, in chapter 4, something happens that has little parallel in the writings of the prophets. Isaiah's prophecy of the end of days is repeated by Micah almost word for word, with very slight textual variations. It is as if Micah had committed it to memory, was haunted by it, and made it his own. Moreover, Micah seems to be saying that here is the ultimate truth about the destiny of his people and of the human race. By doing so, he becomes the cofounder of what might be called the Utopian School of Prophecy. Once this vision has taken hold, the Jewish faith and monotheism as a whole will no longer be the same.

A Lover's Quarrel

The main difference between Isaiah and Micah is what might be considered the difference between a patrician and a commoner. Isaiah is a member of the upper class who is able to transcend his high social position and denounce the haughtiness of his people. He himself can be aloof and detached, and he always seems to be in control of the situation. When King Hezekiah needs advice, he is ready to help and his word is respected. With Micah it is the exact opposite. In one passage he seems to be confronting what appear to be court prophets who might have challenged his authority with the following words:

Thus says Adonai concerning the prophets
Who lead my people astray,
Who cry "Peace"
When they have something to eat,
But declare war against those
Who put nothing into their mouths.
Therefore it shall be night to you, without vision,
And darkness to you, without revelation.
The sun shall go down upon the prophets,
And the day shall be black over them;
The seers shall be disgraced,
And the diviners put to shame;
They shall all cover their lips,
For there is no answer from God.
But as for me, I am filled with power,
With the spirit of Adonai,
And with justice and might,
To declare to Jacob his transgression
And to Israel his sin. (Mic. 3:5–8)

All the literary prophets attack what they call "false prophets." This includes court prophets and all those who might be called "prophets for hire," as evidenced by the words "when they have something to eat." But none seems to be as hard-pressed as Micah to prove that these so-called prophets are wrong while he is right, as we see in Micah's statement "But as for me, I am filled with power, / With the spirit of Adonai." One almost senses here feelings of insecurity and inadequacy on the part of Micah, who has to reassure himself that indeed his is the right message.

Micah, like his older contemporary Hosea, is very emotional and given to excess in his utterances and his understanding of both his prophetic mission and of the nature of God's relationship with the people of Israel and Judah. When he speaks of God's disappointment in the people's behavior, it is hard to tell whether he speaks of his own disappointment or that of God. One passage in particular is extremely moving.

Hear what Adonai is saying:
Rise, plead your case before the mountains,
And let the hills hear your voice.
Hear, you mountains, the quarrel of Adonai,

And you enduring foundations of the earth;
For Adonai has a quarrel with his people,
And God will argue with Israel.
My people, what have I done to you?
In what have I wearied you?
Answer me
For I brought you up from the land of Egypt,
And redeemed you from the house of slavery;
And I sent before you Moses, Aaron, and Miriam.
O my people, remember now
What King Balak of Moab devised,
What Balaam son of Beor answered him,
And what happened from Shittim to Gilgal,
That you may know the righteous acts of God. (Mic. 6:1–5)

God seems to be on the verge of tears. God is heartbroken. God is turning to the mountains and to the hills, pleading with them to listen to how God was betrayed by thankless children. God has a quarrel with those wayward offspring. How could they betray their God? Micah recalls the history of the Exodus from Egypt in greater detail than most prophets have. He mentions the three leaders of the Exodus—Moses, Aaron, and Miriam. He alludes to the story of King Balak and his pagan prophet Balaam, who sought to curse and destroy the wandering Israelites but instead had to bless them because of divine intervention, and he alludes to the trek from Shittim east of the Jordan to Gilgal, west of the Jordan, during which time the people sinned but God forgave them and allowed them to enter the Promised Land. In those few words the prophet relates an entire history that shows how God literally raised the Israelites as a forgiving father, the Israelites who in return have turned their backs on God and have completely failed to live by the laws of the covenant.

And so it seems we hear someone crying. Is it God or is it Micah, or both? And then Micah turns to mocking his misguided people, having them say the following words:

With what shall I come before Adonai,
And bow myself before God on high?
Shall I come before Him with burnt-offerings,
With calves a year old?
Will God be pleased with thousands of rams,
With tens of thousands of rivers of oil?

> Shall I give my firstborn for my transgression,
> The fruit of my body for the sin of my soul? (Mic. 6:6–7)

This is a very extreme statement, making the people sound as though they themselves are mocking God and God's prophet. They seem to be saying, Why are those two so angry at us? After all, we do bring sacrifices to the Temple. How much *should* we bring? How much is enough? Should we drown the Temple in rivers of oil? And what follows is the most extreme statement of all: Should I offer my firstborn child as a sacrifice to ingratiate myself to God, that same God who almost made our ancestor Abraham sacrifice his only child? This last statement may also allude to certain kings of Israel who did exactly that, pass their firstborn son through the fire, which the prophets considered the greatest of abominations. And then, almost in the same breath, Micah turns from this extreme language of fire and brimstone to a calm conclusion, which represents his most oft-quoted words.

> He has told you, O man, what is good;
> And what God requires of you,
> But to do justice, and to love mercy,
> And to walk humbly with your God. (Mic. 6:8)

Nowhere in the Bible do we have such a radical shift from extremely emotional, fiery and erratic language to calm and rational words that continue to resonate throughout the ages.

When all is said and done, what comes through this torrent of words is the aching heart of someone who deeply loves his people, and who deeply believes that God loves them more than they can imagine. In this Micah is not alone. He reflects the feelings of all his colleagues, and later on, as we shall see, his words will be echoed in the prophecies of Jeremiah. Both men are nearly crushed by the terrible burden God has laid on their shoulders, yet both lift themselves up and reaffirm their undying faith. Micah concludes with

> Who is a God like you, pardoning iniquity
> And passing over the transgression
> Of the remnant of your possession?
> He does not retain his anger forever,
> Because he delights in showing clemency.
> He will again have compassion upon us;
> He will tread our iniquities under foot.

You will cast all our sins
Into the depths of the sea.
You will show faithfulness to Jacob
And unswerving loyalty to Abraham,
As You have sworn to our ancestors
From the days of old. (Mic. 7:18–20)

A TIME WITHOUT PROPHETS

Between the time of Micah and Jeremiah we have a time gap of seventy years during which period we have no record of any literary prophet. During most of that time, for a period of fifty-five years, the Kingdom of Judah was under the rule of Manasseh, the longest reigning king in the history of the two kingdoms. What makes it particularly odd that voices like those of Micah or Isaiah were not heard during all that time is that we are told in the second book of Kings that Manasseh turned his back completely on the God of Israel and introduced into the Temple all the pagan forms of worship he could possibly assemble. His actions seemed to seal the fate of the kingdom, and one would have expected a prophet like Micah to come along and predict the fall of Judah. The author of the book of Kings makes this prediction anonymously.

> Therefore thus says Adonai, the God of Israel, I am bringing upon Jerusalem and Judah such evil that the ears of everyone who hears of it will tingle. I will stretch over Jerusalem the measuring line for Samaria, and the plummet for the house of Ahab; I will wipe Jerusalem as one wipes a dish, wiping it and turning it upside down. I will cast off the remnant of my heritage, and give them into the hand of their enemies; they shall become a prey and a spoil to all their enemies, because they have done what is evil in my sight and have provoked me to anger, since the day their ancestors came out of Egypt, even to this day.
>
> Moreover, Manasseh shed very much innocent blood, until he had filled Jerusalem from one end to another, besides the sin that he caused Judah to sin so that they did what was evil in the sight of God. (2 Kings 21:12–16)

It is quite possible that the innocent blood Manasseh shed included the blood of the prophets of his time, and that any written prophecies during his reign were destroyed by order of the king (we will see how a later king slashes and burns a scroll containing Jeremiah's prophecies). While this may be implied in the biblical record, we do know that a few short years after Manasseh's death, during the reign of his grandson Josiah, a scroll of the Torah was found hidden in the Temple. This can be taken as an indication that priests or prophets whose loyalty rested with the God of Israel rather than with the idolatrous king had to hide the written word of God from Manasseh's spies. It was, indeed, the impact of his grandfather's sins that prompted the young Josiah, Judah's last righteous king, to launch an all-out campaign against idol worshipping that ended two years later with the elimination of countless pagan places of worship.

3

THE LATER PROPHETS OF THE WORD

The long years of King Manasseh's reign seemed to erase the teachings of the great prophets and put an end to the prophetic era. But the turning point came during the reign of his grandson, Josiah, who was the last righteous king of Judah. Josiah launched a major religious reform that did away with the worship of foreign pagan gods in Jerusalem and throughout the land. It was during that time that a new generation of great prophets began to emerge, most notably the prophet Jeremiah who, as we shall see, played a critical role in the history of biblical prophecy. Jeremiah lives before and during the destruction of the Kingdom of Judah by the Babylonians. His teachings help the exiles of Judah grasp the universality of the God of Israel, and in due time they will return to their land with their new Torah-centered faith that will mark the beginning of post-biblical Jewish faith.

A younger contemporary of Jeremiah is the prophet Ezekiel, who is exiled to Babylon as a young man and, though completely different from his older colleague in his manner and prophetic approach, helps his fellow exiles remain loyal to their God in the midst of the pagan splendor of Babylon.

This generation of great prophets will be followed after the exile by one last group of prophets. Most notable among them will be the so-called Second Isaiah, whose identity is unknown to us, but whose teachings will raise monotheistic faith to its highest level.

JEREMIAH: THE PROPHET OF NATURE
AND HUMAN HISTORY

It was during Josiah's religious reform that a young new prophet, cast in
the mold of the four great prophets of the previous century, made his
appearance in Jerusalem. His name was Jeremiah, son of Hilkiah the
priest, of the village of Anathoth, north of Jerusalem. He was destined
to play a decisive role in the history of biblical prophecy and world
civilization, a role that only now, centuries later, we are beginning to
fully appreciate.

Like the book of Micah, the book of Jeremiah is extremely hard to
decipher. It is out of chronological order; it covers a long period of
some forty years of intense prophetic activity; and it is not always clear
which prophecy belongs in which particular period. Jeremiah lives
through the reign of five kings, during which time Judah comes under
the yoke of Egypt and later Babylon, and he witnesses the destruction
of the kingdom by the Babylonians and the end of the monarchy. He
survives the catastrophe and attempts to work with the survivors and
start over, but internal strife among them forces him to go into exile in
Egypt, where he disappears from the pages of history. Through it all he
continues to have his prophecies and his teachings recorded by a loyal
and very able scribe named Baruch ben Neriah and distributed to the
exiles in Babylon, and as a result his long book of fifty-two chapters has
been preserved. It provides a wealth of information about his life and
about his activities as a prophet as well as his interaction with other
prophets of his time. It is indeed a gold mine of information for our
search for the meaning of prophecy, and we shall attempt to see how
much we can learn from it.

More than any other prophet, Jeremiah is a prophet of nature and
human history. One can believe in or reject God's existence. But one
cannot reject the existence of nature or of human history. The physical
universe is something we experience every minute. Our human past
affects us and guides our every step. As a young lad, Jeremiah first hears
the voice of God as he observes a blossoming almond tree in early
spring. He also sees a boiling pot with the steam blowing to the north.
He is told that calamity will befall his people from the north. From that
moment on he will continue to receive divine messages from nature,
and he will apply them to the unfolding history of his people. In other

words, Jeremiah's prophetic milieu is nature rather than the supernatural. Unlike previous prophets, Jeremiah never sees angels. He does not
perform miracles, and he does not heal the sick or resurrect the dead.
When Zedekiah, the last king of Judah, asks him to pray to God for a
miracle to save Jerusalem from the Babylonians as Isaiah did in the time
of King Hezekiah when the Assyrians came to conquer the city, Jeremiah refuses. He seems to be saying that the time for divine intervention
is over. The king must take personal responsibility for his actions and
turn himself over to the enemy before it is too late.

Jeremiah is clearly the spiritual heir to his four great predecessors—
Amos, Hosea, Isaiah, and Micah. Like Amos, who begins to prophesy
when he hears the lion roar in the desert, Jeremiah discovers God in
nature. Like Hosea, he likens the covenant between God and Israel to a
marriage contract in which Israel is the bride who becomes the unfaithful wife. Like Micah, he feels God's pain at the waywardness of God's
children. Like Isaiah, he chastises his people for their idolatry and immorality, but like his great predecessor he also envisions a time when
"Jerusalem shall be called the throne of Adonai, and all nations shall
gather to it, to the presence of Adonai in Jerusalem, and they shall no
longer stubbornly follow their own evil will."

Elsewhere he says,

> The days are surely coming, says Adonai, when I will make a new
> covenant with the house of Israel and the house of Judah. It will not
> be like the covenant that I made with their ancestors when I took
> them by the hand to bring them out of the land of Egypt—a cove-
> nant that they broke, though I was their husband, says Adonai. This
> is the covenant that I will make with the house of Israel after those
> days, says Adonai: I will put my law inside of them, and I will write it
> on their hearts; and I will be their God, and they shall be my people.
> (Jer. 3:17; 31:31–33)

What we have here is Jeremiah's vision of the end of days, which makes
him a member of the above-mentioned Utopian School of Prophecy
along with Isaiah and Micah. It is not as majestic and far-reaching as
Isaiah's vision of the end of days, but it adds a new element regarding
writing God's law on people's hearts which, as we shall see, is a critical
addition that will impact the destiny of the people of Judah after the
time of Jeremiah.

But most intriguing is the similarity between Jeremiah and Micah, a prophet who is actually quoted in the book of Jeremiah when the latter is put on trial for his life. We recall how Micah refers to God in the most intimate and emotional terms when he speaks of God pleading with the wayward people of Judah as a parent who is deeply hurt by his children. Ironically Jeremiah, who is a student of nature and of history and a prophet who avoids the supernatural, seems to have, like Micah and also like Hosea, except even more so, a most intimate personal relationship with God. Not enough has been written about the nature of this prophet's personal relationship with God and its impact not only on Judaism but also on Christianity and Islam. In my book on Jeremiah (*The Man Who Knew God: Decoding Jeremiah*), I go into this critical relationship in some detail. Here I will try to summarize it and apply it to our discussion.

Jeremiah has no peer in the Bible in his total dedication to God and to his prophetic mission. Unlike Isaiah or Hosea, he never takes a wife. Unlike Amos, he does not have an occupation. Born to a priestly family, he does not pursue the priesthood. From the moment he hears God's call at age twelve or thirteen, his every waking moment (and also his sleep) is dedicated to God. His mission is to bring God's word to his people and to the world. He loves his people more than anyone else in the Bible because he knows God loves them beyond measure. He says,

> Isn't Ephraim [Israel] my beloved son,
> The child of my delight?
> Though I rebuke him he is on my mind,
> Therefore I tremble for him,
> I will surely take pity on him, says Adonai. (Jer. 31:19)

In Christianity, God's love for the world is the centerpiece of that faith. This belief has its origins in the life and teachings of Jeremiah. One could go a step further and argue that this also applies to the way the monotheistic religions understand God. For Muslims, God is al-Rahman al-Rahim, "the merciful and the compassionate." For Christians, it is a God who "so loved the world." To Jews, it is a God who loves the House of Israel for all eternity (*ahavat olam*). All three believe in a God who is both personal and universal. Prior to Jeremiah's time, the Hebrew tribes believed in a God who was tribal and territorial. The God of Abraham became the God of Ephraim, the God of Judah, and so on. God resided at the Temple in Jerusalem, or even at other temples in places like Beth El or Shiloh. As the end of the Kingdom of Judah drew near, Jeremiah taught his people that God was everywhere, even in Babylonian Exile. It was God who made the Babylonian emperor, Nebuchadnezzar, destroy Jerusalem for its sins, and who sent the people of Judah into exile. And it was God who would watch over them while they were away from their land and who would bring them back in due time. It was this belief that sustained the exiles for some seventy years until finally they began to return to their land. The other lesson the exiles learned from Jeremiah was that God knows each and every one of God's creatures, regardless of family or tribe, and that each person is responsible for his or her own actions. Jeremiah says,

> In those days they shall no longer say:
> "The parents have eaten sour grapes,
> And the children's teeth are set on edge."
> But all shall die for their own sins; the teeth
> Of everyone who eats sour grapes
> Shall be set on edge. (Jer. 31:28–29)

These words, which will be later reiterated and taken a step further by the prophet Ezekiel, represent a departure from the old biblical belief, which states that God visits the iniquity of the parents upon the children and the children's children, to the third and the fourth generation (Exod. 34:6–7). Once the people go into exile, all this will change. Each person must assume personal responsibility for his or her own actions. Each from now on has a personal relationship with God. This idea, which is first tossed into the world by Jeremiah, is the cornerstone of monotheism. It may be the most important idea of all time, for it universalizes monotheism and makes it the faith of every person instead of the faith of a particular people.

As we shall see in the prophecies of the Second Isaiah, Jeremiah is a pivotal prophet in the history of his people and of the world. Along with Moses and Samuel, who play a critical role in the formation and the unification of their people, respectively, Jeremiah plays a critical role in the restoration of his people. Moses turns slaves into a liberated people and gives them laws to live by. Samuel unites the tribes and establishes the kingdom. Jeremiah transitions his people from tribal and territorial people to a community of faith that is able to survive exile. When the exiles return from Babylon, they come back not as Hebrews or Judeans but as Jews. As Jeremiah has predicted, the Torah is now engraved in their hearts, and under the leadership of Ezra and Nehemiah they enter into a "new covenant." This covenant remains in effect to this day.

As was mentioned earlier, the three monotheistic religions are commonly referred to as the Abrahamic Religions because of the common ancestry of Jews and Arabs who are descendants of Abraham's sons, Isaac and Ishmael, respectively, and the ancestry of Jesus, himself a Jew. This author maintains that it is more proper to refer to them as the Jeremiac Religions, since it was Jeremiah who transitioned the Jews from syncretism and monolatry (the worship of one god without excluding belief in other gods) to monotheism, thus enabling new monotheistic religions to form. While Jeremiah is not mentioned by name in the Qur'an, his influence is in evidence in its style and its fervent monotheism. As for Jeremiah's influence on Jesus, this will be examined in chapter 4 when we discuss the Second Isaiah.

Jeremiah and the Meaning of Prophecy

While in the book of the first Isaiah I only found the word "prophet" used eight times, in the book of Jeremiah I found it used sixty-two times, far more than in any other book in the Bible. Jeremiah himself is referred to over and over again by the title of "prophet." It is interesting to note that throughout his lifetime people doubted Jeremiah's words and disagreed with him constantly, and yet deep down they knew he was a true prophet, as evidenced by the fact that when they put him on trial for predicting the destruction of the Temple—or later on during the siege of Jerusalem when the king's counselors wanted to eliminate him for sedition—they could not bring themselves to kill him because they feared divine retribution. (In 2008, archeologists digging in Jerusalem found clay seals belonging to the two counselors who are mentioned in the book of Jeremiah as the ones who secured the king's permission to dispose of Jeremiah. Discoveries of this nature in recent years have added significant material evidence regarding the historicity of Jeremiah.)

Additionally, Jeremiah himself keeps referring to two kinds of prophets—genuine ones, who represent the word of God, and false ones, who only pretend to do so. Invariably, he keeps mentioning the true prophets as the ones whom the people keep persecuting, some of whom are even put to death, as in the case of the prophet Uriah whom King Jehoiakim executes with his own hands (Jer. 26:23). At the same time Jeremiah keeps chastising the court prophets and those prophets who seek to curry favor with the court. In one of his confrontations with this kind of a prophet, Jeremiah provides a rare insight into his understanding of true prophecy.

> In that same year, at the beginning of the reign of King Zedekiah of Judah, in the fifth month of the fourth year, the prophet Hananiah son of Azzur, from Gibeon, spoke to me in the house of Adonai, in the presence of the priests and all the people, saying, "Thus says Adonai of hosts, the God of Israel: I have broken the yoke of the king of Babylon. Within two years I will bring back to this place all the vessels of the Lord's house, which King Nebuchadnezzar of Babylon took away from this place and carried to Babylon. I will also bring back to this place King Jeconiah son of Jehoiakim of Judah, and all the exiles from Judah who went to Babylon, says Adonai, for I will break the yoke of the king of Babylon."
>
> Then the prophet Jeremiah spoke to the prophet Hananiah in the presence of the priests and all the people who were standing in the house of Adonai; and the prophet Jeremiah said, "Amen! May Adonai do so; may Adonai fulfill the words that you have prophesied, and bring back to this place from Babylon the vessels of the house of Adonai, and all the exiles. But listen now to this word that I speak in your hearing and in the hearing of all the people. *The prophets who preceded you and me from ancient times prophesied war, famine, and pestilence against many countries and great kingdoms. As for the prophet who prophesies peace, when the word of that prophet comes true, then it will be known that Adonai has truly sent that prophet."*
> (Jer. 28:1–11; emphasis added)

This narrative speaks volumes about the meaning of prophecy as understood by Jeremiah and by the rest of the prophets. It is important to note that the prophet Hananiah is treated here as a true prophet of God, and one who uses the same formal prophetic phrases used by Jeremiah, such as "thus says Adonai." But Jeremiah knows that Hananiah's prediction about the return of the captives and of the vessels of the Temple from Babylonian captivity in two years' time is false. Hananiah is telling the people what they want to hear. And then Jeremiah makes his categorical statement about the litmus test of true prophecy, namely, prophecies of doom versus prophecies of good tidings. He tells Hananiah that prophecies of doom have always been common and are self-evident. On the other hand, prophecies of good tidings can only be trusted once they have been fulfilled. The general presumption here is that true prophets are not afraid to be critical of their contemporaries and to present them with dire prophecies. Indeed, it is the common task of the prophet to do just that. Good tidings are legitimate only after the people have been chastised and have paid for their wrongdoing, not before. This pattern seems to apply to all of Jeremiah's predecessors, such as Amos, Hosea, Isaiah, and Micah. All of them chastise their people, and all of them predict redemption only after the people have been duly punished.

What seems to differentiate prophets like Jeremiah from wishful prophets like Hananiah is the way Jeremiah arrives at his insights. It is too simplistic to assume that Jeremiah simply hears the voice of God and therefore has a direct channel to the Great Boss whose bidding he does without questioning. Jeremiah does question God on several occasions, and even accuses God of "seducing" him. His relationship with God is of the most intimate nature. But what Jeremiah actually does is piece together messages he receives from nature and from the unfolding of historical events. Those two processes, which are interrelated, enable him to gain insights into the future course of events, much in the same way a visionary pundit or leader would today.

Jeremiah as the Bible's Pivotal Prophet

Historically, Jeremiah has been marginalized by both Judaism and Christianity. He has been seen as a tragic figure living during a tragic time. He witnesses the fall of Jerusalem to the Babylonians, the destruction of the Holy Temple, the end of the Davidic monarchy, and the exile of his people. His prophecies of doom are fulfilled, and the only thing left is the hope for an improbable miracle that will bring down Babylon and restore the people to their land at some future time. Jeremiah has been portrayed by great artists like Rembrandt as an old man sitting among ruins, crying and lamenting over the destruction, and composing the book of Lamentations.

This portrait only represents one facet of Jeremiah's life and teachings. It misses the critical role this prophet played in teaching his people how to overcome exile by resisting the idolatry of their conquerors, bolstering their own faith, and preserving that faith in the one God that would eventually spread around the world. In this, Jeremiah is the vital link between the first Isaiah who, as we saw, universalizes monotheism, and the Second Isaiah, who provides the final stage in the development of the monotheistic idea. Jeremiah was the right man at the right time. When all seemed lost, he was able to personalize the God of the first Isaiah and instill in the exiles of the Babylonian diaspora (but not those of the somewhat earlier Egyptian diaspora, who were too far gone in their idolatrous practices) an abiding faith in this personalized God that enabled them to overcome exile and return to their land, as we can see in the psalm celebrating that event.

> When the God brought back the exiles of Zion,
> We were as if in a dream.
> Then our mouth was filled with laughter,
> And our tongue with shouts of joy;
> Then it was said among the nations,
> "God has done great things for them."
> God has done great things for us,
> And we rejoiced.
> Restore our fortunes, Adonai,
> Like the streams in the desert.
> May those who sow in tears
> Reap with singing.
> Those who go out weeping,
> Bearing the seed for sowing,
> Shall come home with shouts of joy,
> Carrying their sheaves. (Psalm 126:1–6)

But Jeremiah is not only the pivotal prophet in the history of his own people; he is a pivotal prophet in the history of the world. Civilization as we know it might not have come to exist if it were not for this suffering prophet who more than any other prophet before him brought God closer to man and made the belief in a personal and caring God the central belief of people around the world. Great prophetic ideas only survive when they are put into practice by people who believe in them. Otherwise, they only last as ancient texts studied by a few scholars or kept in a museum to remind us of times gone by. Because of Jeremiah, the biblical prophets are not a thing of the past. They continue to inform and influence our lives, and they will continue to do so for generations to come.

We shall return to Jeremiah in chapter 4 when we discuss the Second Isaiah and see Jeremiah's impact on that major prophet.

JEREMIAH'S LESSER-KNOWN CONTEMPORARIES: HULDAH, ZEPHANIAH, HABAKKUK, NAHUM, AND OBADIAH

The biblical canon has preserved the prophecies of five contemporaries of Jeremiah, albeit the dating of some of them is not completely clear. The first, Huldah, the only woman in the group, is also the only one who does not have a book bearing her name, and she is only mentioned briefly in the books of Second Kings and Second Chronicles. Three of them—Zephaniah, Habakkuk, and Nahum—only have three short chapters to their name, and the last, Obadiah, only one small chapter. Even people who are well versed in the Bible find it difficult to tell them apart. Yet they are not insignificant, and they do contribute to the overall impact of biblical prophecy. Like some of their predecessors, they are not always easy to decipher, as they use words and phrases that are not always clear. But their core message is clear, and it complements the message of their great forerunners.

Huldah

During Jeremiah's youth we hear about a woman prophet named Huldah. She is the only woman in the Bible who has left us a prophecy (2 Kings 22:15–20). It consists of five short verses, but it plays a critical role in the history of biblical prophecy. Huldah was consulted by the young king Josiah following the discovery of the scroll of the law in the precincts of the Temple in Jerusalem. She lets the king know that all the punishments mentioned in the scroll (which most likely was the book of Deuteronomy) will befall the people of Judah for their evil deeds, but that the king himself will be spared because he humbled himself before God.

She said to them, "This is what Adonai, the God of Israel, says: Tell the man who sent you to me, 'This is what Adonai says: I am going to bring disaster on this place and its people, according to everything written in the book the king of Judah has read. Because they have forsaken me and burned incense to other gods and provoked me to anger by all the idols their hands have made, my anger will burn against this place and will not be quenched.' Tell the king of Judah, who sent you to inquire of Adonai, 'This is what Adonai, the God of Israel, says concerning the words you heard: Because your heart was responsive and you humbled yourself before Adonai when you heard what I have spoken against this place and its people, that they would become accursed and laid waste, and because you tore your robes and wept in my presence, I have heard you, declares Adonai. Therefore I will gather you to your fathers, and you will be buried in peace. Your eyes will not see all the disaster I am going to bring on this place.'" So they took her answer back to the king.

This one prophecy shows her to be a true prophet in the mold of the great literary prophets, and one could deduce that she must have uttered other important prophecies. Why more of her messages were not preserved is an open question, most readily attributable to her being a woman. She did, however, exert a decisive influence on Jeremiah, who quotes her at least twice during his long prophetic career (Jer. 1:16; 19:4). Here again we learn about the impact prophets had on one another, as we saw in the case of Isaiah and Micah, Hosea and Jeremiah, and so on. The impact is not always apparent, and we can only speculate about it. But here and there we can find concrete proof of it.

Zephaniah

Like Isaiah, Zephaniah is a prophet of the Assyrian period, which lasted until the fall of Assyria in 605, when Jeremiah was already well into his prophetic career. Zephaniah speaks in his opening verses about those in Jerusalem who "prostate themselves on the roofs to the hosts of heaven" (Zeph. 1:5), which reminds us of Jeremiah referring to the "hosts of heaven" (Jer. 8:2), clearly the same pagan practice of their time. Disloyalty to the one God is Zephaniah's main theme, more so than immorality. He denounces Israel's enemies who "taunted the people of God" (Zeph. 2:10), and then he turns to Assyria that tyrannizes the world, and

he predicts its imminent fall. Thus, God is shown disloyalty by all—
Judah, its neighbors, and the ruling world empire, Assyria. This, according to Zephaniah, will result in a most horrendous day of Adonai, which
will bring about total devastation.

> The great day of Adonai is near,
> Near and hastening fast;
> The sound of the day of Adonai is bitter,
> The warrior cries aloud there.
> That day will be a day of wrath,
> A day of distress and anguish,
> A day of ruin and devastation,
> A day of darkness and gloom,
> A day of clouds and thick darkness,
> A day of trumpet blast and battle cry
> Against the fortified cities
> And against the lofty battlements.
> I will bring such distress upon people
> That they shall walk like the blind;
> Because they have sinned against Adonai,
> Their blood shall be poured out like dust,
> And their flesh like dung.
> Neither their silver nor their gold
> Will be able to save them
> On the day of the God's wrath;
> In the fire of God's passion
> The whole earth shall be consumed;
> For a full, a terrible end
> God will make of all the inhabitants of the earth. (Zeph. 1:14–18)

The theme of the day of Adonai (or day of the Lord) runs through
practically all the literary prophets, with the notable exception of Jeremiah. We do not know whether or not Jeremiah believed in this concept, but it does occupy a prominent place in biblical prophecy. It
seems to have been born out of the oppression suffered by Israel and
other nations from the tyranny of the Assyrians. The common belief
among the people of Israel and Judah at that time was that it was a time
when God would avenge them of their enemies, but the prophets believed otherwise. It was a time when God would punish everyone, including the People of the Covenant. In time this belief would be transformed into a messianic belief. Zephaniah, however, does not speak of a

messianic time but rather of a day in the not far-off future. Clearly, such a day of an end "of all the inhabitants of the earth" did not come about, but Assyria did fall, Israel's neighbors did disappear one by one, and the kingdom of Judah was destroyed in Jeremiah's lifetime. Zephaniah, like his predecessors, ends his prophecies with Isaiah's vision of a "saving remnant" of Israel surviving the devastation, and of a time when Israel once again will live in peace and unafraid.

Habakkuk

This prophet is a later contemporary of Jeremiah. While Zephaniah is one of the last prophets of the Assyrian period, Habakkuk is one of the first prophets of the Babylonian period. He lives and prophesies at the time when Assyria falls and Babylon becomes the new world power. Unlike Jeremiah, who sees the rise of Babylon as God's way of punishing Judah for her sins before in turn destroying the Babylonian giant, Habakkuk seems to have expected that after the fall of Assyria a new era of peace would dawn on his people. Habakkuk raises a timeless question: Why does evil continue to have the upper hand, while good is not rewarded? One tyrant is replaced by another, and there is no end in sight. Jeremiah raises the same question, and we could certainly ask it regarding any age, including our own. Habakkuk appears to be a tormented soul who fails to understand the ways of God. His message, however, is far from clear. His prophesying is a poetic outburst that defies any straightforward interpretation. He does not make any reference to moral decay in his own country, which the other prophets are so deeply concerned about, and he only mentions paganism in passing. But he is confident that Babylon will fall to its enemies. In the end, he turns out to be a man of great faith. He makes the famous statement "The righteous shall live by his faith" (Hab. 2:4), and he concludes his prophecies by stating,

> Though the fig tree does not blossom,
> And no fruit is on the vines;
> Though the produce of the olive fails
> And the fields yield no food;
> Though the flock is cut off from the fold
> And there is no herd in the stalls,
> Yet I will rejoice in Adonai;

I will exult in the God of my salvation.
Adonai Elohim is my strength;
Who makes my feet like the deer's,
And makes me tread upon the heights. (Hab. 3:17–19)

Nahum

While Habakkuk is agonizing over the persistence of evil in the world, Nahum focuses on one issue, namely, God's anger at the evil empire of Assyria, whose total downfall Habakkuk predicts in great detail. In discussing Isaiah we suggested that Assyria, which was the most powerful empire in the world in the eighth and seventh centuries BCE, was the originator of ethnic cleansing, and that its savagery matched that of Nazi Germany. It carried within itself the seeds of its own destruction. Divine anger against such evil is a common theme with the Hebrew prophets. With Nahum it is the only theme. We have no biographical data about this prophet, but he is commonly considered to have lived during the time of King Josiah and the early career of the prophet Jeremiah. It is hard to believe that God's anger and divine retribution against Israel's archenemy were this prophet's only concerns. More likely, what we have here is only a fragment of his prophecies. Quite possibly, he shared the concerns of Huldah, Jeremiah, Zephaniah, and Habakkuk regarding the spread of paganism and immorality among the people of Judah. All of this, however, remains in the realm of speculation.

Obadiah

This is the shortest book in the Bible, consisting of one chapter containing twenty-one verses. Here again as we have seen in Nahum, the prophet addresses one issue that is even narrower than the issue of Assyria. Obadiah takes to task Israel's neighbor east of the Dead Sea, namely, Edom. The Edomites were considered descendants of Esau, Jacob's older brother, hence cousins of the Israelites. They were, however, merciless enemies of Israel, and after the destruction of Jerusalem in 586 BCE, they took part in attacking and plundering the fallen Kingdom of Judah. (The rabbis of the Talmudic period often refer to the Roman Empire, the archenemy of Israel in the time of the Second

Temple, as "Edom.") This places Obadiah around the time when the prophet Jeremiah's career was coming to an end. Verses 1:1–4 and 1:5–6 in Obadiah bear a strong resemblance to Jeremiah 49:14–16 and 49:9–10a, respectively.

> The vision of Obadiah.
> Thus says Adonai Elohim concerning Edom:
> We have heard a report from Adonai,
> And a messenger has been sent among the nations:
> "Rise up! Let us rise against it for battle!"
> I will surely make you least among the nations;
> You shall be utterly despised.
> Your proud heart has deceived you,
> You that live in the clefts of the rock,
> Whose dwelling is in the heights.
> You say in your heart,
> "Who will bring me down to the ground?"
> Though you soar aloft like the eagle,
> Though your nest is set among the stars, From there I will bring you down,
> Says Adonai.
> If thieves came to you,
> If plunderers by night—how you have been destroyed!—
> Would they not steal only what they wanted?
> If grape-gatherers came to you,
> Would they not leave gleanings?
> How Esau has been pillaged,
> His treasures searched out! (Obad. 1:1–6)

In Jeremiah the text is nearly parallel.

> I have heard tidings from Adonai,
> And a messenger has been sent among the nations:
> "Gather yourselves together and come against her,
> And rise up for battle!"
> For I will make you least among the nations,
> Despised by humankind.
> The terror you inspire
> And the pride of your heart have deceived you,
> You who live in the clefts of the rock,
> Who hold the height of the hill.
> Although you make your nest as high as the eagle's,
> From there I will bring you down,

Says Adonai. (Jer. 49:14–16)

> If grape-gatherers came to you,
> Would they not leave gleanings?
> If thieves came by night,
> Even they would pillage only what they wanted.
> But as for me,
> I have stripped Esau bare,
> I have uncovered his hiding-places,
> And he is not able to conceal himself.
> His offspring are destroyed, his kinsfolk
> And his neighbors;
> And he is no more. (Jer. 49:9–10)

We do not know whether Jeremiah borrowed this prophecy from Obadiah or vice versa. As we saw in the case of Isaiah's prophecy of the end of days and its repetition by Micah, some prophetic text appears more than once and it is never quite clear which one is the original. But clearly the two prophets shared the same view regarding Edom.

Here again as we have suggested in regard to Nahum, it is hard to believe that Obadiah's entire prophetic career consisted of excoriating Edom. In both cases the book appears to be a fragment of a longer work, and it leads us to conclude that what has been preserved in the Bible is but a portion of a much greater body of prophetic literature.

In taking this brief look at the other prophets of Jeremiah's time, we learn two things. On the one hand, they have much in common in regard to their main concerns and their main message. They are all concerned with Israel's enemies, and they all strive to understand the divine plan for their people's trials and suffering. They invariably see it as divine punishment for their people's transgressions, which makes the enemy an instrument of God's retribution. At the same time, they see God as turning around and punishing that instrument. On the other hand, while all of them live during the time of the fall of Assyria and the rise of Babylon, some, like Nahum, focus on the fall of Assyria, while others, like Jeremiah, look further to the rise of Babylon and its eventual fall. Another major prophetic theme, the day of Adonai, gets much attention from Zephaniah, and little attention from the others, especially Jeremiah. In short, the prophets of this period, as we have seen with the prophets of the previous period, namely, Isaiah, Hosea, Amos, and

Micah, share a common message about the preeminence of God and the failure of God's covenanted people to live up to the covenant, but at the same time they are individual voices with their own personal message, as well as their own personality, which, as we shall see, is also true of the next and last generation of great prophets.

EZEKIEL: THE VISION OF THE DRY BONES

Ezekiel, a younger contemporary of Jeremiah, is exiled to Babylon as a young man along with King Jehoiakim and the Judean elite a few years before the destruction of Jerusalem and the final exile. There, among the exiles, he establishes himself as a prophet of God. In some ways, he is a disciple of Jeremiah and his predecessors. All their predictions about the fall of Judah are now coming true, and Ezekiel takes it upon himself to make sure that the exiles' spirit is not broken by the cataclysmic events. He goes out of his way to make it clear that the fall of Judah was preordained and inevitable; he predicts the revival of his people and their restoration in his famous vision of the valley of the dry bones that come back to life; and he provides a detailed plan for the restored Temple and the reunited tribes of Israel.

But all this hardly sums up the prophetic career of Ezekiel. This prophet is nothing if not original. He is so original in his visions, predictions, and behavior that it is never quite clear what he is up to. One wonders how his contemporaries dealt with his actions and his message, since we do not hear about their reactions to what he does and says as we do in the case of other prophets, particularly Jeremiah. We have to assume that they took him at his word, and that he was effective in delivering his timely message.

The Judean exiles now residing in Babylon are surrounded by the great monuments, temples, buildings, and hanging gardens (one of the seven wonders of the ancient world) of the greatest metropolis in the world at that time, which dwarf their native land by comparison. Their national deity is invisible and, in the eyes of the Babylonians, has now been defeated, while here the gods of Babylon are represented by gigantic, triumphant, composite creatures that are part man, part animal, with the likenesses of lions, bulls, and eagles. Jeremiah was the first one to understand the seductive nature of the Babylon civilization, and he cautioned his people not to fall prey to it. Ezekiel lives in the midst of that culture, and he needs a strong response to it. And so the book of Ezekiel opens with a vision in which God appears to Ezekiel surrounded by divine creatures, each with four faces—that of a man, a lion, a bull, and an eagle.

Isaiah's vision of the divine court at the Temple in Jerusalem is tame by comparison to Ezekiel's vision. In Isaiah's vision, God dwells in one place, surrounded by the seraphim, or fiery angels, and other than the brief description of those six-winged angels, little more detail is provided. Here in Ezekiel's vision, God is traveling on a mysterious chariot carried by the creatures with four faces and many eyes that see in all directions (later on we are told they are cherubim, or angels of a class different from Isaiah's seraphim). The chariot has wheels that gyrate, wheel within wheel. This is an awesome, mysterious chariot that reaches from heaven to earth and can move in any direction. It is described in minute detail, and it gives the impression of an otherworldly vehicle. Jewish and Christian mystics have found a profound meaning in the description of this chariot, and it became one of the foundations of Jewish mysticism. Here Ezekiel is letting his listeners know that God no longer dwells in Jerusalem as reported by Isaiah, but has gone into exile, just like them. God is traveling the world in this fiery chariot that sees and hears everything that is happening throughout the world. Quite obviously, Ezekiel is using his eloquence to create in his listeners' minds an image of a divinity far more awesome than the monumental Babylonian gods, and he delivers a critical message: God can be found anywhere, even in Babylon. No need to despair.

In Ezekiel we have the culmination of all the biblical accounts regarding the visual and verbal encounters between God and the prophet. To Moses, God first appears in a burning bush, and later we are told that "there has never arisen a prophet in Israel like Moses, whom God knew face to face" (Deut. 34:10). To Samuel, God first speaks as the boy Samuel is about to fall asleep (1 Sam. 3:1–10). To Elijah, God appears at the end of a storm in the desert and speaks to him in a "still small voice" (1 Kings 19:12). To Isaiah, God appears on a heavenly throne in the Temple (Isa. 6:1). To Jeremiah, God appears in the blossoming of an almond tree (Jer. 1:11). In all of these epiphanies we have an element of human fear and hesitation, recalling Amos's words, "When a lion roars, / Who is not afraid? / Adonai Elohim speaks, / Who will not prophesy?" (Amos 3:8). With Ezekiel, it is altogether different. He communicates no emotions. He tells us about his revelation, and he proceeds to relate how God begins to talk to him, addressing him as "son of man," a term never used before by any other prophet. From here on Ezekiel does exactly as God commands him to do without questioning or showing any emotions and without deviating one iota. His experiences have little to do with common human reality, but nothing seems to surprise him. A hand appears out of nowhere and gives him a scroll. He is told to eat the scroll down to the last bite, which he does, not knowing what to expect. The scroll is easy to swallow and tastes sweet. To use the language of our digital age, Ezekiel has now been programmed to deliver divine messages, and he does so in a more decisive and effective way than any other prophet. Moreover, he seems to have also been programmed to engage in space travel. He tells us about a wind that lifts him up and transports him from place to place. He is sent to Jerusalem as part of his prophetic mission, and he is flown back to Babylon. In short, he now possesses magical powers or, put differently, he has now been empowered to be God's ubiquitous "watchman" (Ezek. 3:17) over the last days of the Kingdom of Judah and over the Babylonian diaspora. He passes harsh judgment over Judah, which, according to him, can no longer repent, as its inevitable end is near. And he also chastises the exiles in Babylon, particularly the false prophets among them, who are doomed because they misled their people. But he does not stop there. He passes harsh judgment over Israel's neighbors, whom prophets like Amos and Jeremiah also excoriated, and he reaches a climax of condemnations with his prediction of a future war between God and the mythical northern enemy Gog and Magog in which evil will finally be vanquished, the tribes of Israel (including the ten lost tribes) will be restored to their land, and God will rule over all the nations.

> On that day, when Gog comes against the land of Israel, says Adonai Elohim, my wrath shall be aroused. For in my jealousy and in my blazing wrath I declare: On that day there shall be a great shaking in the land of Israel; the fish of the sea, and the birds of the air, and the animals of the field, and all creeping things that creep on the ground, and all human beings that are on the face of the earth, shall quake at my presence, and the mountains shall be thrown down, and the cliffs shall fall, and every wall shall tumble to the ground. I will summon

the sword against Gog in all my mountains, says Adonai Elohim; the swords of all will be against their comrades. With pestilence and bloodshed I will enter into judgment with him; and I will pour down torrential rains and hailstones, fire and sulfur, upon him and his troops and the many peoples that are with him. So I will display my greatness and my holiness and make myself known in the eyes of many nations. Then they shall know that I am Adonai. (Ezek. 38:18–23)

The last section of the book of Ezekiel provides a blueprint for the restored Temple and the restored tribes of Israel who return to their allotted parts of the Land of Israel. In this section this prophet does something no other prophet since Moses had ever done, namely, he provides specifications for the rebuilding of the Temple, and he also provides the ritual laws of the Temple cult which he, as a priest, must have been familiar with during his youth in Jerusalem. Here, as in the other sections of his book, Ezekiel overstates matters and seems to go far beyond actual events in the present and events of the future. For one thing, the tribes of the Northern Kingdom, the so-called ten lost tribes, never come back. The war of God and Magog remains in the realm of myth. The horrific description of moral corruption and rampant paganism in Jerusalem on the eve of its fall is greatly exaggerated. All of this raises a question: Did Ezekiel believe everything he said to be factual, or did he exaggerate on purpose to drive his point home because of the extraordinary times he was living in that required extreme dramatization?

Ezekiel's Visions: Fantasy and Reality

After dealing with Jeremiah and the other prophets of his time, one is baffled when confronting the book of Ezekiel. While none of those prophets are easy to understand, in Ezekiel we have the added problem of telling reality from fantasy. Are we to believe that Ezekiel actually traveled through space? Did he eat a scroll? Did he perform all the other bizarre acts mentioned in his book? When he has the vision of a valley full of dry bones that arise and come back to life, does he talk about actual physical resurrection, or is he relating an allegory?

One clue can be found in Ezekiel's own words when he says, "Son of man, put forth a riddle, and speak a parable to the house of Israel" (Ezek. 17:2). He goes on to describe a "great eagle," which will come and destroy the roots of the "grapevine." The great eagle turns out to be Nebuchadnezzar, the Babylonian king, who comes to Jerusalem and takes away its "roots," namely, the king of Judah and his ruling class. In other words, Ezekiel likes to speak in riddles and parables. When he speaks of the valley of the dry bones, he is using a metaphor to describe the state of mind of many of the exiles around him. They say, "Then God said to me: Son of man, these bones are the whole house of Israel. They say, Our bones are dried up and our hope is gone. We are cut off" (Ezek. 37:11).

Clearly, the whole house of Israel has not died, and the term "dry bones" refers to the drying up of hope for redemption and restoration. The impression one gets from reading the book of Ezekiel is that this prophet has undertaken the enormous task of restoring hope to his exiled people, and he does it by stirring up their imagination with his highly dramatic visions. We keep hearing of the elders of the exiled community coming to him for prophecies, and we never hear of any dissent or displeasure among them after they hear him speak or see him perform his outlandish stunts. His behavior, which appears ecstatic yet not erratic—since he is always in full control of his actions—is something they seem to accept, making allowance for his fiery nature and his close and constant communication with the divine.

It is quite remarkable how different Ezekiel is from Jeremiah, his older contemporary. They both hail from priestly families; they are both natives of the Jerusalem area; and they both pursue the same goal of bringing their people back to their God and to the path of righteousness. Ezekiel adopts Jeremiah's belief that the sins of the parents will no longer be visited upon their children; rather, from now on each person is responsible for his or her own actions. Yet the personalities of these two prophets, their approach to prophecy, and their treatment at the hands of their contemporaries are totally different. Jeremiah is all heart. He loves his people, and he describes God as a loving parent whose heart cries out for his wayward children. To the very last moment before the fall of Jerusalem, Jeremiah hopes that his people will be saved from their dire fate. Not so Ezekiel. He shows his people no sign of caring or compassion. They have sinned, and they will be punished.

With him everything is foreseen and preordained. His God is a harsh
God who will not flinch as the punishment is meted out. When the time
comes for redemption, it will be carried out in a meticulous fashion,
without any emotions. One gets the impression Ezekiel operates as a
detached law-enforcer who does everything by the book. In this he is
different not only from Jeremiah but from all the other literary prophets, who invariably are men of strong yet tender emotions. Ezekiel says,
"Then the word of Adonai came to me: O son of man, set your face
toward Jerusalem and preach against her sanctuaries and prophesy
against the land of Israel" (Ezek. 21:7).

Preach—indeed, Ezekiel is a preacher rather than a poet. The beautiful poetry of an Isaiah or an Amos or a Jeremiah is here replaced by
prose, harsh, relentless prose. And yet, while Ezekiel may not be particularly likable, he is widely accepted as one of the prophetic giants of the
Bible and of all time. He tends to exaggerate and overstate; all his
prophecies may not have been fulfilled; and hardly anyone in the Bible
can match his strange and outlandish behavior. But he does play a
critical role in the restoration of his people to their God and in their
eventual return to their land, and he has exerted an enormous influence
on both Judaism and Christianity, opening the door for the belief in the
ultimate judgment that has influenced all the monotheistic religions.

How Do We Assess Ezekiel?

Ezekiel seems to provide a climactic high point for all the literary
prophets, who have been the focus of our search. He is a very difficult
prophet to assess. I have no trouble with Isaiah's vision of the end of
days, and I feel an emotional attachment to Jeremiah. But Ezekiel
leaves me puzzled and confused. I am not the only one who feels this
way. The early rabbinic sages were perplexed by his book and sought to
exclude it from the biblical canon. We are told in the Talmud, "Rabbi
Judah said in Rav's name: In truth, that man, Hananiah son of Hezekiah
by name, is to be remembered for blessing. If it were not for him, the
Book of Ezekiel would have been hidden" (Shabbat 13b).

For people of a more mystical bent than I, Ezekiel may have great
appeal. In Jewish tradition there is a term, *mechashvey kitzim*, or "those
who seek to figure out the end of time," or the apocalypse and the
messianic era. In our time, Jewish mysticism, or Kabbalah, is enjoying a

revival, and among several Christian groups there is a tendency today to anticipate the coming of the messianic end-time. I would tend to believe that among those of my readers who share such views, Ezekiel may find favor. As for me, I am looking for a resolution prior to any apocalyptic end (as I pointed out in discussing the prophet Elijah), and I take the biblical term "end of time" to mean, as first enunciated in Jacob's blessing to his sons, a later period here on earth rather than a "new earth" (Rev. 21:1) that transcends the world as we know it. For my own modest expectations, I find Ezekiel lacking. Here on earth I believe we need love and compassion, forgiveness and self-generated redemption, elements that are absent in the book of Ezekiel. His God is too stern for me, too unforgiving, and more concerned with "God's greater glory" than human welfare. Perhaps I am speaking out of ignorance, since I am perfectly willing to admit I am unable to fully fathom this prophet.

4

THE LAST PROPHETS OF THE WORD

We have now considered the three giants of the literary prophets' era—Isaiah, Jeremiah, and Ezekiel. To these three, however, we must add a fourth giant, namely, the so-called Second Isaiah. We call him the Second Isaiah or "Deutero-Isaiah" because his prophecies were attached to the book of Isaiah. But the events he refers to take place two centuries later, at the time of King Cyrus of Persia, who allows the Judean exiles to return to Jerusalem from Babylonia. Here the evolution of the monotheistic faith of Israel reaches its highest point. Here the purpose and the mission of the reborn nation are defined for all time. One could argue that the teachings of the Second Isaiah are the culmination of the teachings of all his predecessors.

Four lesser-known prophets will follow the Second Isaiah, and with them the era of biblical prophecy will officially come to an end. After we consider this last group of prophets, we will address the question of why biblical prophecy came to an end when it did.

THE MYSTERY PROPHET: THE SECOND ISAIAH

We have no biographical data whatsoever about the Second Isaiah, and he remains the nameless mystery prophet of the Bible. He lived in the mid-sixth century BCE, two centuries after the time of the first Isaiah, during the fall of Babylon to the Persian king Cyrus, who allowed the

Judean exiles to return to their land and rebuild their city and their temple. This nameless prophet appears suddenly in chapter 40 of the book of the first Isaiah, welcoming the return to Zion with the words

> Be comforted, be comforted my people,
> Says your God. [2]
> Speak tenderly to Jerusalem,
> And call out to her.
> For she has served her term,
> For her penalty is paid.
> For she has received from God's hand
> Double for all her sins. (Isa. 40:1–2)

There is something symbolic and mysterious about the namelessness of this prophet. Unlike his predecessor Ezekiel—who puts himself front and center in his prophecies, and to whom his people seem to be altogether unworthy of redemption—the Second Isaiah removes himself completely from the narrative and puts his people back on the stage of history as the ones who are now worthy of God's grace and of the great mission that awaits them. "Be comforted my people." They are God's people, or God's nation. The moment of redemption has arrived. The great and enlightened King Cyrus, anointed by Israel's God, ushers in a new age for Israel and for the world even though he, a pagan king, does not know God (Isa. 45:1–5). While the prophet praises Cyrus, he does not expect him to redeem Israel or the world. Nor does he look for a leader among the returning exiles who will redeem his people. Instead, the Second Isaiah presents us with a new reality that will become critical in the course of time for both Israel and the world, namely, the direct relationship between Israel and the only God of the universe— and, by extension, between God and every individual person—and the redemptive role of Israel in the world.

The God of the Second Isaiah

We ought to realize by now that everything in the Bible evolves, just as it does in nature and in history. The people of Israel evolve, prophecy evolves, and even God evolves. Better put, God per se does not evolve, but man's understanding of God does. With the Second Isaiah the understanding of God reaches its peak. After Moses and the Israelites cross the Red Sea we hear them sing,

> Who is like you, Adonai, among the gods?
> Who is like you, majestic in holiness,
> Awesome in splendor, doing wonders? (Exod. 15:11)

In other words, they acknowledged the existence of other gods besides Adonai, as did their descendants down to the time of the Second Isaiah. This was a major reason why all throughout biblical times, idolatry kept cropping up among them. It is not until the return from Babylon in the sixth century BCE that we no longer hear about idol worshipping among them, and some biblical scholars, such as Andre Lemaire in his book *The Birth of Monotheism*, credit the Second Isaiah with helping establish this new reality. The prophet mocks idol worshipping in the following words:

> To whom then will you liken God,
> Or what likeness compare with him?
> An idol?—A workman casts it,
> And a goldsmith overlays it with gold,
> And casts for it silver chains.
> As a gift one chooses mulberry wood—
> wood that will not rot—
> Then seeks out a skilled artisan
> To set up an image that will not topple.
> [2]Have you not known?
> Have you not heard?
> Has it not been told you from the beginning?
> Have you not understood from the foundations of the earth?
> [2]It is God who sits above the circle of the earth,
> And its inhabitants are like grasshoppers;
> Who stretches out the heavens like a curtain,
> And spreads them like a tent to live in;
> Who brings princes to naught,
> And makes the rulers of the earth as nothing. (Isa. 40:18–24)

God says,

> I am the first and I am the last,
> Besides me there is no god. (Isa. 44:6)

Elsewhere we hear,

> For I am God, and there is no other,
> I am God, and there is no one like me,
> Declaring the end from the beginning

And from ancient times things not yet done. (Isa. 46:9–10)

This may be the most critical development in all of biblical prophecy. God is not the greatest of all the gods. God is the only God. "There is no God but God," the Muslim proclaims. The trinity is one God, Christianity teaches. Our God is one, the Jew affirms in the *Shema* prayer, the watchword of the Jewish faith. And all three believe they are addressing the same God. While this is common knowledge, it was first fully enunciated by the prophet we call the Second Isaiah.

Israel as "Light to the Nations"

Whoever the Second Isaiah was, he was certainly an unabashed visionary. When the exiles begin to return to the new Persian province of Judea, they are few in number, poorly organized, set upon by new enemies who are now living in their land, and unprepared to rebuild the Temple. Gone is the former glory of the kingdom of David and Solomon. Gone is the Hebrew monarchy. And yet, the prophet does not hesitate to proclaim that this pitiful remnant of a people is about to become "a light to the nations" (Isa. 42:6; 49:6). He uses the metaphor *eved adonai*, or "God's Servant," in referring to Israel's role in the world. He says,

> Here is my servant, whom I uphold,
> My chosen, in whom my soul delights;
> I have put my spirit upon him;
> He will bring forth justice to the nations.
> He will not cry or lift up his voice,
> Or make it heard in the street;
> A bruised reed he will not break,
> And a dimly burning wick he will not quench;
> He will faithfully bring forth justice.
> He will not grow faint or be crushed
> Until he has established justice in the earth;
> And the coastlands wait for his teaching.
> Thus says God, Adonai
> Who created the heavens and stretched them out,
> Who spread out the earth and what comes from it,
> Who gives breath to the people upon it
> And spirit to those who walk in it:

> I am God,
> I have called you in righteousness,
> I have taken you by the hand and kept you;
> I have given you as a covenant to the people,
> A light to the nations. (Isa. 42:1–6)

In this passage the prophet defines the role of Israel in the world. Like the prophet himself who has no choice when called upon by God to prophesy, Israel, God's servant (the Hebrew word *eved* actually means "slave"), has no choice but to become God's witness and God's messenger to the nations. Here the prophet is echoing the prophecy of the first Isaiah concerning the end of days, which is also voiced by other prophets such as Micah and Jeremiah, envisioning a world of justice and enlightenment, a world without war and without strife.

A careful reading of the prophecies of the Second Isaiah shows that the prophet was overcome with an eschatological fervor as a result of the return to Zion, and he believed that the vision of his great namesake was about to be fulfilled. Disillusionment, however, would soon set in. Zechariah, a prophet of the same time, says regarding reality in the newly established community as he tries to lift the spirits of the people, "He who despises the day of small things shall rejoice" (Zech. 4:10). And when the Temple is finally rebuilt, we are told that the elders who remembered the old Temple wept because the new house did not come close to capturing the splendor of the old one (Ezra 3:12). Furthermore, the pagan empire of Persia was greater than either Assyria or Babylon, and monotheism would remain the faith of the few. The vision of both Isaiahs had to be deferred, and the role of Israel as a "light to the nations" would evolve and be fulfilled indirectly, centuries later, through the birth of Judaism's two daughter religions. I am reminded of my experience as an eight-year-old child in my native town of Haifa, when the State of Israel was born after two thousand years of exile. We children thought that the long-awaited-for messiah was about to come. But our second-grade teacher disabused us of such thoughts, and told us that hard times were ahead, and the struggle would be long and hard. Her prediction was soon fulfilled.

God's Servant

There are several references in the Second Isaiah to what the prophet calls "my servant," which means God's servant. The most prominent references are referred to by scholars as the "songs of the servant." Jewish and Christian commentators have struggled for centuries with these poetic descriptions of the servant. The prophet starts out by speaking of "Jacob my servant" (Isa. 41:8). Later on, he speaks of a mysterious person who takes on the sins of his people and brings them healing through his suffering (Isa. 53:1–7). This last passage has been commonly accepted by believing Christians as foreshadowing the passion of their savior. To Jews it has meant their own suffering throughout history as God's witnesses. But yet a third view has been offered in Jewish and other sources identifying a historical personality, either a biblical king or a prophet, perhaps even the Second Isaiah himself.

Isaiah 53:1–7 reads,

> Who can believe what we have heard?
> And on whom was Adonai's power revealed?
> He rose like a child before Him
> And like a tree trunk in an arid land;
> He had no rank and was given no respect,
> We did not find anything attractive about him.
> He was despised, shunned by all,
> A great sufferer, greatly afflicted,
> He seemed to hide from us,
> Despised, we took no account of him.
> Indeed, he carried our affliction,
> And he suffered our pain,
> And we thought him diseased,
> God stricken, tortured.
> But he was stricken
> Because of our sins,
> Oppressed because of our iniquities,
> The lesson of our welfare is upon him,
> And in his bruises we were healed.
> We all went astray like sheep,
> Each going our own way,
> And upon him God visited the guilt of us all.
> He was attacked, yet he remained submissive,
> He did not open his mouth.

He was led like a sheep to the slaughter,
Silent as a ewe about to be sheared.

No one who has read the New Testament can fail to identify the subject of this poem, and no one who believes the New Testament to be the word of God can fail to believe that the prophet refers to the future Christian savior. This, clearly, is a matter of faith. But a textual study of these seven verses shows that our mystery prophet has embedded a well-known prophet in these verses, namely, Jeremiah. In my book on Jeremiah, I make the case that Jesus considered himself a disciple of Jeremiah and emulated this prophet's example of putting his life on the line for his faith.

Why did the Second Isaiah choose to speak of Jeremiah as God's suffering servant?

As we mentioned before, no one in the Bible loved his people more than the prophet Jeremiah. No one, that is, with perhaps the one exception of the Second Isaiah. To begin with, the Second Isaiah is a great comforter of his people who starts out by saying, "Be comforted, be comforted, my people" (Isa. 40:1). Over and over again, he keeps reassuring the suffering and bewildered remnants of his people who return from Babylonian captivity that God's love for them is undying and eternal. He says,

But Zion said,
"God has forsaken me,
My God has forgotten me."
Can a woman forget her nursing-child,
Or show no compassion for the child of her womb?
Even these may forget,
Yet I will not forget you.
See, I have inscribed you on the palms of my hands;
Your walls are continually before me.
Then you will know that I am God;
Those who wait for me shall not be put to shame. (Isa. 49:14–23)

Later on he says,

For the mountains may depart
And the hills be removed,
But my steadfast love shall not depart from you,
And my covenant of peace shall not be removed,
Says Adonai, who has compassion on you. (Isa. 54:10)

In the Second Isaiah we almost find the reincarnation of Jeremiah.

Moreover, the Second Isaiah tells us in Isaiah 53:1–7 that through his personal sacrifice Jeremiah enabled his people to overcome destruction and exile and return to their land—an act unparalleled in human history—and thereby confirm the eternal covenant between them and their maker. He thus positions Jeremiah as the Bible's pivotal prophet, the one we should pay very close attention to in our search for the prophet.

Why doesn't he mention Jeremiah by name?

For two reasons. First, he never mentions himself by name. He seems to be implying that the identity of the individual prophet is not important. What is important is God and the people. Second, he does not wish to turn Jeremiah into an object of worship. For that matter, he never uses the word "prophet." And yet it is quite clear that he speaks in the name of all the prophets when he says,

> Seek God while he may be found,
> Call upon him while he is near;
> Let the wicked forsake their way,
> And the unrighteous their thoughts;
> Let them return to Adonai,
> That he may have mercy on them,
> And to our God, for he will abundantly pardon. (Isa. 55:6–7)

This prophet seems to reflect a new reality that transcends his predecessors. The era of the biblical prophets is about to come to an end. The people whom those prophets chastised during the time of the monarchy are no longer the same, and the monarchy is gone. There is a shift of emphasis here, from the king and the prophet to the people. The people are God's servant, and God is their only true king. We shall return to this critical change later on when we consider the implications of the teachings of this prophet for our search for the meaning of prophecy.

THE LAST PROPHETS: JOEL, HAGGAI, ZECHARIAH, AND MALACHI

Joel

In a way, Joel is also a mystery prophet, except for the fact that we do know his name. There is absolutely no agreement as to when he lived and prophesied. He has been shifted around by the traditional Jewish sources and by modern scholars from 800 BCE to 500 BCE and even later. He seems timeless and placeless. As such, he is somewhat lost in the shuffle and does not get enough attention. His main vision is about a plague of four different kinds of locust that invade the land and cause total devastation. It is not clear whether he speaks of an actual plague or uses symbolic language to describe the enemies of Israel. The use of the number 4 regarding Israel's enemies will appear again in the prophecies of Zechariah (see below), and whether or not Joel speaks of an actual plague, the symbolism here is strong. In four short chapters, Joel alludes to the prophecies of several of his colleagues, as when he reverses Isaiah's words in the vision of the end of days about beating swords into ploughshares, or when he uses Amos's image of God roaring like a lion. And like most of the literary prophets, he has his own vision of the day of Adonai, which includes the following prediction that deserves a very close reading:

> Then afterwards I will pour out my spirit on all flesh;
> Your sons and your daughters shall prophesy,
> Your old men shall dream dreams,
> And your young men shall see visions.
> Even on the male and female slaves,
> In those days, I will pour out my spirit. (Joel 3:1–2)

This passage is paraphrased in the New Testament.

> In the last days, God says, I will pour out
> My Spirit on all people.
> Your sons and daughters will prophesy,
> Your young men will see visions,
> Your old men will dream dreams. (Acts 2:17)

The words "I will pour out my spirit" have become well known and commonly used among Christians, but not so much among Jews. The traditional Jewish commentators, notably Rashi, do not pay much attention to them. They relegate them to the messianic era and offer vague explanations as to what "pour out my spirit" and "your sons and daughters shall prophesy" mean. They base their views on the words "in those days," which they link to the words "the end of days," ergo, the messianic age.

The above passage from the book of Joel has great significance for our search for the meaning of prophecy. It is part of one of the shortest chapters in the Hebrew Bible, and I would like to quote this chapter in its entirety:

> Then afterwards I will pour out my spirit on all flesh;
> Your sons and your daughters shall prophesy,
> Your old men shall dream dreams,
> And your young men shall see visions.
> Even on the male and female slaves,
> In those days, I will pour out my spirit.
> And I will show wonders in the heavens and in the earth,
> Blood and fire and pillars of smoke,
> The sun shall be turned into darkness,
> And the moon into blood,
> Before the coming of the great and terrible day of Adonai.
> But everyone who invokes the name of Adonai will escape,
> For there shall be a remnant in Mount Zion and Jerusalem,
> As God has spoken,
> And among the remnants those whom God shall call. (Joel 3)

The power and the mystery of this chapter were not lost on the Jewish sages who incorporated the phrase "blood and fire and pillars of smoke" in the Passover Haggadah to dramatize the story of the deliverance from Egyptian bondage. Similarly, it was not lost on the rabbis who canonized the biblical text when they provided the final version of the Bible as they concluded the last book of the books of the prophets with the words "Before the coming of the great and terrible day of Adonai" (Mal. 3:24). But the pouring out of the spirit of God on all flesh and the subsequent prophetic movement that would emerge, a rather momentous event, have been disregarded by the Jewish sages and scholars.

It has been suggested that Joel is alluding to the time of the first formal prophet of the people in their land, namely, Samuel. We recall how during that time, which marked the beginning of the consolidation of the Hebrew tribes and the birth of the Hebrew monarchy under Saul and later David, prophecy was a popular movement that gave rise to "schools of prophets" who roamed the countryside, looking for inspiration with the aid of musical instruments, dance, and other physical means to induce a trance in the hope of invoking the spirit of God and hearing God's message. This movement continued for some two hundred years through the time of the prophets Elijah and his disciple Elisha, but as the age of the literary prophets dawned with prophets like Amos, Hosea, and Isaiah, the movement seems to have subsided or perhaps even ended altogether. Now, at what seems to be the end of the prophetic era, Joel, our elusive prophet, is predicting a future time of redemption when prophecy will no longer be the domain of the chosen few, but will spread to "all flesh."

When the biblical period ended, the rabbis of the Mishnah and the Talmud determined that the prophetic era was over and one should no longer expect to hear a divine voice. Prophecies such as chapter 3 of the book of Joel were relegated to a messianic future. When the Hebrew Bible was canonized in the second century CE, the word of God was sealed for all time. And yet in our search for the prophet, Joel's words give us pause. Why does he predict that "your sons and your daughters shall prophesy?" And why does he go even further and include "male and female slaves"?

This question, along with the question of hearing the voice of God, will be revisited when we come to the end of our search.

Haggai

Two prophets are clearly associated with the time of the return from Babylonian Exile and the rebuilding of the Second Temple, namely, Haggai and Zechariah. They both play a central role in lifting up the spirits of the returned exiles and preparing them for the new reality of small beginnings in their ancestral land. With only two chapters, Haggai makes a brief appearance in the Bible as a "one issue" prophet. We are told,

In the second year of King Darius, in the sixth month, on the first day of the month, the word of God came by the prophet Haggai to Zerubbabel son of Shealtiel, governor of Judah, and to Joshua son of Jehozadak, the high priest, saying: Thus says the God of hosts: These people say the time has not yet come to rebuild God's house. Then the word of God came to the prophet Haggai, saying: Is it a time for you yourselves to live in your paneled houses, while this house lies in ruins? (Hag. 1:1–4)

That Haggai succeeds admirably in fulfilling his mission as evidenced in the following report:

Then Zerubbabel son of Shealtiel, and Joshua son of Jehozadak, the high priest, with all the remnant of the people, obeyed the voice of Adonai their God, and the words of the prophet Haggai, as Adonai their God had sent him; and the people feared God. Then Haggai, the messenger of God, spoke to the people with God's message, saying: I am with you, says God. And God stirred up the spirit of Zerubbabel son of Shealtiel, governor of Judah, and the spirit of Joshua son of Jehozadak, the high priest, and the spirit of all the remnant of the people; and they came and worked on the house of the God of hosts, their God. (Hag. 1:12–14)

When we look back on all the other prophets, who seldom seemed to get their people's attention, let alone their compliance, it would appear that all of them would have envied Haggai, who was able to deliver a clear and unequivocal message and accomplish the historical task of moving his people forward by having them rebuild the Temple that ushered in a new phase of Jewish history, namely, the era of the Second Temple, which would last for six hundred years. Surely this accomplishment should elicit our admiration.

Zechariah

A younger contemporary of Haggai, Zechariah was also accepted by the returning exiles as a prophet of God and, like his older colleague, was able to lift up their spirits and ease them into the new age they were now facing. He clearly continues in the traditions of the great literary prophets like Amos, Isaiah, and Jeremiah when he reminds the people that the rebuilding of the Temple is not enough. Along with the rituals of the Temple the people must heed the divine command to live and act righteously, for only then will the good life be established. He says,

> Thus says the God of hosts: Let your hands be strong—you that have recently been hearing these words from the mouths of the prophets who were present when the foundation was laid for the rebuilding of the temple, the house of the God of hosts. [10]For before those days there were no wages for people or for animals, nor was there any safety from the foe for those who went out or came in, and I set them all against one another. [11]But now I will not deal with the remnant of this people as in the former days, says the God of hosts. [12]For there shall be a sowing of peace; the vine shall yield its fruit, the ground shall give its produce, and the skies shall give their dew; and I will cause the remnant of this people to possess all these things. [13]Just as you have been a cursing among the nations, O house of Judah and house of Israel, so I will save you and you shall be a blessing. Do not be afraid, but let your hands be strong.
>
> [14]For thus says the God of hosts: Just as I plotted to bring disaster upon you, when your ancestors provoked me to wrath, and I did not relent, says the God of hosts, [15]so again I have plotted in these days to do good to Jerusalem and to the house of Judah; do not be afraid. [16]These are the things that you shall do: Speak the truth to one another, render in your gates judgments that are true and make for peace, [17]do not devise evil in your hearts against one another, and love no false oath; for all these are things that I hate, says Adonai. (Zech. 8:9–17)

When there is righteousness in people's hearts, there is tranquility in the land and people prosper. This is the sum and substance of the prophetic message, which Zachariah captures in the above passage. But he also adds a new perspective that reflects the lessons people like him had learned from the bitter experience of the destruction and the exile. This new perspective is captured in the following words:

> He said to me: "This is the word of the Lord to Zerubbabel: Not by might, nor by power, but by my spirit, says the God of hosts. What are you, O great mountain? Before Zerubbabel you shall become a plain; and he shall bring out the chief stone amid shouts of Hurrah, hurrah!"

Moreover, the word of Adonai came to me, saying: "The hands of Zerubbabel have laid the foundation of this house; his hands shall also complete it. Then you will know that the God of hosts has sent me to you. For who despises the day of small things?" (Zech. 4:6–10)

Two great new lessons are contained in these words. The first lesson is "Not by might, nor by power, but by my spirit" (Zech. 4:6). Great empires rise and fall. Human might is not right. The only might that is right is the might of God. The might of God is manifested in the righteous acts of people. Doing what is right is man's way of establishing God's kingship on earth. The destiny of this people, who have left their land as Hebrews and returned as Jews is to be witnesses to God's will on earth. They have now become a "kingdom of priests and a holy people" (Ex. 19:6). This is the spiritual message of Zechariah, which will help shape the character of his newly redeemed people.

Zechariah's second great lesson is "For who despises the day of small things?" Men seek glory, fortune, and fame, but real greatness resides in the small acts of kindness performed by ordinary people every day of the week. This will become the central teaching of a great spiritual movement in Judaism started in modern times and known as Hasidism, which has put an emphasis on such acts; it will also become a key teaching of Christianity. This is a lesson that still resonates today.

Less important for our purpose are Zechariah's visions, which are reminiscent of some of Ezekiel's visions. Ezekiel has his four-headed divine creatures, and Zechariah has his colorful horses. Why horses of different colors are chosen as God's messengers scouting the earth is hard to say. Like Ezekiel, Zechariah also has a mysterious scroll of unusual proportions. The difference, though, between the two scrolls, is that, unlike Ezekiel, Zechariah does not eat his. As a general rule, Zechariah does not engage in the bizarre acts that characterize Ezekiel, but rather has passive dreams and visions, which include a scene of four horns representing the various enemies of Israel. (Here we may recall Joel's four kinds of locust, which may also represent the same thing. The number 4 alludes to the "four corners of the earth," or the four points of the compass, conveying the idea of being surrounded by enemies on all sides.) We also have here a vision of a seven-branched candelabra that represents God's watchfulness and which is the most authentic symbol of the Jewish people, more so than the so-called Star of David. This candelabra was prominently displayed in the Holy Temple in Jerusalem, and its bas-relief can be seen to this day inside the Arch of Titus in Rome in a scene showing Roman soldiers carrying it in their victory procession after destroying the Temple in the year 70 CE. Its modernized replica can be seen today in front of Israel's parliament building, the Knesset, in Jerusalem.

We need not join the controversy as to whether Zechariah is also the author of the second half of his book, which bears little resemblance to the first. Here we have no visions, but rather prophecies against the nations reminiscent of those of previous prophets, as well as an eschatological vision of the day of Adonai when Jerusalem will be delivered and its God will reign supreme.

> On that day there shall not be either cold or frost.
> And there shall be continuous day, it is known to God,
> Not day and not night, for at eveningtime there shall be light.
> On that day living waters shall flow out from Jerusalem,
> Half of them to the eastern sea and half of them to the western sea;
> It shall continue in summer as in winter.
> And God will become king over all the earth;
> On that day Adonai shall be one and His name one. (Zech. 14:6–9)

Malachi

Who is Malachi? Is he the last of the Hebrew prophets?

There are good reasons to doubt such a prophet ever existed. The name means "my [God's] messenger" or "my [God's] angel," a term used twice in the stories of the Exodus (Exod. 23:23; 32:34). It does not appear elsewhere as a person's name. The book, consisting of three chapters, sounds like a compendium of prophetic statements and ideas pieced together somewhat awkwardly. It does, however, provide a fitting conclusion to the prophetic era. In fact, it serves a dual purpose: it speaks to its own time, which is the period after the rebuilding of the Temple under the initiative of Haggai and Zechariah, and it serves as a summary of the message of all the previous prophets.

The book opens with a discussion of God's relationship with the people of Israel, and it continues with God's role in the world in relation to all people. Even though the author's contemporaries seem to have doubts about God's love for Israel, the author reassures them that

God loves Israel, and he borrows Jeremiah's idea that God is a loving parent to the People of the Covenant. The author goes on to affirm the universality of God.

> For from the rising of the sun to its setting
> My name is great among the nations,
> And in every place incense is offered to my name,
> And a pure offering; for my name is great among the nations,
> Says the Lord of hosts. (Mal. 1:11)

This is by no means an easy passage to understand, since the nations of the world at that time did not worship the God of Israel. But the intent is clear: whether the rest of the world knows the true God or not, God is indeed worshipped by all creation since God is the creator of all. This is the message all the prophets sought to impart to their people. It reaches its full realization with the Second Isaiah who, as we saw, articulated what we may consider to be pure monotheism. It is here, at the end of the prophetic period, that the full eradication of polytheism among the Judeans begins to take place.

It is interesting to note that, unlike most of the other literary prophets, the author of the book of Malachi does not discuss prophets, either true ones or false. Instead, he speaks at length about the priests who are now ministering once again at the Holy Temple. The prophetic era is now coming to an end. For the next several centuries the province of Judah, no longer a sovereign monarchy, will be led by the priestly class. The author seems to provide instructions for the priests as to how to conduct themselves as leaders of their people. He says,

> And now, O priests, this command is for you. If you will not listen, if you will not lay it to heart to give glory to my name, says the God of hosts, then I will send the curse on you and I will curse your blessings; indeed I have already cursed them, because you do not lay it to heart. I will rebuke your offspring, and spread dung on your faces, the dung of your offerings, and I will put you out of my presence.
>
> Know, then, that I have sent this command to you, so that My covenant with Levi may hold, says the God of hosts. My covenant with him was a covenant of life and well-being, which I gave him; this called for reverence, and he revered Me and stood in awe of my name. True instruction was in his mouth, and no wrong was found on his lips. He walked with me in integrity and uprightness, and he turned many from iniquity. For the lips of a priest should guard

knowledge, and people should seek instruction from his mouth, for he is the messenger of the God of hosts. But you have turned aside from the way; you have caused many to stumble by your instruction; you have corrupted the covenant of Levi, says the God of hosts. (Mal. 2:1–8)

This passage marks a turning point in biblical history. The biblical prophets have completed their mission. It is now time for the priests to take over. Along with the priests come the scribes, most notably Ezra the Scribe, who plays the key role in introducing Torah-centered Judaism, which will eventually replace the Temple sacrificial cult. The priests and the scribes will eventually be replaced by the scholars and the rabbis, who will become the authority on the Torah and its interpretations. The prophets, who were the original "messengers of God," are now being replaced by the new guardians of their words.

The book of Malachi concludes with the words

Remember the Torah of my servant Moses, the statutes and ordinances that I commanded him at Horeb for all Israel.

Lo, I will send you the prophet Elijah before the great and terrible day of Adonai comes. He will turn the hearts of parents to their children and the hearts of children to their parents, so that I will not come and strike the land with a curse. (Mal. 3:22–24)

These words are both a promise and an admonition. When the Israelites first enter the Promised Land under the leadership of Joshua, God tells Moses's successor, "Let not this book of the Torah depart from your lips, and meditate upon it day and night" (Joshua 1:8). Now these words have come full circle. Here, however, a new dimension is added, namely, the prophetic idea of the future day of Adonai. When exactly it is supposed to take place, we are never told. What we do learn here is that the prophet Elijah, who according to the biblical story did not die but instead went up to heaven, will return to usher in that "great and terrible day," which in time will become the day of the coming of the messiah.

WHY DID PROPHECY CEASE IN ISRAEL AFTER THE BABYLONIAN EXILE?

The classical rabbinic view on prophecy is that after the Babylonian Exile prophecy comes to an end. In the Talmud we read, "Said Rabbi Johanan: Since the day the Temple was destroyed, prophecy was taken away from the prophets and given to fools and little children" (Baba Batra 12b). This is a rather harsh statement, and it should be understood in the context of its time. Rabbi Johanan lived around 200 CE, the time when the Hebrew Bible was canonized in its final form for all time. Nothing could be added or taken out. The words of the prophets that appeared in the canon became sacrosanct. The most sacrosanct part of the Scriptures is the Torah, which contains the divine commandments. The second-most is the prophetic books, and the third-most is the Writings, which form the third division of the Hebrew Bible, or Tanakh. A statement from the Torah carries more weight than one from the prophets, and a statement from the prophets carries more weight than one from the Writings. A similar process seems to take place in all world religions. They all have their prophetic figures who cannot be surpassed or replaced. They all have their scriptures that are set for all time. They all resist changing this set order, which is considered valid for all time.

Another reason for considering Hebrew prophecy an exclusive phenomenon of pre-exilic time, which comes to an end with the Babylonian Exile, is the profound change that took place when the exiles returned from Babylon under the leadership of Ezra and Nehemiah in the fifth century BCE. As was mentioned earlier, the role of the prophets during the time of the monarchy was to bring the people back to their God and to the teachings of the Torah. During the four centuries of the monarchy the tribes of Israel were ridden with pagan practices and moral decay. The prophets were not able to change this state of affairs during their lifetime. But they did bequeath to their people a legacy that the people carried with them into exile, and when the exiles of Zion came back, they became changed people. They no longer practiced any pagan rituals, and they became committed to living by the laws of the Torah. Now the work of the prophets was completed. They were replaced by the Sages, namely, the scholars and later rabbis who were the interpreters and guardians of the law. There was no longer a need for signs and wonders or miracles; now the word of God was set for all time and became an object of ongoing explication and interpretation.

Some have suggested that the strong stand taken by rabbinical authorities like Rabbi Johanan against the acceptance of new prophets or prophecies was a reaction to the new faith that began to emerge at that time among Jews, namely, Christianity. There were always those among the Jews of post-biblical times who continued to believe that new prophets were making their appearance in their midst. The best-known new prophets were John the Baptist and Jesus of Nazareth who, after all, were Jews. I am inclined to accept two other reasons as more compelling explanations. Christianity at the time of the canonization of the Hebrew Scriptures was still a small movement, and it did not appear as threatening to Judaism as it became later on. Its prophets were not the only ones confronting post-biblical Judaism. They were part of a phenomenon rooted mainly in folk religion that had to be dealt with in order for rabbinical oral law—also known as the Talmud and represented by sages like Rabbi Johanan who sought to build a strong fence around the law to protect it from unwanted views and beliefs—to become the established authority in Judaism.

Yet another reason for taking such a strong stand against the possibility of new prophets and new prophecies was a new kind of belief that emerged during that time, namely, messianism. While in the day of the biblical prophets the concept of a messiah meant a human king who descended from the House of David, it now became a belief in a supernatural savior. A major rabbinical figure preceding Rabbi Johanan, namely, Rabbi Akiba, was tempted by this belief into proclaiming a military leader named Bar Kokhba a messianic leader who would redeem his people. Bar Kokhba's uprising against the Romans brought only a short period of independence, and its suppression by the emperor Hadrian resulted in the massacre of hundreds of thousands of Jews and the end of Jewish dreams of independence for the next eighteen centuries. What happens at this point in time is that the two concepts of prophet and messiah become interrelated. The messiah is a prophetic figure, a messenger of God, who comes to redeem his people. The rabbis, following the Bar Kokhba rebellion (132 CE), which followed the earlier uprising against Rome in the year 70 CE that resulted in the destruction of Jerusalem and the Second Temple, realized that the time for messianic and prophetic fervor was over and had to be relegated to the distant future in order for the remnants of the people to survive. Theirs was no longer a time for heroic action. It was a time for turning inwardly and "giving Caesar what is Caesar's" while "giving God what is God's."

This, then, is the official Jewish belief. But the rest of the world has had its own views on the matter. Prophets and prophecies have continued to be part of the human culture to this day.

5

PROPHETIC TRUTH

What have we learned so far from our exploration of biblical prophecy?

Most importantly, the prophets, from Moses to Malachi, as the Bible makes it amply clear, were not divine but rather flesh and blood. Like all mortals, they made mistakes, they overreacted, they tried to walk away from their mission, and, on the verge of total despair, as happened with Jeremiah, they even cursed the day of their birth. Not only were they human, they were, to use Nietzsche's phrase, all too human. Therein perhaps lies their greatness. They confronted kings and they put their life on the line, but they were not mighty warriors. What animated them was not physical courage but an overwhelming sense of right and wrong. Hypersensitive souls that they were, they were not able to keep their silence in the face of injustice. Elijah confronts the king for stealing the vineyard of one of his subjects. Amos cries out against the rich people of Samaria, who sell the poor for a pair of shoes. Jeremiah attacks King Jehoiakim for robbing the people to build himself a luxurious palace. In the blessing chanted before the *haftarah,* the reading from the prophets, the prophets are referred to by the Jewish liturgy as "the prophets of truth and justice." They taught the world the divine truth about justice as the supreme value in human affairs. "Justice, justice you shall pursue" (Deut. 16:20). Without justice for all, society cannot endure.

Another lesson we derive from examining the history of biblical prophecy is that the prophets' lofty ideals and great aspirations fell short of being fully realized. Isaiah and Micah dreamed of a world without war and conflict and governed by divine law. Such a world did not come about in their time, and it still remains a seemingly unattainable goal today. Neither they nor the founders and prophets of the other religions of the world or of any of the nontheistic ideological movements, whether political, economic, spiritual or intellectual, past or present, have been able to bring about utopia. The Greek philosopher Epicurus (whose name became synonymous among the ancient rabbis with heresy) taught his disciples that all that matters in life is pleasure, inner peace, and self-fulfillment, and that the gods do not reward or punish human actions, so we may as well seize the moment and not worry about the state of the world because, to use the words of Ecclesiastes, what was will be, and there is nothing new under the sun (here Greek philosophy and biblical wisdom have a rare meeting of the minds). So what were the Hebrew prophets so worked up about?

This is what we need to examine. Those who still believe in the possibility of a better world, whether religionists or secularists, believers or nonbelievers, need to carefully consider what these relentless emissaries of the divine message were trying to tell us. When they said, "The day will come," it could have been next week, or next year, or even centuries later. They did not have a timetable for ultimate salvation. God only knows. And God did not give them the date, much less is it given to mere mortals like us. But people have always dreamed of paradise, and the day people stop dreaming will be the day all hope is lost. And so we continue with the search for the meaning of prophecy.

THE VOICE OF GOD

The most common phrase used by the Hebrew prophets is "Thus says Adonai." The key question regarding the Hebrew prophets, which no biblical scholar has ever been able to answer, is whether they actually heard the voice of God or whether they were listening to the voice of their own conscience. In our inability to answer this question, we posit that it is a matter of faith, which places the question beyond objective discussion. Let us revisit this question, now that we have taken a close look at the full range of biblical prophecy.

My point of departure is that the Hebrew prophets expressed truths that were both universal and unique. God as understood by most people today is the God of Amos, Isaiah, Jeremiah, and, most importantly, the Second Isaiah. When they say, "Thus says Adonai," I take it to mean that they convey a message they know is emanating from the source of all being, namely, the one true God. That source never lies, and its pronouncements are never relative or debatable. They are eternal truths. That these prophets had their human limitations makes them even more credible. That they were dreamers who did not accept human behavior as sufficient and excusable and that they reached beyond our common reality does not in any way diminish them. They did not deal with "what is" but with what, to quote Micah, "your God asks of you." The exact manner in which they heard the voice of God is immaterial. As we pointed out in the beginning, there are many different ways of hearing and many different ways of verbal and nonverbal communication. We measure these prophets not by their method of communication, but by the magnitude of their message.

We may be coming now closer to answering the question about hearing the voice of God, but there seems to be more to it that still needs to be explored. Before we can take our stand in this matter, we need to examine the nature of prophetic truth and the meaning of the biblical narrative. One thing I have absolutely no doubt about: To the prophets, "Thus says Adonai" was no mere figure of speech or hypothetical statement. The word of God was the central reality of their lives. Everything else paled by comparison. However we are to understand it, each prophet might have been thought to say, to use Jeremiah's expression, the word of God "burned like a fire in my bones" (Jer. 20:9). Here we have an overwhelming mental and even physical experience, the like of which most of us never experience. Something enters the soul of the person known as a prophet and does not let go. The prophet becomes possessed, unable to go about his daily personal affairs. The prophet hears a voice not his; it comes from somewhere else. Trying to resist it is futile. The voice takes full possession of the prophet's will and makes him go out and speak in public to let people know that "thus says Adonai." More often than not, those who happen to listen shrug their shoulders and dismiss the message as a rant or idle talk. But the prophet does not let go. He goes elsewhere and speaks again. He keeps repeating his message despite the unwillingness of his listeners to believe him. If his message is indeed as compelling as he believes it is, it will find its way into some people's hearts and eventually become acknowledged as the word of God. This, more or less, is the process by which the Hebrew prophets delivered their message, which remains with us to this day.

DIVINE TRUTH

In his vision of the end of days and the peaceable kingdom, Isaiah says,

> They will not hurt or destroy
> Throughout my holy mountain;
> For the earth will be full of
> The knowledge of Adonai
> As the waters cover the sea. (Isa. 11:9)

The concept of knowledge in general and the knowledge of God, or *da'at adonai*, in particular, is one of the most complex concepts in the Bible. The common meaning of the word "knowledge" is "information acquired through either learning or experience." In the biblical stories of creation, however, we learn about the existence in the Garden of Eden of a tree of the knowledge of good and evil, conveying the idea of knowledge not as information but as the ability to make a moral judgment. God orders Adam not to eat of the fruit of the tree of knowledge of good and evil, for "the day you eat it you will surely die" (Gen. 2:9, 17). Later on, when the serpent tempts Adam and Eve to eat the forbidden fruit, the tempter argues that rather than die, they will become godlike in their knowledge of good and evil. We then learn that God decides to expel Adam and Eve from the Garden of Eden because "now man is like one of us [God and the angels], knowing good and evil, and now he may reach out and also partake of the fruit of the tree of life [another presumably forbidden tree] and live forever" (Gen. 3:22).

These stories have puzzled classical biblical commentators as well as modern biblical scholars and still continue to elicit innumerable commentaries. The immediate question is this: Why does God tell Adam he will die on the day he eats from the tree of knowledge, when in effect

Adam does not die the day he eats from it? It is the serpent, rather than God, who makes the more credible statement, namely, that eating the forbidden fruit makes Adam godlike, as we soon learn when we hear God repeat exactly what the serpent said.

Another compelling question is this one: Why is God averse to man acquiring the knowledge of good and evil?

One possible answer is that God knows that this kind of knowledge implies self-awareness as well as awareness of the world, which inevitably leads to pain and suffering. Man becomes aware of his own mortality, which may well be the actual meaning of the phrase "you will surely die," which we can take to mean "you will surely become aware of your mortality." Here we may have a rare insight into the prophets' understanding of God. Theirs is not a remote and unfeeling God, a God found in other cultures and religions (of which Heschel, the contemporary Jewish theologian, wrote so eloquently in his book on the prophets). Rather it is a God who feels and suffers the pain of the world. It is the God the prophets bequeathed to Christianity (a God who "so loved the world") and to Islam (a God who is "the merciful and the compassionate"). It is the God Jews believe in to this day as the God who "waits for man to return."

Be this as it may, what we further learn from these stories of creation is that the knowledge of good and evil, or the ability to make a moral judgment, is a divine attribute. Thus, to be able to tell good from evil is to know God. In this light, Isaiah's above-quoted statement, namely, "They will not hurt or destroy / Throughout my holy mountain; / For the earth will be full of / The knowledge of Adonai / As the waters cover the sea," is self-evident.

The next time the word "knowledge" is used in the stories of creation, it takes on the meaning of carnal knowledge, when Adam "knows" his wife sexually and she gives birth to their sons, Cain and Abel (Gen. 4:1). Here the first human couple also acquires a godlike attribute by creating life.

The last use in the Torah of the verb "to know" appears in the story of the death of Moses. We are told that there never arose another prophet in Israel "whom God knew face to face" (Deut. 33:10). Here again, knowledge is related to the relation between the human and the divine.

The prophets present us with a dichotomy of two kinds of knowledge: the knowledge of God, which they call *da'at*, and human knowledge, which they call *hochmah*, or "wisdom." Jeremiah says,

> Let not the wise glory in his wisdom . . .
> But let him who glories
> Glory in understanding
> And knowing me,
> For I am Adonai. (Jer. 9:22–23)

The prophets do not reject human wisdom, but they make it clear that it cannot replace *da'at*, which is a higher form of wisdom. Our common understanding of the term "wisdom" seems to be different from theirs. To us, wisdom is a faculty that people possess to a greater or lesser degree. Knowledge is acquired, and the wiser one is, the more knowledge one is able to acquire. We do not ordinarily think of knowledge as being superior to wisdom, but rather subordinate to it. And yet the prophets present us with a form of knowledge that is superior to wisdom. Herein we may find a clue to what they mean when they talk about hearing the voice of God. It is not by dint of being wiser than other people that the prophet can hear God's voice. No prophet in the Bible is referred to as being the wisest of men, a title the Bible reserves for King Solomon. Hearing the divine voice is not a function of human intelligence. Instead, it is the deep-seated feeling we referred to early in our discussion as *moral compulsion*, which reaches beyond reasoning and all the categories of human knowledge. It comes from a place beyond our conscious mind, the same place from where we derive our faith, our dreams, our hopes, the place where we know there is something greater than our own self, something which many of us call God and others may call by other names. It is from that place that the prophet hears a voice, either a "still small voice" or one accompanied by thunder and lightning. In short, this is not a phenomenon we can discuss in the cool light of reason, but one of which we can only hope to catch a glimmer of understanding in the depths of our innermost feelings.

In discussing the knowledge of God, one may argue that God did not create man in His own image, but rather man created God in *his* own image. What if we humans invented God because we could not cope with the terrible reality of life? To begin with, whatever we might have invented because of our human needs and through our human understanding, the ultimate reality of God remains outside our reach. Our search here is not for the ultimate reality of God, but for God in relationship to man, if indeed such a relationship exists. No matter how much we may speculate about it, the ultimate reality of God remains beyond our comprehension. But the question of our interaction with God is a valid and necessary one. It is not a matter of speculation but of personal experience and intuition. People who seek to interact with God do so commonly through prayer, which the twentieth-century Jewish religious thinker Martin Buber refers to as a dialogue rather than a monologue. The idea of dialogue implies a response from the one who listens, in this case God. It should be mentioned that in the time of the prophets the main way of communicating with God was through the offering of animal sacrifices rather than prayer. This raises the question whether God expects or needs this kind of sacrifice. Throughout human history, bringing food offerings to the gods has been a common practice, and in some religions it is still practiced in some form. Jewish philosophers have debated the validity of animal sacrifices, and while Maimonides maintains that the sacrificial cult was a concession the Jewish faith in biblical times made to the common practices of the religions of the time, Yehuda Halevi insists that God indeed expects such sacrifices. Here we may have an example of something that may have grown out of a human need rather than a divine decree, and which over time has declined and ceased to be in common use. Similarly, prayer may also be the fulfillment of a human need rather than something God expects of man. But prayer is our human way of acknowledging our relationship with God, and it seems to be in perfect step with the prophetic idea of God as one who communicates with man through some form of speech, and with the practice of the biblical prophets who also prayed to God.

THE ROLE OF MIRACLES

Let us tentatively say that the prophets did hear the voice of God. This raises an interesting question: Are we also to believe that they believed in or even performed miracles?

To answer this question, we first need to ask ourselves, What is the nature and function of miracles in the biblical narrative?

The main age of miracles in biblical times is the time of Moses. The story of the enslavement of the Hebrew tribes in Egypt, followed by the liberation and the Exodus, and finally the conquering of the Promised Land, remained engraved in the collective memory of the people as the time when God became known to their ancestors; performed mighty acts on their behalf that forced the Egyptians to let them go; gave them the law at Mount Sinai; and sustained them for forty years, enabling them to cross the Jordan and inherit the land promised to their ancestor, Abraham. This story must have been told in many different ways and versions, and along the way events took on new dimensions. The purpose of the miracles, from the time Moses hears God's voice coming out of the burning bush to the time the voice of God is heard at Mount Sinai by the people as they receive the Ten Commandments, is that of "signs and wonders," namely, supernatural acts that establish the supremacy of the one true God over all the other gods of the nations and their rulers, particularly the pharaoh. At that time, Egypt had already existed for millennia as a powerful nation worshipping powerful gods. The pharaoh's priests had magic powers, enabling them to perform such acts as turning sticks into snakes (most likely by trickery). The Hebrew slaves hardly stood a chance against such powerful masters. It is against this backdrop that God appears on the scene, and the only way to persuade the pharaoh to let the children of Israel go is by supernatural acts, which culminate in the splitting of the Red Sea.

Looking back, what becomes clear is that the real miracle is not turning the waters of the Nile into blood or bringing water out of a rock. Rather, it is the ability of an enslaved people to free themselves and survive a long trek through the desert, in the process entering into a covenant with an invisible God and a set of laws and beliefs that endure to this day. Whether an event such as the splitting of the Red Sea was a divine miracle or a natural phenomenon is immaterial. The enduring results of that actual or presumed event is what matters.

It is important to emphasize that it is not Moses who splits the Red Sea, takes the Israelites out of Egypt, and brings down the law, but rather God. The biblical text attributes those momentous miracles not to man but to God. Moses is not a miracle worker. He is an ordinary mortal who is picked by God to serve as God's emissary to the pharaoh and to the Hebrew slaves. Each time Moses performs one of those miraculous acts, we are told that God tells him exactly what to do and, when necessary, speaks words of encouragement to him to help him overcome his fear and hesitation. It is a common misconception shared by many that Moses is the one who performed the miracles.

The second major age of miracles in prophetic history is the time of Elijah and his disciple Elisha. Here miracle working takes on an altogether different character. Unlike Moses, Elijah is not picked by God to free his people and give them the law. He appears in the Northern Kingdom of Israel in the days of King Ahab and his Phoenician wife, Jezebel, as a folk healer and miracle worker who performs the miracle of making food last longer than expected and revives a deathly ill child, much in the same way Jesus does several centuries later. Elijah's greatest miracle is his challenge to the prophets of Baal, the Canaanite god of fertility, whereby he causes the "fire of God" (most likely lightning) to come down from heaven and consume the offering on the altar. We do not hear of God asking him to perform such an act; he seems to do it on his own initiative. Elijah, then, remains in the collective memory of his people as a bona fide miracle worker. This, together with the story about his going up to heaven rather than dying (one may wonder why this happens to him and not to Moses), raises questions as to whether Elijah is presented in the Bible as flesh and blood or as a semi-mythological figure. One way of understanding his powers as a miracle worker is by looking at the time he lives in. The people of the Northern Kingdom are steeped in idolatry mainly because of their Baal-worshipping queen. There seems to be a need for a powerful representative of the faith of the God of Israel, one whose personal faith is so strong that he takes on supernatural powers. That person is Elijah, followed by his disciple Elisha. However we are to understand their powers, one thing remains unchanged, as was pointed out earlier when we discussed the time of those prophets. Unlike Moses, who succeeded in liberating his people and giving them the law, Elijah and his disciple do not succeed in eradicating paganism from among their people. The kings of the Northern Kingdom remain steeped in idol worshipping, and at the end of the following century the kingdom falls to the Assyrians and ceases to exist.

This brings us to the time of the literary prophets, beginning with Hosea, Amos, and Isaiah, and ending with Jeremiah, Ezekiel, and Malachi. Here we see a great decline in the performance of miracles. Essentially, the literary prophets are not miracle workers. Unlike an Elijah who roams the countryside and performs miracles, Amos travels from his native southern town of Tekoah to Samaria, the capital of the Northern Kingdom, to deliver his ethical message. He and his colleagues are orators and poets who deliver God's word and who have visions of God that they communicate to their people. On one particular occasion, Isaiah intercedes with God on behalf of King Hezekiah, who fears the onslaught of Sennacherib, king of Assyria. God sends an angel during the night who slaughters what seems to be the entire Assyrian army (2 Kings 19:15–35). A century later, however, when Nebuchadnezzar of Babylon lays siege to Jerusalem, the prophet Jeremiah rejects King Zedekiah's plea to intercede with God and ask for a similar miracle (Jer. 37:17). By now the prophets seem to have forgone this kind of miraculous intervention altogether.

Ezekiel, Jeremiah's younger contemporary, who seems to have the same fiery personality as Elijah, reports visions and actions that appear to be miraculous, such as being flown from Babylon to Jerusalem. But Ezekiel does not perform miracles like Elijah, much less like Moses. He does not heal the sick or revive the dead, his vision of the dry bones notwithstanding. His visions and "out of body" experiences are not part of common reality; they are extrasensory perception that has little to do with actual events.

In our search for the meaning of prophecy, we do not look to miracles as a yardstick to measure the prominence or relevance of a given prophet. Miracles seem to belong to the realm of what we referred to earlier as folk religion, which is part of every formal religion and is practiced for the most part outside the purview of the religion itself. We take our cues from prophets like Jeremiah or the Second Isaiah, who sought to teach us truths that go beyond the performance of physical miracles.

ANGELS AND OTHER DIVINE BEINGS

How prominent are angels in prophetic teachings? What role do they play, and what does the Bible actually have in mind when it tells us about angels and other divine beings?

To answer these questions, let us begin with a biblical personality we did not touch on in our discussion of the prophets, namely Daniel. The book of Daniel is not included among the books of the prophets in the Hebrew Bible; rather, it is found in the non-prophetic Writings section. In Christianity, on the other hand, Daniel is considered a full-fledged prophet. A good case can be made for either view, since the book includes prophetic pronouncements, and Daniel is described as some-one who receives divine messages. Still, he does not play a prophetic role similar to the classical prophets, and furthermore, while Daniel is presented as a contemporary of Jeremiah, the book was written four centuries later, in the second century BCE, and does not fit into the mold of the classical prophets.

The distinction between the Jewish and the Christian views of the book of Daniel is important for understanding the different roles angels play in the two religions. In this late biblical book we learn for the first time about the existence of individual angels who are identified by names such as "Gabriel" and "Michael." Here we have the beginning of what will eventually become a well-established hierarchy of angels in Christian theology. Gabriel and Michael will become archangels, and they will be assigned specific roles. Other angels will be added to this hierarchy, and they will continue to play important roles in the church to this day.

While the same angels appear in post-biblical Jewish lore and faith as well, rather than form part of the core official faith they remain in the realm of folk belief. There are many stories and legends in rabbinical and post-rabbinical literature about angels, and during the Middle Ages Jewish liturgical poets enriched the traditional Jewish prayer book with beautiful prayers depicting angels, prayers that are still popular today, such as the Sabbath song *Shalom Aleichem*, welcoming the Sabbath angels of peace. But unlike Christian belief, where angels take on a reality all their own, the Jewish view is more allegorical than dogmatic. The medieval Jewish philosopher Maimonides sought to intellectualize the belief in angles in his following comment:

> God, glory and majesty to Him, does not do things by direct contact. God burns things by means of fire; fire is moved by the motion of the sphere; the sphere is moved by means of a disembodied intellect, these intellects being the "angels which are near to Him," through whose mediation the spheres [planets] move . . . thus totally disem-

bodied minds exist which emanate from God and are the intermediaries between God and all the bodies [objects] here in this world.
(*Guide for the Perplexed* 2:4)

It is interesting to note that while the Hebrew Bible posits the existence
of angels from the stories of creation onward, it refuses to divulge the
names of individual angels. Thus, for example, after Jacob wrestles with
an angel who is not able to subdue him, he asks for the angel's name but
the mysterious stranger refuses to reveal his identity (Gen. 32:24–29).
Later on, when Samson's father is visited by an angel, he also tries to
find out the stranger's name but is told that it is "too wondrous" (Judg.
13:17–18). There seems to be a deliberate vagueness in the Bible when
it comes to identifying angels or providing too many details about their
nature. In fact, the word "angel" in Hebrew simply means "messenger,"
rather than a divine being, and quite often it is not clear in the biblical
narrative whether the mysterious stranger who appears before biblical
characters like Abraham or Samson's father is indeed an angel or a
mere mortal.

Most importantly, however, while some of the classical prophets
have visions of angels, some, like Jeremiah, never mention angels at all.
If indeed God is surrounded by an entourage of angels, and if we are to
follow Maimonides' explanation of angels as the intermediaries between God and the world, it is rather puzzling that the prophets repeat-
edly report being addressed directly by God rather than by any intermediaries. Nor, for that matter, do the prophets, with the exception of
Zechariah (Zech. 3:2), mention Satan, the leader of the fallen angels in
Christian lore. Satan's role becomes much more prominent in post-
biblical times. The impression one gets from reading the classical
prophets is that they were reluctant to attach too much importance to
creatures with supernatural powers for fear of creating polytheism. On
the other hand, they never dismiss the belief in divine beings such as
angels, which undoubtedly was deeply ingrained among their contemporaries. To this day, many of the believers of the world's religions
espouse some kind of a belief in angels, while perhaps just as many
either doubt or reject their existence. Be this as it may, the Hebrew
prophets did not put a great emphasis on such belief. As in the case of

miracles, the prophets' main concern was not with events or beings that exist outside common human experience, but rather with ethical human behavior and the welfare of society.

GOD IN THE REAL WORLD

When we examine the stories of the founders and prophetic figures of the world's religions, we discover two themes that seem to run together. The first theme is instruction; the second theme is transcendence. By instruction I mean teaching one's followers the right way that leads to living the good life. By transcendence I mean the ability of the prophetic person to go beyond common human experience and tap into a higher source of knowledge and power. Instruction is rooted in common human experience, while transcendence is a belief in the unknown, something that one accepts on faith. One question we need to ask when we examine our own faith is how does it balance the two? Is the main emphasis in our belief system on instruction or on transcendence? Which of the two is more important? Which gives us a better chance to better ourselves and our world?

In the teachings of the Hebrew prophets, the answer is instruction. Other religions may put the emphasis on transcendence, or belief. Micah's famous dictum comes to mind: "He has told you, O man, what is good; / And what God requires of you, / But to do justice, and to love mercy, / And to walk humbly with your God" (Mic. 6:8). The emphasis here is on instruction, namely, teaching man to act justly and mercifully to other people. God comes third, and the demand is not to believe in God but to walk humbly. One is reminded of the Talmudic statement "Would that they forsake Me but observe my Torah" (Jerusalem Talmud Haggigah 1:7). In other words, what matters to God in the real world is not that one profess a belief in God but rather that one live according to God's instruction, namely, the Torah. The Hebrew prophets liken God to a parent who loves his or her children. In his opening words Isaiah says,

> Hear, O heavens, and listen, O earth;
> For Adonai has spoken:
> I reared children and brought them up,
> But they have rebelled against me.

The ox knows its owner,
And the donkey its master's crib;
But Israel does not know,
My people do not understand.
Ah, sinful nation,
People laden with iniquity,
Offspring who do evil,
Children who deal corruptly,
Who have forsaken Adonai,
Who have despised the Holy One of Israel,
Who are utterly estranged! (Isa. 1:2–4)

What does Isaiah mean by knowing God? We heard him say, "They will not hurt or destroy / Throughout my holy mountain; / For the earth will be full of / The knowledge of Adonai / As the waters cover the sea" (Isa. 11:9). Knowing God is healing and building rather than hurting and destroying. What does the prophet mean by God rearing and bringing up children? Here we go back to the story of creation, when Adam is instructed by God, and to the stories of Moses and the Exodus, when God gives the Torah to the Children of Israel. In short, whatever else one may or may not believe about God, what really matters to the prophets is how one behaves toward others, who are all God's children.

The Hebrew prophets were not Greek philosophers, nor were they theologians. They did not spend their time speculating about God as the prime mover, or the first cause. They did not agonize over the nature of God. They accepted their human limitations and said, in the words of the Second Isaiah, "For My thoughts are not your thoughts, and My ways are not your ways, says Adonai" (Isa. 55:8). What preoccupied them was the manifestation of God in God's creation, namely, nature and human history. The guiding principle running through all of their utterances is this: God did not just make the world and then walk away. God is involved in every atom of the universe. God is aware of every breath each living being takes, and God is concerned with every word one utters and every act one performs, no matter how small and seemingly insignificant.

GOD IN NATURE

From Amos to Jeremiah and beyond, God appears to the prophets in nature. The natural world is the textbook the prophets use to learn about God. What is remarkable about what they learn from nature is that although the world's religions until their time—from the most simple and innocent cults practiced in Polynesia or Peru to the most sophisticated religions practiced by the great civilizations of their time (i.e., Egypt, Greece, and Rome)—all deify nature itself and believe the sun, the moon, the stars, and the earth to be gods, the prophets realize that nature itself is not divine but rather the handiwork of a force outside nature that is reachable through nature. They grasp the existence of a life force in nature that renews life continuously. In the book of Psalms we read,

> Adonai, how manifold are Your works!
> In wisdom You have made them all;
> The earth is full of Your creatures.
> Behold the sea, great and wide,
> Teeming with creeping things and
> Living creatures both small and great . . .
> There go ships,
> And Leviathan that You formed to sport with.
> These all look to you
> To give them their food in due season;
> When You give it to them, they gather it up;
> When You open Your hand,
> They are filled with good things.
> When You hide your face, they are dismayed;
> When You take away their breath, they die
> And return to dust.
> When You send forth Your spirit, they are created;
> And You renew the face of the ground. (Ps. 104:23–30)

The ancient Egyptians and Babylonians, in fact, all the nations of antiquity, wrote hymns of praise to the sun, the moon, and the stars, which they worshipped as gods. In the following hymn, Aton, the sun god (or a related deity) is praised by the Egyptian pharaoh Ikhnaton for the work of creation:

Your dawning is beautiful / In the horizon of the sky / O living Aton, / Beginning of life. / When you rise in the eastern horizon / You fill every land / With your beauty.
You are beautiful, Great, Glittering, / High above every land, / Your rays, / They encompass the land, / Even all that you have made. (Ikhnaton Songs to Aton)

The contrast between the biblical psalm and the Egyptian hymn is palpable. In the psalm, nature is at the mercy of an unknowable power that continues to replenish it and give it new life. In the Egyptian hymn, nature itself has divine powers and becomes an object of worship for the ruler of Egypt, who himself is worshipped by his people as a deity. The prophets, in other words, saw nature as nature, not as a divinity. They looked upon nature as a gift from God to man, as attested to by the stories of creation, where God tells the first human couple to have dominion over every living thing (Gen. 1:28).

A recurring motif in the stories of the prophets is the encounter between the prophet and the divine that occurs while the prophet is alone, communing with nature. Moses is alone in the desert when he hears God's voice speaking to him out of the burning bush. Elijah escapes to the same desert where he experiences a mighty storm, after which he hears God speak to him in a "still small voice." Amos is alone in the wilderness when he hears the lion roar, followed by the voice of God. Jeremiah is alone in a field watching the blossoms of an almond tree when he is addressed by God for the first time. In all of these stories, nature is the venue where man, alone and undistracted by the hustle and bustle of life, appears to get in touch with his own soul and with the author of creation; it is where revelation takes place.

Prophetic poetry is rich in imagery, similes, and metaphors borrowed from nature. When Isaiah decries man's arrogance, he compares it to the magnificence of nature.

> For Adonai of hosts has a day
> Against all that is proud and lofty,
> Against all that is lifted up and high;
> Against all the cedars of Lebanon, Lofty and lifted up;
> And against all the oaks of Bashan;
> Against all the high mountains,
> And against all the lofty hills;
> Against every high tower. (Isa. 2:12–15)

It is not the magnificent cedars of Lebanon or the oaks of Bashan that arouse the anger of God. It is man comparing himself to those wonders of nature, worshipping them, and failing to acknowledge that they are God's handiwork. Isaiah goes on to say,

> The haughtiness of people shall be humbled,
> And the pride of everyone shall be brought low;
> And Adonai alone will be exalted on that day.
> And the idols will completely disappear. (Isa. 2:17–18)

The prophets are deeply aware of the harmony between God and nature, particularly between God and the animal kingdom, which stands in sharp contrast to the disharmony between God and man. Jeremiah, who draws on natural imagery more than any other prophet, makes the following comparison:

> Even the stork in the heavens
> Knows its time cycles;
> And the turtle-dove, swallow, and crane
> Observe the time of their coming;
> But My people do not know
> The law of Adonai. (Jer. 8:7)

To this day, migratory birds arrive regularly in the land of Judah where Jeremiah lived and prophesied 2,600 years ago. The regularity of their migrations must have struck the prophet as proof that nature is not erratic or arbitrary but rather orderly and governed by the "law of Adonai," a law he felt his own people failed to observe. When he says, "Even the stork in heaven," it is clear that he expects better from man, the "crown of creation," whom God made but "a little less than God" (Ps. 8:5). How great God's disappointment must be, the prophet seems to suggest, when the animals, who were made for man's benefit, behave better than man himself.

When the prophets envision a time of redemption, they describe it with images taken from nature. In his vision of the end of days, Micah speaks of a time when people "shall dwell under their vine and under their fig tree, and none shall make them afraid" (Mic. 4:4). In his vision of redemption for the people of Israel returning from exile, Amos predicts,

> The time is surely coming, says Adonai,
> When the ploughman shall overtake the reaper,

And the treader of grapes the one who sows the seed;
The mountains shall drip sweet wine,
And all the hills shall flow with it.
I will restore the fortunes of my people Israel,
And they shall rebuild the ruined cities and inhabit them;
They shall plant vineyards and drink their wine,
And they shall make gardens and eat their fruit.
I will plant them upon their land,
And they shall never again be plucked up
Out of the land that I have given them,
Says Adonai your God. (Amos 9:13–15)

The prophets see nature as a divine trust, a gift from God to man. God expects man to treat nature with respect, not by worshipping it as a divinity but by caring for it and sharing its bounty with others. Nature, according to the prophets, is where we can read the language of God. It is in nature, more than in anything else, that man can find God, and it is through nature that man can commune with God and discover the meaning of life. The prophets do not see nature as an arena for the survival of the fittest. They see it as a place for the survival of right over wrong.

THE PROPHETS' LIMITED COSMOLOGY

One could argue that the prophets had a very limited view of nature. They believed the earth was flat and that it was the center of the universe. They thought man was the crown of creation and that God dwelled up in the sky, which was the roof of the world. They had no idea of light years and black holes and the millions of years it took to form the earth. They thought the sea was populated with gigantic mythological creatures they called by fanciful names. Isaiah inveighs,

On that day Adonai with his cruel and great
And strong sword will punish Leviathan the
Fleeing serpent, Leviathan the twisting serpent,
And he will kill the dragon that is in the sea. (Isa. 27:1)

Clearly Isaiah, living inland before there were any deep-sea explorations, had little knowledge of marine life. He might have heard stories told by mariners about monstrous sea creatures such as a giant octopus or a whale or the "big fish" in the story of Jonah, and he must have heard mythological stories that contained the names of the sea creatures he mentions in his series of prophecies about "that day," or the day of Adonai. In a book titled *The Grand Design*, the English cosmologist Stephen Hawking seeks to unlock the secret of the creation of the universe. A reviewer of the book rhapsodizes,

> On a larger scale, in order to explain the universe, the authors write, "We need to know not only how the universe behaves, but why." While no single theory exists yet, scientists are approaching that goal with what is called "M-theory," a collection of overlapping theories (including string theory) that fill in many (but not all) the blank spots in quantum physics; this collection is known as the "Grand Unified Field Theories." This may all finally explain the mystery of the universe's creation without recourse to a divine creator. (*Publishers Weekly*)

The term "unified field theory" was coined by Albert Einstein, who spent the last twenty years of his life trying to find a theory that explains all the forces and particles of the physical universe in one unified field, thereby unlocking the secrets of the universe. For the past sixty years this pursuit has attracted many scientists as well as nonscientists who seem to be fascinated by such a formidable proposition. One may wonder: Even if man finds a way to decipher the secrets of our universe and how and why it came about, would that preclude a force outside physical reality, or perhaps even inside, that operates in a totally different dimension that the prophets grasped intuitively or by some sort of inspiration?

In other words, the prophets were not scientists. They did not approach nature as a science, the way a naturalist or a physicist would. They did not study marine biology or the theory of relativity or any other scientific discipline or theory. They were aware of the fact that there was more to nature than met the eye. In the words of the psalmist,

> Adonai, how manifold are your works!
> In wisdom you have made them all;
> The earth is full of your creation. (Ps. 104:24)

When the prophets speak of God's creation, they do not think in terms of the world they know, but in terms of worlds beyond their knowledge. When they look at nature, they know that very little is revealed to them and that there is much more they do not know. By the same token, with all of our scientific knowledge in the twenty-first century, there is a great deal we do not know. The statement in the review of Hawking's book "This may all finally explain the mystery of the universe's creation without recourse to a divine creator" seems somewhat premature.

GOD IN HISTORY

The prophets see human history as having a reason and a purpose. Man is not an accidental creature who happens to have evolved on planet Earth and is now struggling to find his place in the sun. In history they discern the hand of God. Other civilizations have a much longer history than Israel, but Israel has a long historical memory, which is the legacy of the biblical prophets. There are key events they always evoke, beginning with the stories of the patriarchs, which took place a thousand years before their time, and the story of the liberation from Egypt and the giving of the Torah at Mount Sinai, which happened centuries before their time. They read the will of God in historical events, and they use those events to constantly remind their listeners that life is not a free-for-all but rather a reality guided by what is known in Christian thought as "God's plan," in which a relationship between God and man is at work, whereby human actions have far-reaching consequences, either positive or negative. This puts an enormous responsibility on man, and particularly on the people of Israel, who have entered into a direct covenant with God. Nothing seems to trouble the prophets more than seeing their people break the covenant that was entered upon at Sinai. God always remembers the covenant, but the people keep forgetting. Jeremiah says,

> Hear the word of Adonai,
> O house of Jacob,
> And all the families of the house of Israel.
> Thus says Adonai:
> What wrong did your ancestors find in me
> That they went far from me,

And went after worthless things,
And became worthless themselves?
They did not say,
"Where is God
Who brought us up from the land of Egypt,
Who led us in the wilderness,
In a land of deserts and pits,
In a land of drought and deep darkness,
In a land that no one passes through,
Where no one lives?"
I brought you into a plentiful land
To eat its fruits and its good things.
But when you entered you defiled my land,
And made my heritage an abomination.
The priests did not say,
"Where is Adonai?"
Those who handle the law did not know me;
The rulers transgressed against me;
The prophets prophesied by Baal,
And went after things that do not profit.
Therefore once more I accuse you,
Says Adonai,
And I accuse your children's children.
Cross to the coasts of Kitim and look,
Send to Kedar and examine with care;
See if there has ever been such a thing. (Jer. 2:4–10)

Here Jeremiah gives his people a lesson in history. They are the descendants of slaves who lived under Egyptian bondage. They had no national identity. They were a group of desert tribes who went down to Egypt during a drought looking for food to survive. They became enslaved and were persecuted by their masters, who sought to reduce their numbers by throwing all their newly born male children into the Nile. Their future looked bleak. They had been reduced to the most miserable condition imaginable. But they had one advantage. Five centuries earlier God had entered into a covenant with their common ancestor, Abraham, and promised him that he would give rise to a great nation, and that through him "all the nations of the world will be blessed" (Gen. 22:18). And so when it seemed that all was lost, God empowered an Egyptian-born Hebrew shepherd named Moses to liberate them from the pharaoh through "signs and wonders."

The liberated slaves were able to cross the Red Sea (or the Sea of Reeds), and found themselves back in the desert. For forty years they wandered through the wilderness that separated Egypt from the land God had promised to Abraham, during which time they faced many hardships, such as hunger and thirst, a scorching sun by day and frost by night, and hostile tribes who kept harassing and decimating them. But the hand of God kept guiding them and enabled them to reach the Promised Land. When they entered what was then the Land of Canaan, they discovered a fertile country flowing with milk and honey. They also discovered that this fertile land had attracted many other settlers, such as Amorites, Jebusites, Canaanites, the list goes on and on, some of whom had built fortified towns and were militarily far superior to the twelve tribes of Israel. But here again God, through the able leadership of Joshua, enabled them to overcome all their adversaries and take possession of the land.

One would have expected that once settled in their land, the people would recognize all the many blessings God had showered upon them (the famous Passover song, *Dayeynu*, or "It Would Have Been Enough," referring to those blessings, comes to mind) and become faithful to their heritage and to God's law, the Torah. Instead, they and their leaders—the priests, the teachers of the Torah, the rulers, and even the official prophets—turned their backs on their law and on their history and worship other gods. Jeremiah concludes his history lesson by pointing out that even the pagan nations of his time—the Greeks ("Kitim" is a reference to the Greek Isles) in the west and the Arabs ("Kedar" is a reference to Arabian tribes) in the east—were faithful to their own gods, who were false gods, while his people, who had the one true God, had broken the covenant.

The key to understanding the prophets' view of history is the idea of the covenant. The God of the universe had entered upon two covenants, the first with the entire human race, and a second with the people of Israel. The first covenant occurred in the time of Noah after the flood that destroyed the entire human race with the exception of Noah and his family. God makes the promise never again to destroy the human race, and as a reminder God creates the rainbow (Gen. 9:9–13). The second covenant takes place at Mount Sinai when Moses brings the two tablets of the covenant inscribed with the Ten Commandments to the people waiting at the foot of the mountain. Whatever we may choose to believe about the historicity of those events, they do represent a philosophy of history affirming the survivability of humanity and the mission of the Jews as God's covenanted people.

The prophets' view of history is nondeterministic. According to a saying attributed to Rabbi Akiba, God may know all future events, but man is still able to exercise free will (Avot 3:19). Here again as we saw in the story of the tree of the knowledge of good and evil, man is not a passive actor on the stage of history but rather has the godlike ability to choose a course of action and to influence events. When Moses explains the meaning of God's commandments to the Israelites about to enter the Promised Land, he says,

> I call heaven and earth to witness
> Against you today that I have set
> Before you life and death, the blessing
> And the curse. Choose life so that you
> And your descendants may live. (Deut. 30:19)

The freedom to choose is a key element in the prophetic understanding of history. The other cultures of their time did not accord man the same kind of freedom. When the kings of Israel became like all the other kings of their time and sought to take away their people's freedom, prophets like Nathan, Elijah, and Jeremiah spoke out against the kings and warned them of the dire consequences of their actions. The prophets greatly valued human freedom as a God-given right. They looked upon the foreign rulers and emperors of their time as tyrannical and self-serving, depriving their subjects of their rights and treating their neighbors with extreme cruelty. The book of Amos begins with prophecies against the nations of his time that present a brief historical survey of the cruelty of their rules.

> Thus says Adonai:
> For three transgressions of Damascus,
> And for four,
> I will not revoke the punishment;
> Because they have threshed Gilead
> With threshing-sledges of iron.
>
> So I will send a fire on the house of Hazael,
> And it shall devour the strongholds of Ben-hadad.
> I will break the gate-bars of Damascus,

And cut off the inhabitants from the Valley of Aven,
And the one who holds the scepter from Beth-eden;
And the people of Aram shall go into exile to Kir,
Says Adonai.
Thus says Adonai:
For three transgressions of Gaza,
And for four, I will not revoke the punishment;
Because they carried into exile entire communities,
To hand them over to Edom.
So I will send a fire on the wall of Gaza,
Fire that shall devour its strongholds.
I will cut off the inhabitants from Ashdod,
And the one who holds the scepter from Ashkelon;
I will turn my hand against Ekron,
And the remnant of the Philistines shall perish,
Says the Adonai Elohim.
Thus says Adonai:
For three transgressions of Tyre,
And for four, I will not revoke the punishment;
Because they delivered entire communities over to Edom,
And did not remember the covenant of kinship.
So I will send a fire on the wall of Tyre,
Fire that shall devour its strongholds.
Thus says Adonai:
For three transgressions of Edom,
And for four, I will not revoke the punishment;
Because he pursued his brother with the sword
And cast off all pity;
He maintained his anger perpetually,
And kept his wrath for ever.
So I will send a fire on Teman,
And it shall devour the strongholds of Bozrah.
Thus says Adonai:
For three transgressions of the Ammonites,
And for four, I will not revoke the punishment;
Because they have ripped open pregnant women in Gilead
In order to enlarge their territory.
So I will kindle a fire against the wall of Rabbah,
Fire that shall devour its strongholds,
With shouting on the day of battle,
With a storm on the day of the whirlwind;

> Then their king shall go into exile,
> He and his officials together,
> Says Adonai. (Amos 1:3–15)

The prophets were keenly aware of the rise and fall of empires and of the wars that kept plaguing the human race. A common designation the emperors of the ancient Near East applied to themselves was "king of kings" (Dan. 2:37). The kingdoms of Israel and Judah often came under the yoke of a foreign empire such as Egypt, Assyria, or Babylon whose ruler considered himself a king of kings. The prophets, however, regarded such a ruler a temporary instrument in the hands of God. To Jeremiah, the Babylonian emperor Nebuchadnezzar was God's instrument sent to punish the Kingdom of Judah for its sins. With Nebuchadnezzar thus empowered, Jeremiah argued, there was no point in resisting him since the king of Judah could not go against the will of God. To the Second Isaiah, Cyrus, the emperor of Persia, was God's instrument in allowing the Judean exiles to return to Jerusalem. Emperors invariably considered themselves invincible, and expected their empires to last for a long time. The prophets understood that their great military power was short-lived and their end was always predictable. To them, the power of right was always superior to the power of might, a concept that would take their people a long time to internalize.

The reality of war as an ongoing phenomenon in human affairs gave rise, as we pointed out before, to what might be seen as the Utopian School of Prophecy. Its main proponents were Isaiah and Micah, who predicted an age of world peace. All the prophets were aware of the evils of war, and all sought to look beyond the wars of their time to a time of redemption, return, and restoration for their people and the world. They never doubted that the covenantal relationship between God and the people of Israel ensured their survival, and that no matter how hopeless things might look at a given moment, the people would eventually be restored to their land and enjoy a time of peace and prosperity. When Jerusalem is about to fall to the Babylonians, Jeremiah, an old man without hope, performs the symbolic act of purchasing a field in his native village of Anathoth. He explains his strange action in the following words:

For thus says Adonai: Just as I have brought all this great disaster upon this people, so I will bring upon them all the good fortune that I now promise them. Fields shall be bought in this land of which you are saying it is a desolation without human beings or animals; it has been given into the hands of the Chaldeans. Fields shall be bought for money, and deeds shall be signed and sealed and witnessed, in the land of Benjamin, in the places around Jerusalem, and in the cities of Judah, of the hill country, of the coast, and of the south; for I will restore their fortunes, says Adonai. (Jer. 32:42–44)

The nineteenth-century British prime minister Benjamin Disraeli once observed that people like the Jewish people, who continued to celebrate harvest holidays centuries after they had lost their land, will one day return to their land.

6

THE GREAT QUESTIONS OF LIFE

The great questions of life that faced the prophets still confront us today. Every person at one time or another wonders about such imponderables as the meaning of life, the afterlife, the role of evil in the world, and the role of organized religion, only to name a few. Over time, many answers have been offered and many beliefs embraced. Let us take a look at what the prophets believed and how their views may or may not apply to the realities of today's world.

THE MEANING OF LIFE

Is life a punishment or a reward? In the stories of creation God punishes Adam and Eve for eating the forbidden fruit and sends them out of the Garden of Eden to live a life of hardship. The psalmist bewails man's fate:

> O God,
> What is man that you take account of him,
> What is a mortal that you think of him?
> Man's life is vanity, his days are like a passing shadow. (Ps. 144:3–4)

The author of Ecclesiastes adds,

> Vanity of vanities, says Koheleth,
> Vanity of vanities! All is vanity.
> What do people gain from all their toil under the sun?
> A generation goes, and a generation comes,

But the earth endures forever. (Eccles. 1:2–4)

The prophets did not live in happy times. They had many reasons to despair and feel bitter. As we saw in the accounts of their lives and times, they lived during the decline and destruction of the kingdoms of Judah and Israel, and they were not able to influence the course of events. But the prophets were people of great faith, perhaps more so than anyone who has ever lived. Their faith continues to sustain the majority of the human race to this day. They did not live in the moment. They lived in eternity. They understood that each person's life is part of a greater life. Habakkuk said, "The righteous shall live by his faith" (Hab. 2:4). In other words, faith equals life. Many years ago I visited a Catholic nun who was dying of cancer at a hospital on Long Island. She looked at me with radiant eyes. She said, "I am going to meet my beloved." She taught me a lesson in faith.

Life constantly offers us the bitter and the sweet, the sting and the honey. Jeremiah prophesied doom and destruction, and at the same time he offered words of consolation and reassurance of a better future. The prophets understood the cycles of time. They saw rebirth in nature, and they saw it in human history. They knew they did not have all the answers, but they had faith. Without faith, life is indeed bleak and hopeless.

My mother once wrote to me in a letter, "I lost my entire family in Europe because of Hitler's hell. But God gave me a new family here in the reborn State of Israel." My mother was not an observant Jew. But she had faith.

The prophets understood that life is with people. One does not live in a vacuum. One lives in and through the lives of those one loves and connects with. When the Judeans returned from Babylonian Exile under the leadership of Ezra and Nehemiah, they returned as a community of faith. They were not allowed to reestablish the monarchy of the House of David, or to restore the Holy Temple to its former glory. They were few in number and beset by enemies. But they had internalized the teachings of the prophets, and they had given up idolatry. They began to transition their faith from the temple cult of animal sacrifices to a life of "Torah study, prayer, and good deeds," the formula of the Jewish faith practiced to this day. This was indeed the great accomplishment of the prophets. They were rejected in their lifetime, but their teachings outlived them. They bequeathed to their people a legacy of faith that has sustained a Jewish people who for centuries walked through fire and water, through a long night of exile that lasted for almost twenty centuries, and who prevailed. It is not a faith one carries alone, but one that is shared with one's community and even reaches beyond.

The prophets also taught their people self-reliance. Isaiah said, "If you do not stand firm in your faith, you shall not stand at all" (Isa. 7:9). They did not tell their people to rely on miracles or on divine intervention. For life to have meaning, they seemed to suggest, one has to give it meaning. Man is not a helpless creature, and life is not a vanity of vanities. Life is a gift, and it is up to man to treasure it and make the most of it. It is always easy to blame others for our misfortunes, and ultimately to blame God. But those who do so are bound to suffer. During the time of the prophets, the Hebrew people were tribal, and both blame and praise were often imputed to the tribe rather than to the individual. Typically, the prophets addressed the group rather than the individual. Prophets like Jeremiah and Ezekiel, however, were the first to teach their people personal responsibility when they rejected the ancient teaching of God visiting the sins of the fathers on the children. Jeremiah says,

> In those days they shall no longer say:
> "The parents have eaten sour grapes,
> And the children's teeth are set on edge."
> But all shall die for their own sins; the teeth
> Of everyone who eats sour grapes
> Shall be set on edge. (Jer. 31:28–29)

While Jeremiah speaks these words before the fall of Jerusalem and the start of the Babylonian Exile and puts them in the future tense, Ezekiel repeats them after the exile begins, and puts them in the present tense (Ezek. 18:2). In taking responsibility for one's own life and actions, one can find meaning in life.

AFTERLIFE

One of the most difficult things for people to accept is that physical death means the end of one's life. The Bible states the finality of death unequivocally: "For you are dust and to dust you shall return" (Gen.

3:20). Over time, religions and belief systems around the world, including Judaism and notably Christianity, have developed many theories about life after death. Perhaps the quaintest of all is the belief, found in Eastern religions, in multiple resurrections of every individual person through both human and animal bodies, resurrections known as reincarnation. The beauty of this belief, from my outsider's viewpoint, is that it teaches us that we are all part of nature, and that every form of life on the planet is interrelated.

Two beliefs emerged in Rabbinical Judaism around the time of Jesus that are related to the afterlife: the belief in some form of life after death, and the belief in the eventual physical resurrection of the dead. These beliefs are based on post-biblical beliefs in the existence of an *olam habah*, or next world, also known as heaven and hell, where human souls dwell, and when, in a messianic age, a physical resurrection of the dead will take place.

It is important to note that while in Judaism these beliefs remain somewhat vague and speculative (as attested to by Talmudic stories on this subject), in Christianity they become central to the creed and inseparable from the essence of being a Christian. At the center of Christianity we find a messiah who himself was resurrected, and who offers a life beyond this life. This makes Christianity a much more otherworldly religion than Judaism.

Where do the prophets stand on all of this?

The biblical prophets, from Moses to Malachi, do not seem to be preoccupied with life after death. It clearly belongs in the category established by the Second Isaiah when he speaks about the things that are known to God and not to man. The Torah puts it as follows: "The hidden things belong Adonai our God and the revealed things belong to us and to our children" (Deut. 29:28). When King Saul asks the woman of En-Dor to conjure up the spirit of the dead prophet Samuel, King Saul learns that the prophet is very displeased for being awakened from his eternal rest. The prophets, in other words, focus all their attention on life here and now, and not on life beyond the grave. They do not promise the individual person any rewards beyond this life. To them the definition of a fulfilled life is living a long and productive life, and dying surrounded by many offspring. To them, one's life continues through one's children or loved ones, and through the good name one leaves behind.

To those like me whose faith is rooted directly in the biblical prophets and who question some post-prophetic beliefs, the prophets' stance is quite satisfying because they neither affirm nor reject the various forms of belief in an afterlife. It seems to me that this is best left to each person to decide. There is something awesome about believing oneself to be immortal, and I for one am not quite ready to think myself worthy of immortality. I do believe that we are all part of a greater life. To follow the thinking of our friends who practice Eastern religions, our life is connected to all of nature, and when we return to the ground we are transformed into the greater life of space and time.

THE ROLE OF EVIL IN THE WORLD

According to the medieval Jewish Bible commentator Abraham Ibn Ezra, some commentators considered the serpent in the story of the temptation of Adam and Eve to be the devil. Yet the prophets prior to the Babylonian Exile never mention the devil. In early biblical history the word "satan," which later becomes the name of the devil, simply means "adversary," or "enemy," either human or nonhuman. After the return from exile, the prophet Zechariah for the first time identifies an evil angel by the name of "Satan" (Zech. 3:1). Most likely, the Jews in the Persian Empire at that time became exposed to the new religion of Zoroastrianism, which introduced the dualistic concept of the prophet Zoroaster of two separate deities, a good god and an evil god. In Judaism, and later in Christianity and Islam, the evil god was transformed into an evil angel or agent of God who represents the evil forces in the world.

The monotheistic faiths, in other words, believe that the world is ruled by the forces of good, forces to which evil is subordinate. But they also believe that evil has a reality all its own, and that man is a constant prey to this reality. All of them seem to struggle with the question of evil, which is one of the most central questions of philosophy and theology, and which defies any simple answer. Most difficult of all is the question of the suffering of the righteous and the innocent, which seems to contradict the supremacy of good in the world.

The prophets, as we have seen, struggle with these questions and do not seem to have definitive answers for them. It appears that there is an element of mystery about evil, and quite often man fails to understand it. When the prophets raise the question of why the righteous suffer and evildoers prosper, one can hear the pain in their voices:

> You are righteous, Adonai, that I may quarrel with You,
> Yet I will call You to judgment:
> Why do the evildoers prosper
> Why do all the treacherous thrive? (Jer. 12:1)

The prophets do not regard evil as a permanent condition in a person. They often talk about the dichotomy of the *tzaddik*, or "righteous person," and the *rasha*, or "evil person." But they always make it clear that it is within man's capacity to overcome evil. Ezekiel makes this point forcefully when he says,

> Say to them, As I live, says Adonai, I have no pleasure in the death of the wicked, but that the wicked turn from their ways and live; turn back, turn back from your evil ways; for why will you die, O house of Israel? (Ezek. 33:11)

The book of Psalms opens with the following description of the righteous vis-à-vis the evildoers:

> Happy are those
> Who do not follow the counsel of the wicked,
> Or stand in the path of the sinners,
> Or sit in the seat of scoffers;
> But their delight is in the law of Adonai,
> And on His law they meditate day and night.
> They are like trees
> Planted by streams of water,
> Which yield their fruit in their season,
> And their leaves do not wither.
> In all that they do, they prosper.
> The wicked are not so,
> But are like chaff that the wind drives away.
> Therefore the wicked will not stand in judgment,
> Nor sinners in the congregation of the righteous;
> For Adonai knows the way of the righteous,
> But the way of the wicked will perish. (Ps. 1)

In Judaism, man is endowed with both a good and an evil inclination. Christianity goes a step further and maintains that because of Adam and Eve's sin of eating the forbidden fruit, man henceforth is born in sin. But both believe man can overcome evil. To use Freud's phraseology, man has to learn how to sublimate the evil drive and turn it into a force for good. But the capacity to do evil is always there, and life is a constant struggle to overcome that drive.

FREEDOM AND HUMAN AUTHORITY

It is commonly accepted that ancient Greece invented democracy. A good case, though, can be made for the biblical prophets as the first to recognize the rights of every member of society, no matter how humble. The prophets understood that the role of the ruler is to serve the people, not the other way around. Throughout time, from the pharaohs to many of today's leaders, rulers have acted as though the people were there to serve them. Even in Western and other democracies today that have a good record of taking care of their citizens, good leadership is difficult to come by, and many social problems persist.

Why is it so difficult to establish and maintain a just and honest social system that takes care of all the members of society, and why is leadership such a problem?

We can answer this question in two ways. First, we can point to the inherent weaknesses of the person, who may have the necessary qualifications to lead, but who at the same time may either have a flaw of character or may be seduced by power and adulation and as a result take advantage of the office. Second, we may argue that any political system, no matter how enlightened, is flawed. To borrow Winston Churchill's famous words, "It has been said that democracy is the worst form of government except all the others that have been tried." In some ways, the state, rather than seen as the ultimate good, can be regarded as a necessary evil designed to protect its members from greater evils.

The prophets understood all of this many centuries before anyone else did. Their singular insight regarding a force in the universe that transcends human authority made them realize that human authority is both limited and subordinate to a higher authority. One of the most illustrative stories in prophetic literature that exemplifies this concept is

found in the book of Jeremiah. During the siege of Jerusalem, as the
city was about to fall to the Babylonians, the rich people in the city were
ordered to free their Hebrew slaves so that they might be added to the
ranks of the defenders of the city. According to the biblical law, a
Hebrew slave could only be kept for six years and had to be set free on
the seventh year. The slave owners in Jerusalem were lax in keeping this
commandment, and they had to be ordered by the king to free their
slaves. At one point the enemy seemed to be lifting the siege, and the
former slaves were no longer needed to man the fortifications. Their
owners did not waste any time and pressed them back into service.
Jeremiah, himself imprisoned at that time on charges of sedition for
opposing the war, spoke out in the harshest terms against those in
authority who put themselves above the higher authority and deprived
their own people of their freedom.

> Therefore, thus says Adonai: You have not obeyed Me by granting a
> release to your neighbors and friends; I am going to grant a release to
> you, says Adonai—a release to the sword, to pestilence, and to fa-
> mine. I will make you a horror to all the kingdoms of the earth. (Jer.
> 34:17)

When the tribes of Israel first decide to become a unified nation and
select a king to rule over them, the prophet Samuel warns them that it
is the nature of kings to oppress their people and to take advantage of
them. He warns them that

> these will be the ways of the king who will reign over you: he will
> take your sons and appoint them to his chariots and to be his horse-
> men, and to run before his chariots; and he will appoint for himself
> commanders of thousands and commanders of fifties, and some to
> plough his ground and to reap his harvest, and to make his imple-
> ments of war and the equipment of his chariots. He will take your
> daughters to be perfumers and cooks and bakers. He will take the
> best of your fields and vineyards and olive orchards and give them to
> his courtiers. He will take one-tenth of your grain and of your vine-
> yards and give it to his officers and his courtiers. He will take your
> male and female slaves, and the best of your cattle and donkeys, and
> put them to his work. He will take one-tenth of your flocks, and you

shall be his slaves. And in that day you will cry out because of your king, whom you have chosen for yourselves; but Adonai will not answer you in that day. (1 Sam. 8:11–18)

Samuel understood that at best a king is a necessary evil. He realized that he could not stop the people from crowning a king, but he wanted them to be prepared for what was in store for them. The first to warn the people against the excesses of a king and to set limits on what a king could do was Moses, who said to the people while preparing them to enter the Promised Land,

When you have come into the land that Adonai your God is giving you, and have taken possession of it and settled in it, and you say, "I will set a king over me, like all the nations that are around me," you may indeed set over you a king whom Adonai your God will choose. One of your own community you may set as king over you; you are not permitted to put a foreigner over you, who is not of your own community. Even so, he must not acquire many horses for himself, or return the people to Egypt in order to acquire more horses, since Adonai has said to you, "You must never return that way again." And he must not acquire many wives for himself, or else his heart will turn away; also silver and gold he must not acquire in great quantity for himself. When he has taken the throne of his kingdom, he shall have a copy of this law written for him in the presence of the levitical priests. It shall remain with him and he shall read in it all the days of his life, so that he may learn to fear the Lord his God, diligently observing all the words of this law and these statutes, neither exalting himself above other members of the community nor turning aside from the commandment, either to the right or to the left, so that he and his descendants may reign long over his kingdom in Israel. (Deut. 17:14–20)

What Moses's and Samuel's admonitions have in common is their objection to the king's tendency to build a military power and to become implicated in military adventures. The history of the kingdom of Israel makes it clear that it was not the destiny of the Hebrew people to become empire-builders. The one exception—and here historicity is yet to be proven—are the reigns of David and Solomon, which together only lasted eighty years and ended in the splitting and the decline of the divided kingdom. It was indeed the great Solomon who acquired many horses and many wives in defiance of the Deuteronomic law, and whose reign proved fatal for his people.

In the prophets' view, empire-building is a great evil. While the state by necessity restricts the freedom of the individual, the empire subjugates and enslaves other nations. In the Bible, the one exception to this rule is Cyrus the Great, the founder of the Persian Empire, who respected the customs and religions of the nations he conquered, reversed the policies of his Babylonian predecessors, and let the Judean exiles return to their land. Throughout time we find a few other exceptions to the rule (I was born in Palestine under the rule of the British Empire, and although we Jews were at odds with the British as we sought to establish our own free state, we had great respect for them and learned a great deal from them), but the general rule to this day is that occupying another people goes against what the prophets believe to be the sanctity of human freedom.

In our search for the meaning of prophecy, we should keep in mind that there is much we can still learn from the biblical prophets about freedom and human authority.

ORGANIZED RELIGION

The spiritual life of Israel in biblical times was entrusted not to the prophets but to the priests. The priests officiated at the Temple in Jerusalem or other places where official worship took place, such as Shiloh or Bethel. They accepted offerings from the people, acted as intermediaries between man and God, and were in charge of preserving and teaching the law of Moses. Prior to the time of the literary prophets, the priests practiced a form of divination or communication with the divine in matters of state and even in personal questions. This was done by consulting the *urim* and *thummim*, two obscure terms related to a breastplate worn by the high priest in which twelve precious stones were embedded, the stones representing the twelve tribes of Israel. The prophets never make mention of this type of practice, and it could well mean that they did not think much of it. After all, divination was a pagan practice, which was unacceptable to the prophets. By the time of the Babylonian Exile and the end of the prophetic era, this practice seems to have stopped. What is significant about it is that it shows how at one time priestly duties overlapped prophetic powers. A very telling mention of this overlap appears in the following verse from the time of Samuel: "When Saul inquired of God, Adonai did not answer him, not by dreams, nor by the urim, nor by prophets" (1 Sam. 28:6).

Unlike the prophets, who could come from any walk of life, the priestly post was hereditary. There were two dominant priestly families during the time of the prophets, the House of Abiathar and the House of Zadok. Both Abiathar and Zadok served as high priests during the time of King David. Abiathar, however, fell out of favor with Solomon, David's son and successor, and was exiled to the priestly town of Anathoth, north of Jerusalem, where three centuries later the prophet Jeremiah would be born. The House of Zadok became dominant, and after the return from Babylon when the priests took on the mantle of leadership in the absence of a king, its influence continued to grow.

Invariably, the priests during the time of the prophets were officials of the state and were loyal to the king. Besides the priestly class, there was also a class of court prophets, who were also loyal to the king. The prophets whose words and careers we have discussed, however, were not in the employ of the state or the king, and they did not answer to any human authority. These prophets have few kind words to say about either the priests or the court prophets. They seem to be in a state of perpetual conflict with those functionaries to whose hands the teaching and the spiritual life of the people was entrusted, and they constantly criticize the offering of sacrifices at the Temple (which provided sustenance for the priests) as a manifestation of false piety in light of the immorality and corruption that often characterizes the behavior of those who make such offerings.

Yet we never hear the prophets advocate the elimination of the priestly class or of the sacrificial cult. On the contrary, they accept the Temple as the house of God, and they envision a future time when it will be the gathering place for the nations of the world once they all become peaceful and abandon idolatry. The prophet Ezekiel goes a step further at the time of the Babylonian Exile and provides a detailed blueprint for a future temple that will replace the one that has just been destroyed.

The biblical priests represented what today we call organized religion. They were the people's spiritual leaders who worked directly with
the people and took care of their spiritual needs. The prophets, on the
other hand, worked as free agents and seemed to be perennial critics of
the system. Many in our time have come to look upon organized religion as a main source of much of the trouble in the world. To Karl Marx,
religion was the "opiate of the masses." To Sigmund Freud, it was a
"mass neurosis," to cite only two of the best-known definitions denigrat-
ing religion. Years ago I asked a young Episcopalian priest whom I
befriended while serving as a rabbi in Guatemala how he accounted for
all the evil Christianity had committed in recent centuries in the name
of a loving savior. He explained that there is a vast difference between
Christianity and Christendom. The first is a spiritual term, while the
second is political. Much of the time, he argued, so-called Christian
nations and individuals acted not according to the teachings of Christ
but according to the dictates of the state and of self-interest. Be that as
it may, I find it just as easy to make a case against organized religion as
it is to make a case for it. Religion makes great demands of people, and
the biblical prophets are a good case in point. The people in their day
did not live up to the prophets' expectations, nor did their "shepherds."
Much has not changed since those days, as we have learned over and
over again in our own time. Yet priestly or organized religion continued
to exist after the prophetic period, and it still exists today. Political
ideologies in our time have collapsed around the world, but religion
does not go away. If anything, it is experiencing a comeback in countries
around the world. This author looks upon religion as a two-edged
sword. It can bring out the best in people, and it can also bring out the
worst. Nothing is worse than the perversion of religion by fanatics who
have no regard for human values or human life and usually act out of
ignorance. Yet nothing can bring the best out in people like a sincere
and enlightened faith based on a strong sense of justice and compassion. The authors of the prophetic texts understood this when they said,

> I have set before you
> Life and death,
> The blessing and the curse. . . .
> Choose life. (Deut. 30:15, 19)

We should keep in mind that the three most prominent literary prophets, namely, Jeremiah, Ezekiel, and Isaiah, were of priestly descent
(probably, in the case of Isaiah). We should also note that it was the
priests, during the time of the Second Temple, who were the leaders of
the people, and despite the fact that the prophets put the priests in such
a bad light, the priests embraced the teachings of the prophets and
made them the foundation of the faith. It would be safe to say that both
kinds of spiritual leaders were needed to preserve the people and the
word of God—prophets as well as priests. The model represented by
Moses and his brother Aaron, prophet and priest, respectively, working
together, remains the working model of the spiritual history of Israel
and the world.

AM I MY BROTHER'S KEEPER?

"Where is your brother Abel?" God asks Cain after Cain kills his brother. Cain pretends not to know. He says, "Am I my brother's keeper?"
(Gen. 4:9). To the prophets, this must have been the most cynical and
malicious reply God had ever heard. To be human is to be the keeper of
one's brothers and sisters, namely, the human race. In Cain's time, Abel
was the only sibling on earth. In our time, the human race is counted in
the billions and keeps growing at an accelerated pace. We have good
reasons to worry about the future. How will all these people subsist, let
alone thrive? This may well be the most critical question of our time.

In nature, species of animals that overbreed are thinned out by
various natural causes. In human history, a similar process takes place,
often induced by human actions such as war. By some calculations, a
total of some 400,000,000 to 500,000,000 (half a billion!) human lives
were lost in the twentieth century, mostly through violent action such as
war and human-induced starvation and disease. In the Soviet Union
alone, as many as 100,000,000 human lives were destroyed as the result
of communism's efforts to bring about a better world. During World
War II, about 50,000,000 lives were lost worldwide. The twentieth century might well have been the bloodiest century in human history. How
much has the world learned from all of this in the twenty-first century?

The most evil regimes of the twentieth century, such as Nazi Germany, the Soviet Union, Imperial Japan, Fascist Spain, and Fascist Italy, have disappeared. An international organization that was formed in Europe after World War I to bring "peace in our time" only lasted twenty years, and it was replaced after World War II by the United Nations, which continues to operate to this day. A third world war between the two nuclear superpowers, the United States and the Soviet Union, which was feared for years, did not take place. Despite a series of localized wars around the world that still take place, the world in the twenty-first century seems to focus more on economic development than armed conflict. The world's two most populous countries, which account for more than a third of the human race, namely, China and India, have embarked on a path of unprecedented economic growth. After centuries of endless wars, Europe has finally formed a union with a common currency and economy. Most unexpectedly, a social ferment for democratization has begun in the Arab world that promises to have far-reaching consequences.

Is the human race approaching the millennium?

The human race today is in a better place than it was in the previous century. But this is not to say that the millennium is around the corner. It will probably take a long time to get it right, and the road ahead is not clear. Overpopulation continues to be a critical problem. It was dealt with in China, but not in the rest of the world. The preservation of human life remains the highest moral imperative, but it is not enough. A life of poverty and want is not a worthy goal. There are many countries in the world today where most people live below the poverty line. How can the people of the world achieve the good life? How would the prophets answer this question?

The prophets would respond with postulates like righteousness, justice, and being mindful of the welfare of others. The prophets may point to something that many in today's world have already begun to realize. We are all in it together. Poverty, suffering, and oppression in one corner of the world affects the entire world. "No man is an island, entire of itself." We inhabit a small, fragile planet with limited resources, and life is both precious and precarious. Turning on each other never solves anything, least of all today. Good things begin to happen when people put self-interest aside and put their brains and their brawn together for the common good. The great successes of a nation like the

United States of America have been due to its genius for allowing people of all different backgrounds to put their talents to work for the common cause of society.

From the beginnings of human civilization, man has expended most of his talents and resources on producing weapons and making war. If all that mental energy and all that wealth were to be redirected to solving the problems of human welfare, most of society's problems could be solved. Micah understood that long ago when he said in his vision of the end of days,

> They shall beat their swords into ploughshares,
> And their spears into pruning-hooks;
> Nation shall not lift up sword against nation,
> Neither shall they learn war anymore;
> But they shall all sit under their own vines
> And under their own fig trees,
> And none shall make them afraid. (Mic. 4:3–4)

This says it all. Here is the goal the world needs to set for itself today.

WAITING FOR A MESSIAH

All the three major monotheistic faiths express a yearning for a time when the world will be redeemed by supernatural events at the center of which appears a redeemer whose identity varies among the three. The belief in a supernatural messiah emerged after the time of the Hebrew prophets, but it has its origins in their visions of a future redemption of their people and of all people. As was mentioned before, the Hebrew word for "messiah" is derived from the verb "to anoint," which refers to the anointing of the kings of Israel. Isaiah speaks of a future descendant of the House of David who will redeem his people and establish a reign of justice and peace. After the destruction of the Second Temple by the Romans in the year 70 CE, and even more so after the brutal suppression of the Bar Kokhba revolt in 135 CE, it became clear that the Judean monarchy was not going to be reestablished by human action, and the expectation of redemption became sublimated and transformed into a belief in a divinely ordained messiah who, in the fullness of time, would come to redeem his people. This redeemer would be preceded by the reappearance of the prophet Elijah (who never died but rather went to heaven), who would usher in the messianic age.

Here we have a link between prophecy and messianism. The biblical prophet is a messenger of God to the people, and so is the messiah. In biblical history, prophets from Moses to Malachi play the role of redeeming their people, beginning with their liberation from Egyptian bondage and culminating in the establishment of an abiding belief system that ensures their survival as a community of faith. In a sense, the task of the future messiah is understood to be the culmination of the prophetic enterprise of establishing a just and peaceful world. Man has always felt that human reality falls short of human expectations, and especially at times of great trouble, the yearning for such a world is intensified. Along with the belief in the afterlife, this belief in the future coming of a messiah, accompanied by the resurrection of the dead, provides hope and solace in the face of grim reality and an awareness of the brevity of life. At certain times in history, this belief became urgent, and people began to believe the messianic age was around the corner. The most notable example of this in Jewish history was the appearance in Europe of a self-proclaimed messiah named Shabtai Zvi in the mid-seventeenth century, at a time of great persecution of the Jews in Eastern Europe. Shabtai Zvi persuaded thousands of Jews to leave their homes and their sources of livelihood in Europe and follow him to the Land of Israel, where he would launch the messianic era. He traveled to Constantinople to meet the Turkish sultan who at the time ruled over the Holy Land, and he sought to be recognized by the sultan as the messiah. Instead, Shabtai Zvi was imprisoned by the Turks, and he agreed to convert to Islam to save his life. It was a painful and sobering experience for the Jews of that time, and it became common among Jews to say that one could not hurry the coming of the messiah.

For the next two centuries Jews kept praying for the coming of the messiah who would bring them back to their land and redeem the world. But in the late nineteenth century a new movement was started among the Jews of Europe, a movement known as Zionism, or the return to the Land of Israel (or Zion) through political action rather than by supernatural means. The Jews were now divided into three schools of thought regarding the question of a messiah. The ultra-Orthodox camp rejected political Zionism and clung to the old belief in a supernatural messiah. Many of the more moderate Orthodox accepted the idea of a political state as "the beginning of our redemption," while continuing to believe in the eventual coming of the messiah. Jewish secular Zionists made the establishment of a state through political action their central goal, while dismissing the belief in a messiah. In 1948 the State of Israel became a reality, radically changing the status of the Jews in the world.

For several reasons, the messianic tension was always greater among Jews than among Christians. For one thing, according to the Christian faith, the messiah has already made his first appearance on earth, as a result of which salvation has been brought to the world. To the Christian believer, following the Christian savior means finding salvation. Thus, Christian belief in the second coming of the savior takes on a different meaning than the first coming of the Jewish messiah. Moreover, Jews for the past two millennia have lived as a small minority in Christian and Muslim host countries, and they often have experienced severe persecution and even the threat of extinction. During World War II, when Germany was committing genocide against the Jewish people, one of the songs Jews sang in the death camps began with the words, "I believe in perfect faith in the coming of the messiah." Nevertheless, there are many evangelical Christians today who are convinced that the second coming is imminent. Many of them see the birth of the State of Israel as a sign of what they call the End Times, and there is much speculation as to the date of that event.

Biblical prophecy, as we have seen, did not flourish during the glory days of King David or King Solomon, but rather after the breakup of the kingdom and during and after the destruction of the kingdom and the Babylonian Exile. The prophets had every reason to despair of their times and dream of a better future. They yearned for a future king of the House of David who would resemble his illustrious ancestor and who would bring about an ideal order designed to reflect the kingdom of God (*malchuth shaddai*). But to the prophets, the word "messiah" did not mean someone with supernatural powers. It meant a human king who was anointed with oil, hence becoming "the anointed." Here we have the origin of the belief in a messiah who transcends common human reality, a belief that began to emerge after the time of the prophets.

In addition to the belief in an ideal king, the prophets also shared a belief in what they called the day of Adonai. According to Joel and Malachi, it is "a great and awesome day" (Joel 3:4; Mal. 3:23), but it is described in different ways by each prophet, and it is not clear when it is to take place. The common belief among the people at the time was that it would be a day on which God would avenge Israel of its enemies. The prophets saw it differently. They saw it as a day of judgment against all transgressors, including Israel. But they never associated it with any messianic figure, redemption, or resurrection. It was a day on which God alone would pass judgment amid awesome natural phenomena.

> And I will show wonders in the heavens and in the earth,
> Blood and fire and pillars of smoke,
> The sun shall be turned into darkness,
> And the moon into blood,
> Before the coming of the great and terrible day of Adonai. (Joel 3:3–4)

In post-biblical times this vision of a judgment day, or last judgment, will become associated in Christianity and Islam with the time of the coming of the messiah. In Judaism it became an annual event during which every Jew and indeed every living being is judged by God, starting on Rosh Hashanah, the first day of the Jewish year, and culminating ten days later on Yom Kippur, the Day of Atonement.

If we look for a prophetic view of a supernatural messiah, no such view is to be found. Instead, reading Isaiah's and Micah's vision of the end of days, it is safe to say that the prophets believed in a messianic age, a time of peace and righteousness, of prosperity and goodwill. It is the kind of belief that can be accepted by all, religionists and secularists alike. It is the kind of belief that can unify people around the world across all religious and ideological lines rather than create sectarian barriers. It is for this reason that Isaiah's vision of the end of days is carved on the wall of the United Nations building in New York City.

7

JEWISH MESSIANISM

The era of biblical prophecy ends after the return from the Babylonian Exile and before the time of the Maccabees in the second century BCE. By the year 70 CE, Jewish independence in the Land of Israel ends with the Roman destruction of Jerusalem and the Holy Temple. For the next twenty centuries the Jews will become scattered throughout the world and live under Muslim and Christian rulers, during which time they will continue to yearn for and pray for the coming of the messiah of the House of David who will not only return them to their land and restore their sovereignty as of old, but will also fulfill the vision of Isaiah and Micah of ushering in a new era of world peace. During those twenty centuries, certain messianic personalities will emerge and will either proclaim themselves or will be regarded by others as the long-awaited messiah who has come to redeem his people. This will typically occur during a time of great calamity for the Jews. During such times the yearning for redemption will always intensify, and people will be willing to believe in a would-be redeemer, even though there might be good reasons to doubt the credentials of such a person.

The first prominent figure of this kind is the second-century CE warrior Bar Kokhba, who lived in the time of Rabbi Akiba and the Roman emperor Hadrian. The Jews who had remained in the Roman province of Judea had come under the yoke of Rome and faced the prospect of having their religion outlawed. Bar Kokhba was able to organize an uprising against Rome and overthrow their rule for three years. The Romans were not about to give up. Once the Romans had reconquered the province of Judea, the Jews paid dearly for their defiance and Bar Kokhba came to be regarded by many as a false messiah.

The second major cataclysmic period in Jewish history was the time of the Crusades during the Middle Ages when many Jewish communities in Europe and the Middle East were caught in the conflict between Christianity and Islam and suffered great losses in life and property. Messianic fervor ran high during that time and witnessed the appearance of a false messiah named David Alroy who sought to redeem his people by force of arms and reestablish the kingdom of Israel. But once again it was not meant to be.

The third major tragedy of Jewish history was the expulsion of the Jews from Spain in 1492, which gave rise to a false messiah named David Hareuveni and yet another one inspired by him, Shlomo Molcho. They too sought to redeem their people by taking advantage of the conflict between Christian and Muslim rulers, but failed.

The fourth major catastrophe for the Jews were the Khmelnytsky Massacres in Poland in 1648, following which the best-known false messiah of Jewish history, Shabtai Zvi, made his appearance in Europe. Never since the time of Bar Kokhba did Jewish messianic hopes run so high, only to end in disaster and total disillusionment. For the next two centuries, the Jews would turn inward and messianism would become otherworldly. In the nineteenth century, we see the rise of Jewish nationalism under the banner of a new movement known as Zionism, a movement that would eventually result in the birth of the State of Israel in the mid-twentieth century. This event, which would profoundly change the status of the Jews in the world, is regarded by many moderate Orthodox Jews and others as the beginning of the redemption of the Jewish people, but by many ultra-Orthodox Jews as an interference with the divine plan of sending a supernatural messiah.

In recent years a new messianic figure has emerged in the Jewish world among the adherents of a Hasidic movement known as Chabad. Many Chabad Hasidim believe that their late leader, Rabbi Menahem Mendel Schneerson, known as the Lubavicher Rebbe, is the messiah who will return to redeem his people and the world. Here Jewish messianism seems to have come full circle. The concept of a Hasidic rabbi having prophetic or messianic qualities is not new. But the case of

Schneerson is different from all the others because of the activism of his followers, and it is a living proof that messianic expectations are still alive and well among certain segments of Jewry.

It is to be expected that as long as humanity is beset by widespread poverty and by violent conflict, people will continue to yearn for the messianic promise of redemption. The alternative would be to resign oneself to a future of endless conflict.

BAR KOKHBA

In Jewish history, Simon Bar Kokhba is both glorified and maligned. Cast in the mold of biblical heroes like Samson and David, and of post-biblical heroes like Judah Maccabee, he was the last Jew in antiquity to liberate his people from the yoke of a foreign power. One of the great-est rabbinical sages proclaimed him the king messiah. The sages of the Talmud, however, referred to him as a false messiah to discourage the Jews who survived his revolt from resorting to military adventures and from believing in a human messiah. Indeed, his name reflects this dual-ity. His real name was Simon Bar Kosiba, which in Hebrew can be taken to mean "son of a lie," hence false prophet. His followers and admirers changed his name to Bar Kokhba, which means "son of a star," a biblical allusion to a savior. In reality, he was neither a sinner nor a saint. He was the last of the great military leaders who arose in the Land of Israel in ancient times. Like Spartacus, he took on the Roman op-pressor. It took half of the Roman legions and two years of a brutal military campaign to put down Bar Kokhba's uprising. From 132 to 135 CE, Bar Kokhba served as nasi, or president, of a free Judea. He did not proclaim himself a messiah or a king, although many of his followers believed that with the overthrowing of the Roman yoke, the messianic era had begun. No less a luminary than Rabbi Akiba seemed to share this belief. Akiba was not only a great scholar but also a passionately proud Jew who dreamed of national redemption. Clearly he failed to realize that little Judea did not stand a chance against the mighty le-gions of the Roman Empire and that the time of redemption was far off.

The Roman emperor Hadrian exacted a horrendous price for the uprising. According to Roman sources, nearly six hundred thousand Jews were killed, which would be the equivalent today of the six million

Jews killed in the Holocaust. Bar Kokhba was executed, and Rabbi Akiba along with the other great sages of the Sanhedrin were tortured and put to death. Indeed, there is a similarity between Hadrian and Hitler. Both sought to eradicate the Jewish people. Hadrian issued decrees against Jewish religious laws, changed the name of Jerusalem to Aelia Capitolina, erected statues to Jupiter and to himself on the site of the Temple Mount, and changed the name of Judea to Palestine, after the ancient Philistines who had lived along the coast. As far as Hadrian was concerned, Judea had ceased to exist. The Jews were about to become extinct.

But apparently this was not God's plan. By now Judaism was no longer a temple-centered religion, but rather a faith embodied in religious laws and liturgy that transcended the Roman province of Judea or Palestine. As a result of the Bar Kokhba revolt, the center of Jewish life shifted from the Land of Israel to Babylonia, where the Babylonian Talmud began to take shape. In short, Judaism was to outlive the Roman Empire.

The aftermath of the failed Bar Kokhba revolt is one of the great mysteries of human history. By all rights, it should have marked the end of the Jewish people. The surviving Jews had every reason to believe that God had abandoned them. Jerusalem and the Land of Israel were no more. The Jews' short-lived messianic hopes had been dashed against the rocks of harsh reality. Rabbi Akiba's famous words "Happy are you O Israel, for before whom do you purify yourselves, and who purifies you, if not your Heavenly Father" now sounded hollow and cruel. What was it, then, that made the Jews want to go on?

The answer is very simple. The prophets. The Jews had by now internalized the teachings of the prophets, the ones whom they called "the prophets of truth and justice." They were able to say, echoing the prophets, "Because of our sins we have been exiled from our land," and "God is just in all His ways" for "the rock of Israel will never lie." Or, in the words of Job, "Even if He kills me, I will wait for Him." To them, God was real. God was not an abstraction. When Rabbi Akiba was about to die as the Romans were flaying his flesh, he said, "All my life I was hoping to die saying the Shema prayer, and now I get my wish: Hear O Israel, Adonai is our God, Adonai is one." According to legend, he died uttering the word "one."

One might add that Bar Kokhba preferred to die a free man than live under Roman bondage and follow Roman pagan beliefs. Today, in the reborn State of Israel, he is no longer considered a false messiah but rather a hero who, across the ages, continues to send his message to future generations: One must be prepared to die for freedom if one does not wish to live as a slave.

DAVID ALROY

During the long centuries of exile, Jewish scholars and mystics spent a great deal of time and energy searching for the date of the coming of the messiah. In times of persecution and dislocation, those esoteric efforts intensified and had a profound effect on peoples' lives. Such a time was the era of the Crusades from the eleventh to the thirteenth century. Jewish communities throughout Europe were decimated by the Crusaders on their march from Europe to the Holy Land to redeem the Christian holy places from Muslim occupation. The Jews living at the time in the Middle East also felt the impact of the conflict between the Christian and the Muslim worlds. Many believed that the Crusades were the conflict of Gog and Magog, predicted by the prophet Ezekiel, which signaled the coming of the messiah. The time was ripe for someone to appear and proclaim himself messiah of the house of David. History has shown time and again that when people are ready to believe in something they will do so, no matter how removed it may be from reality.

It was against this backdrop that an Iraqi Jew whose real name was Menahem al-Ruhi, but who changed his name to David Alroy, appeared in strife-torn Mosul and Baghdad around 1160 and encouraged his fellow Jews to arm themselves, get rid of the Muslim sultan, and go to Jerusalem to reestablish their independence. Alroy, however, was not as successful as his biblical predecessors. By defying the sultan, Alroy became a threat to the throne and had to be eliminated. Despite Alroy's magical powers, the sultan found a way to dispose of him by bribing his father-in-law to assassinate him.

But the Alroy story does not end with the demise of this self-proclaimed messiah. We are told by a Muslim source that after Alroy's death, two of his followers appeared in Baghdad, which had a large

Jewish community, and presented a forgery that they claimed was a letter from Alroy, in which he announced the date of the coming of the messiah. The letter went on to say that on that particular night the Jews of Baghdad would be flown to the Land of Israel. This story is reminiscent of Ezekiel, the prophet of the Babylonian Exile, who claimed that God enabled him to fly from Babylonia to Jerusalem so that he might prophesy about the destruction of the Temple. The Muslim narrator (a Jew who had converted to Islam and had a score to settle with the Jewish community) goes on to describe how the Jews of Baghdad, who prided themselves on being worldly and shrewd, fell for the story. They squandered their riches, dressed in their finest clothes, and went up on the roofs of their houses to await the moment when they would be flown back to their land. To make a long story short, they waited all night and nothing happened, and as a result they became the laughing-stock of Baghdad. Many, however, continued to believe that someday Alroy's prophecy would be fulfilled.

How much of this story is true is not clear. All the stories associated with Alroy are reminiscent of the stories of the Arabian Nights. But underneath the hyperbole and the flights of imagination we can detect the plight of the Jews of the Middle Ages living in the lands of the crescent and the cross. Whether rich or poor, they were strangers who lived at the mercy of the local ruler, but they refused to give up the dream of returning to their ancestral land. Even during the Golden Age of the Jews of Spain, the great Hebrew poet of the Middle Ages, Judah Halevi, would proclaim, "My heart is in the east, but I am in the far west." Halevi's messianic yearnings prompted him to go in his old age on a pilgrimage to Jerusalem where, according to legend, he was trampled to death by an Arab horseman.

DAVID HAREUVENI AND SHLOMO MOLCHO

Three centuries separate the story of David Alroy from the stories of David Hareuveni and Shlomo Molcho, but they all have common elements of fact and fantasy intermingled, and they all reflect the Jews' deep yearnings for redemption during the long night of the exile. As in the day of Alroy, here again we find the Jewish world in great turmoil after the expulsion of the Jews from Spain and the continuing persecution of the Jews by the Spanish and Portuguese inquisitions. For centuries, the Iberian Peninsula was the battleground of two great civilizations: the Muslim Moorish civilization, then in decline, and the expanding Catholic civilization of Europe, which in 1492 completed the conquest of Spain and put an end to Moorish rule. That same year, made famous by Columbus's discovery of the New World, the Jews, who had enjoyed a Golden Age in Spain under Islam that had given rise to such luminaries as the philosopher Maimonides, the poet Judah Halevi, the Ibn Tibbon dynasty of translators, and many more, were forced to leave and find refuge in places like Holland, Italy, Turkey, and other parts of Europe and the Middle East.

It was against this backdrop that a strange, swarthy dwarf named David Hareuveni, hailing from somewhere in the Arabian Peninsula or India, made his appearance in Rome in 1524 riding a white horse and sought an audience with Pope Clement VII. He was invited to see the pope, and he proceeded to tell his story about a Jewish kingdom in Arabia ruled by his brother Joseph. He brought letters from Portuguese captains who had reached that part of the world and confirmed his claims. The Portuguese at that time needed local allies to help them confront the Turkish sultan Selim I, who had conquered Egypt in 1521 and diverted the valuable spice trade. Hareuveni also asked the pope to make peace between the Catholic kings of Europe so that they might join forces and free the Land of Israel from the Turks. The idea, of course, was to return the Jews to their land. The pope told his Jewish visitor he was not able to do such a thing, but he arranged for him to see the king of Portugal.

With the help of Jewish supporters, Hareuveni was able to pay for his trip to Portugal and meet with King John III of Portugal. He tried to convince the king to provide him with warships to fight the Turkish sultan. The king, who was at the time involved in persecuting suspected Marrano Jews, found it difficult to enter into an alliance with a Jew, but while they were negotiating he refrained from harassing the Marranos—Jews whose conversion to Catholicism was suspected to be insincere.

In Portugal, Hareuveni met a young Marrano Jew named Diego Pires, who was deeply impressed with this exotic coreligionist from the East. Pires, who held a position in the Portuguese high court, took the appearance of Hareuveni as a sign of the imminent arrival of the messiah. He had himself circumcised and reverted to Judaism, changing his name to Shlomo Molcho. While he wanted to join Hareuveni on his mission, the latter told Shlomo Molcho that he had put his life at risk in Portugal, and that he had to leave the country. Molcho went to Turkey, and from there he went to the Land of Israel, which at the time was a province of the Ottoman Empire. He traveled the land as a preacher and predicted that the messiah would arrive in the year 1540. It appears that he made a great impression on the Jewish communities in the Holy Land. This prompted him to believe that he had a messianic task to fulfill, either as the messiah himself or the precursor of the messiah. Apparently Molcho, like Hareuveni, was a charismatic personality who could impress people in high office. He traveled back to Italy and met with the same pope who had given Hareuveni an audience. The pope and several Judeophile cardinals took a liking to this fervent young man. A story has it that he predicted a great flood in Rome, which did occur, thereby enhancing his mystical reputation.

In Italy, Molcho and Hareuveni joined up once again. Both were determined to find a way to redeem their people and bring them back to the Promised Land. This time they went to see Emperor Charles V, ruler of the Holy Roman Empire. Hareuveni offered Charles an alliance with the Jews of the East against the Ottoman Empire. It was at this point that the fortunes of both Molcho and Hareuveni took a turn for the worse. Here again, there is no way of separating legend from fact, but as the story has it, they were brought before the inquisitors. Molcho, who had betrayed his Catholic faith, was given the option to repent and return to the bosom of the church. He refused, and chose martyrdom by fire. As for Hareuveni, he was taken away in chains and probably died soon thereafter.

Both Hareuveni and Molcho have become folk heroes in Jewish history. While both have earned the dubious title of "false messiah," in their own tragic, romantic way they continued to carry the torch of Jewish messianic expectations that gave a glimmer of hope to the Jews during the long night of their exile and would eventually enable them to return to their land.

SHABTAI ZVI

In Jewish history, the name Shabtai Zvi is synonymous with "false messiah." Over a century separates him from the time of David Hareuveni and Shlomo Molcho, but the lot of the Jews in Europe did not improve during that time. Shabtai Zvi was born in Smyrna, Turkey, in 1626, and at a young age he lost interest in his Talmudic studies and became completely absorbed in Jewish mysticism. He became an ascetic and began to have visions that prompted him to conclude at the age of twenty-two that he was the messiah. The year was 1648, another tragic year in Jewish history, marking the beginning of a Cossack revolt in Poland and the Ukraine led by Bohdan Khmelnytsky, which resulted in the death and dislocation of hundreds of thousands of Jews. According to Jewish "end-of-days predictors" of that time, that year marked the beginning of the messianic age. As a learned and charismatic young man steeped in Kabbalistic lore, Shabtai Zvi was convinced he was to play a key role in the imminent redemption of his people.

From this point on the Shabtai Zvi story goes through many twists and turns, all equally bizarre, and all pointing to a very conflicted and delusional person who is clearly a charlatan. Along the way the would-be savior picks up other strange characters who are equally misguided, and together they play out a messianic charade, which, were it not for its tragic consequences, sounds like a third-rate comedy. It begins with a journey to the Land of Israel where the young Jew from Turkey is warmly received by local Jewish mystics. He is now convinced beyond a doubt he is indeed the messiah, and he even finds himself a disciple named Nathan of Gaza who proclaims himself to be Elijah the Prophet, the one who is considered the precursor of the messiah. With the help of Nathan and other disciples, Shabtai Zvi's fame begins to spread throughout the Jewish diaspora in Europe and in the Muslim world. The new redeemer begins to act as though the messianic era has already dawned. He decrees that fast days become days of joy. He marries a woman of ill-repute because "God ordered him to do it, as He had ordered the prophet Hosea to marry a woman of whoredom." He begins to pronounce the forbidden name of God, and he has his followers address him as the king messiah.

What is most remarkable about this improbable story is the fact that the antics of the young savior and his followers are taken seriously by entire Jewish communities and by leading rabbis and scholars throughout the world, who believe they are about to be taken back to the Holy Land where the Holy Temple will be rebuilt and the messiah will rule the world. Many sell their homes and liquidate their affairs as they await the miraculous return to Zion.

And then comes the moment of the great disillusionment. Shabtai Zvi, who has by now managed to convince himself that the whole world is now ready for him, goes to see the Turkish sultan in Constantinople. Meanwhile, another self-styled messiah tells the sultan that his rival is plotting to overthrow the Ottoman Empire. Shabtai Zvi ends up in prison and is given a choice between converting to Islam or facing death. Unlike Molcho, who chose martyrdom instead of apostasy, the messiah from Smyrna agrees to become a Muslim. He justifies his act by claiming it is the will of God. His conversion sends shock waves throughout the Jewish world. The great euphoria turns into depression. Shabtai Zvi's name, once revered in nearly every synagogue, is now no longer mentioned. The age of the false messiahs is now coming to a close.

RABBI MENAHEM MENDEL SCHNEERSON

Of all the Hasidic movements in the world today, the best known is Chabad. In most countries, one can find a Chabad center or emissaries of the Chabad movement. It has a strong presence in the United States and Israel, and it seems to grow in influence throughout the world, even though Hasidism as a whole represents a small segment of the Jewish people. All of this is due to their late leader, Rabbi Menahem Mendel Schneerson, the Lubavicher Rebbe, who died in 1994, and who is yet to be succeeded by a new rebbe.

In the wake of the Shabtai Zvi messianic movement's fiasco, the Jewish masses in Eastern Europe fell into a state of deep despair. Most Jews were poor and ignorant, struggling to survive, and unable to afford the luxury of education. This gave the impetus in the mid-eighteenth century for the birth of a new movement in Judaism known as Hasidism. Its founder, Rabbi Israel, known as the Baal Shem Tov ("He of the good name"), practiced a new form of Jewish piety known as practical mysticism, which emphasized worship through fervent prayer and good deeds as more important than Jewish scholarship and religious legalism, thus making Judaism more accessible to the Jewish masses. In a way, Hasidism succeeded in neutralizing messianism by internalizing it as part of the daily spiritual experience of the Jew rather than leaving it a militant movement. During its early years, Hasidism gave rise to great rabbinical leaders who established several rabbinic dynasties, which, by the late nineteenth century, counted their members in the millions. One of those rabbinical leaders was Rabbi Shneur Zalman of Liadi, the founder of the Chabad movement. Unlike his colleagues, who followed strictly in the footsteps of the Baal Shem Tov, Shneur Zalman reemphasized the importance of study and knowledge ("Chabad" in Hebrew is an acronym for "chochma, bina, daat," or "wisdom, understanding, and knowledge"). Thus, his movement became the more intellectual one among the Hasidic groups.

During World War II many of Europe's Hasidim perished in the Holocaust. After the war, several Hasidic movements were able to reestablish themselves in the United States and Israel. In 1951, Rabbi Menahem Mendel Schneerson became the leader of Chabad, and he proceeded to turn it into a force in world Jewry. Schneerson, known as the Rebbe, was an anomaly among Hasidic rabbis. He had a degree in engineering from a French school, and he had an unusually broad worldview. While all the other Hasidic leaders turned inward and shut themselves and their followers off from the outside world, including the Jewish world, Schneerson taught his followers to reach out to all Jews everywhere. In a sense, his young men became missionaries to the Jewish world, as many of them were sent to live in Jewish neighborhoods throughout the United States and around the world and to offer their homes as Jewish centers of learning and religious experience. Many of them excelled in showing friendliness, extending a helping hand, and attracting Jews of all walks of life by using a tolerant and noncoercive approach. The Rebbe himself became the most sought after Jewish spiritual leader during his later years. He would receive thousands of letters and visitors every year from all parts of the Jewish world seeking his advice and his blessing. To his Hasidim, his word became law.

Over the years, a growing number of Chabad Hasidim began to put forth the idea that their Rebbe was in effect the long-awaited messiah who would redeem the world. They would compose songs that were sung during the large gatherings (Farbrengen) at his world headquarters in Brooklyn, New York, in which they proclaimed him the king messiah. For the most part, the Rebbe objected to this practice that he found divisive and ordered the singing to stop. But in his last year he was reported to approve of it. Upon his death the movement split in two over the issue of his messiahship. It did, however, remain one movement and its worldwide activities did not suffer. One can still see posters in the United States, Israel, and other countries proclaiming him the messiah. While rabbis and scholars across the Jewish religious spectrum have denounced these messianic manifestations as misleading and dangerous, the manifestations seem to continue unabated.

What is ironic is the fact that of all the Hasidic movements, the one that started by emphasizing rational thinking rather than emotionalism has now resorted to a belief that has long been discredited among Jews because of its unfortunate history. How this latest messianic movement will continue to unfold remains to be seen.

PROPHECY AND MESSIANISM

Biblical prophecy gave birth to the idea of messianism. As we have seen, many attempts were made throughout Jewish history to hasten the coming of the messiah. They all failed, but it appears that the last chapter in the story of Jewish messianic expectations is yet to be written. The brutal suppression of the Bar Kokhba revolt, the bitter fate of Alroy and Hareuveni and Molcho, the great disillusionment of the Shabtai Zvi movement, and the negative reactions to the messiahship of Schneerson do not alter the fact that the Jewish people have not only overcome all their misfortunes, they have reclaimed their place in history and are once again a nation among the nations of the world.

The messianic idea of the prophets has spread around the world. People everywhere have found their own teachers and their own belief in a better world. The great religions of the world continue to hold sway over millions of believers. At the same time, history has produced both prophetic personalities who have had a beneficial impact on humanity, and false or misguided or even evil prophets who have caused great harm. In the following chapters we will look at some of these key players and see how they have affected the course of history.

The criteria being used to distinguish between those who have followed in the footsteps of the Hebrew prophets and those who have failed to do so are the same as those we discovered early on in discussing those prophets. Most important among them is the prophet's *moral compulsion*, a total and unconditional dedication to a moral message that transcends human will and is applicable to all people. The second is the question as to what extent their words and actions either benefit or harm their followers. The third is their lasting impact on the human race. Needless to say, much ground is being covered here, and there is room for disagreement and even controversy. Moreover, the judgment of history is an ongoing process, and more knowledge will be added in the years ahead. But, hopefully, there is something to be learned from all those we have chosen to discuss.

8

THE PROPHETS OF THE WORLD'S RELIGIONS

Of the prophets of the world's religions, I have selected five whose teachings I believe have influenced not only their own adherents but also the world at large. Sometimes this influence is not clear or direct, or might have been filtered through the teachings or practices of other religions. But all five display aspects of the moral compulsion we have found in the teachings of the Hebrew prophets, and all five have brought their followers comfort and inner strength. The scriptures of Buddhism, Confucianism, Christianity, Islam, and the Baha'i faith all teach respect for human life, compassion for the weak and the needy, and the pursuit of peace.

One could argue that Buddhism and Confucianism are social philosophies rather than religions. Neither is commonly referred to as a monotheistic religion. Yet both are imbued with the spirit of what in the West we think of as godliness.

Christianity, despite its long history of conflict with Judaism, its parent religion, is rooted in the teachings of the Hebrew prophets, and enlightened Christian leaders have always recognized this kinship. Some scholars question the concept of the "Judeo-Christian tradition," but the two faiths have always influenced each other in more ways than most people realize.

The second-largest monotheistic religion, namely, Islam, is not enjoying great popularity in the West these days because of radical Islamists who have been resorting to violence to advance their agenda.

While representing a small minority in the Muslim world, they have managed to eclipse the vast majority of Muslims who are not violent and who try to live by the teachings of their prophet. We can only hope that the moderate voices of Islam will help repair the image of this great religion that was once a source of enlightenment and progress throughout the civilized world.

Finally, the Baha'i faith, which only has a few million adherents worldwide and is an offshoot of Islam, is not known to most people, but it is included here because its teachings are the most inclusive of all the other religions, and it can serve as a model for a world where all religions work together for the common good.

BUDDHA—BUDDHISM

For centuries, Buddhism has been the dominant religion of the Eastern world. No other prophetlike figure has had a greater impact on the great civilizations of the East than Siddhartha Gautama, known to the world as the Buddha. While there are more Hinduists than Buddhists in India, and while the leading traditional personality in China is Confucius rather than the Buddha, in the broad spectrum of Asian religions or social philosophies, the Buddha is the dominant figure. Buddhist teachings and beliefs have had a growing impact on Western civilization in recent years, and one of the most popular religious leaders in the world today is the exiled Buddhist leader of Tibet, the Dalai Lama. How does the Buddha fit into our prophetic mold?

According to most scholars, the person who eventually became the Buddha, or the Enlightened One, was born in what is modern-day Nepal in the mid-sixth century BCE, around the time of Jeremiah and Ezekiel. One could argue that Jeremiah and Gautama were both inspired by their encounter with human suffering. Jeremiah as a young man left his peaceful town of Anathoth and became exposed to social injustice in the capital city of Jerusalem. The Buddha as a young prince left his sheltered life at his father's palace and discovered human suffering resulting from poverty, disease, and old age. The way these two contemporaries reacted to this exposure, however, was completely different, and it marks a watershed in the history of Eastern and Western civilizations. The Buddha focused on the person, while Jeremiah focused on society. Jeremiah attributed the suffering of the poor, the weak, and the elderly to social injustice, and he believed that such social ills could be corrected by a society that heeded the ethical teachings of what Jeremiah believed to be a just God. The Buddha, on the other hand, looked for a solution to human suffering not in social reform and not in a divine law but in bringing about change from within the person himself. The ideal person in the Buddhist tradition became the ascetic or the monk, the one who gives up the material things of this world and dedicates himself to spiritual pursuits. The ultimate goal of life is to achieve nirvana, a state of total peace, absence of suffering, and becoming one with the world.

In the vast expanses of India and the Far East, Buddhism developed in many different ways, and stories about the Buddha range from the supernatural to folk stories of everyday life. It is very hard to define the Buddha and Buddhism. Is Buddhism a religion or a spiritual philosophy? What is the role of the Buddha in Buddhism? Hinduism and the Ahmadiyya branch of Islam consider the Buddha to be a god. The Baha'i faith believes him to be god-like. Other religions regard him as a prophet. Strictly speaking, the Buddha is a great spiritual teacher.

The original Buddha rejected the idea of a creator, denied the concept of creation, and saw divinity as a hindrance to achieving the state of nirvana. In this regard, the Buddha's view of man and the universe seems to be diametrically opposed to Jeremiah's. Yet there is a certain common ground between the two. Both believe in man's ability to change and improve. Jeremiah calls it *teshuvah*, or "return to God." The Buddha sees it as divesting oneself of all base desires and selfishness. Both are opposed to violence as a way to achieve human goals. Micah's teaching of pursuing justice and loving mercy and walking humbly is in perfect harmony with the teachings of the Buddha. For people who find it difficult to accept the concept of a divinity and a creator, Buddhism can certainly hold great attraction.

In Western religions, particularly in Christianity, the idea of social activism has become a key concept in pursuing a better world. In trying to reconcile Buddhism with this idea, some Western writers who look for ways to make Eastern religions relevant to the West have made several suggestions in this regard. Ken Jones, coauthor of the book *The New Social Face of Buddhism*, writes in his essay "Buddhism and Social Action: An Exploration,"

In modern Western society, humanistic social action, in its bewildering variety of forms, is seen both as the characteristic way of relieving suffering and enhancing human well-being and, at the same time, as a noble ideal of service, of self-sacrifice, by humanists of all faiths.

Buddhism, however, is a humanism in that it rejoices in the possibility of a true freedom as something inherent in human nature. For Buddhism, the ultimate freedom is to achieve full release from the root causes of all suffering: greed, hatred and delusion, which clearly are also the root causes of all social evils. Their grossest forms are those which are harmful to others. To weaken, and finally eliminate them in oneself, and, as far as possible, in society, is the basis of Buddhist ethics. And here Buddhist social action has its place.

The experience of suffering is the starting point of Buddhist teaching and of any attempt to define a distinctively *Buddhist* social action. However, misunderstanding can arise at the start, because the Pali word *dukkha*, which is commonly translated simply as "suffering," has a much wider and more subtle meaning. There is, of course, much gross, objective suffering in the world (*dukkha-dukkha*), and much of this arises from poverty, war, oppression and other social conditions. We cling to our good fortune and struggle at all costs to escape from our bad fortune.

Some may argue that this is an attempt to put a square peg in a round hole. One could further argue that the Buddhist ascetic life is an escape from the ills of the world and a failing to engage in social activism. Much has been said and written about Buddhism and other Eastern religions and spiritual philosophies as being passive rather than proactive. Yet it is precisely Buddhist pacifism that gave the world in our time the philosophy of nonviolence of Mahatma Gandhi, Martin Luther King, and Nelson Mandela, and which has had an enormous impact not only on India, the United States, and South Africa, but also on the entire human race.

Zen

We are all influenced by ideas we know nothing about. This may sound like a paradox, but it is true. In the West today, the most famous school that grew out of Buddhism is known as Zen. During my formative years, I was indirectly influenced by Zen, of which I knew next to nothing. This was in the early sixties, and I was in my early twenties. In college I had a professor of philosophy named Van Meter Ames, who exerted great influence on my young, impressionable mind. He was a Unitarian and a humanist of the best kind. He let his students explore great philosophical ideas in the novels of leading twentieth-century European writers. Unbeknownst to me, he was at work at the time on a book titled *Zen and American Thought*. He was one of the most open-minded people I have ever met. He searched for knowledge everywhere, and he did not take anything for granted. To him, great ideas were something you learn not from a book, but rather from life. This was my first lesson in Zen, albeit I was not aware of it at the time.

The only bit of Zen wisdom I recall from those days was the question "What is the sound of one hand clapping?" It became a fashionable joke among young people like myself. It is only now, years later, that I can appreciate this question. Now I know it is what Zen refers to as a koan, or a question designed to stimulate thought. Over the years it has given rise to endless speculation. The koan is not a challenge to the rational mind, but to one's intuition. Unlike Christianity, which believes that "in the beginning was the word," or Judaism, which believes that the world was created by divine speech, Zen is suspicious of words and of human speech. Let us play for a moment with the "sound of one hand clapping" question. Most obviously, that sound is silence. Zen seems to imply that silence is a higher form of communication than words or the sound made by two hands clapping. Zen emphasizes meditation as superior to speech. It is entirely possible that Zen provides a clue to the question whether the prophets heard the voice of God. Is silence the voice of God? When Elijah hears God, we are told that he hears a "still small voice," better translated as "the voice of a subtle silence." In other words, the prophet, like the Zen disciple, reaches into his inner self, and a silence inside of him, which comes not from his conscious mind but from another source, enables him to receive a message that the prophet recognizes as coming from a divine source.

Zen does not deal with absolutes. It has no god, no scriptures, no rituals, and no doctrine. Zen deals with the flow of life and the constant becoming. The Buddha taught that religion is in a constant state of change. Buddhism believes that religion can interfere with the ability of the individual to reach nirvana. In short, Buddhism, and more so its Zen variety, offers an alternate religious philosophy that does not negate the religions of the West, but rather lets them look at things from another, more individualized, more introspective perspective. It is no wonder that one of the great Catholic thinkers of the twentieth century, the Trappist monk Thomas Merton, whose book *The Seven Storey Mountain* also exerted a great influence on me during my formative years, became a devotee of Zen, as did my professor, Van Meter Ames, the Unitarian philosopher.

The philosophical side of Zen is not easy to explore. But some of its practices, such as meditation, can be taught by a qualified instructor and can greatly benefit anyone who seeks help with stress and anxiety. I should know, because in midlife I once came under great stress because of a career change and I developed hematuria. My doctor, who was the son of a minister, prescribed meditation, which helped me get cured.

The main lesson I have learned from both Zen and Buddhism is that staying within the confines of our own faith or convictions and ignoring or dismissing all others is self-limiting and self-defeating. Every faith and every philosophy has something to teach us and does not necessarily challenge our own beliefs or ideas. The more we know, the better off we are.

CONFUCIUS—CONFUCIANISM

Confucius, who lived in China during the second half of the sixth century BCE, was a contemporary of the last Hebrew prophets. Like the prophets, he gave his people a moral philosophy. He also gave them a quasi-religious tradition that is espoused by millions of people in East Asia. In his article "Confucian Ethic of Death with Dignity," Ping-cheung Lo writes,

> In Confucianism, human beings are teachable, improvable and perfectible through personal and communal endeavor, especially including self-cultivation and self-creation. A main idea of Confucianism is the cultivation of virtue and the development of moral perfection. Confucianism holds that one should give up one's life, if necessary, either passively or actively, for the sake of upholding the cardinal moral values of *ren* [humaneness] and *yi* [proper behavior]. (*Annual of the Society of Christian Ethics* 19 [1999]: 313–33)

Like the Hebrew prophets, Confucius was concerned not only with the conduct of the individual person but also with the nature of society and particularly its rulers. Here he parts ways with the Buddha, who, despite his origins as a member of the ruling warrior class, turned his back on power and focused on the life of the spirit and on moral conduct. Confucius, like the Hebrew prophets, lived in a time of endless wars between feudal states, and like the prophets he yearned for a time of peace and prosperity, a revival of the ordered society of earlier times. He also introduced the concept of a ruling class that would succeed to power on the basis of its moral merits instead of lineage. Such a ruler would spread his own virtues to the people instead of imposing proper behavior with laws and rules.

Unlike the Hebrew prophets, whose vision of a righteous future king of the House of David was not fulfilled, Confucius's teachings were adopted by the Chinese emperors as early as the second century BCE, and a system was instituted for testing the moral character of government officials, who came from different walks of society and gained a higher social and economic status by attaining government positions. Confucianism became the state religion, or social philosophy, of China, and it also spread to other parts of Asia. Confucian thought has shaped the Chinese character throughout the ages. Some of its salient features are loyalty to parents and the worship of one's ancestors; proper and virtuous behavior; obedience to the ruler who himself is expected to be of high moral character; and a strong emphasis on learning and knowledge.

Viewed historically, however, Confucianism did not succeed in establishing an ideal social order in China. As the most populous nation in the world, one of the biggest problems in China has always been establishing an effective central government that can manage the affairs of its vast population and provide a good life to its countless millions. I recall an anecdote about a French ambassador to China who, in recent years, asked a Chinese government official about the size of China's population. The official smiled and said, "Do you mean this morning or this afternoon?" For centuries, China was ruled by powerful emperors who, like the pharaohs, were considered to be the sons of heaven. They were remote and unapproachable to their subjects. A common criticism that has been leveled against Confucianism has been that it became an imperial tool for consolidating the power of China's emperors and perpetuating a feudal system that kept the Chinese masses poor and oppressed. In 1912 imperial rule in China came to an end and was replaced by a republic. The next thirty-seven years saw great political turmoil and a very aggressive war with Japan, and finally in 1949 China came under communist rule, which has remained in place to this day.

With the introduction of communism to China, a Western secular philosophy with messianic overtones replaced Confucianism as the state religion. During the so-called communist Cultural Revolution in the 1960s and 1970s in which countless people were brutally persecuted and murdered, Confucianism was blamed for the ills of China and was portrayed as a negative force holding China back and preventing its people from bettering themselves. While this tragic episode in Chinese history has receded into the past, it is doubtful that Chinese communism can do away with the teachings of Confucius. Communist economic doctrine is no longer practiced in China. Unlike North Korea and Cuba, which chose to stop the hands of the clock despite the failure of communism to create a better world, the Chinese have joined the world economy and are playing a dominant part in it.

This brief review of the place of Confucianism in Chinese history makes it clear that while this major moral and religious philosophy has had an enormous impact on a major portion of the human race, it has always had its ups and downs, and in our time its adherents have begun to look for a new ideology that is better suited to the realities of today's world.

JESUS—CHRISTIANITY

The most dominant religious teacher on the planet is Jesus. It never ceases to amaze me that my fellow countryman and coreligionist, the gentle son of a carpenter from a town not far from the one where I was born, is worshipped in practically every land and every tongue on this earth. I remember my first visit to Nazareth, an Arab Christian town. It was a school trip, and I was a young teenager. I knew next to nothing about world religions, but even then I had an avid interest in what different people believed. It was always clear to me that there is only one God and that all human beings are children of that same God. In those days the Holocaust was a fresh memory. I remember as a child wondering what Jesus would have to say about the murder of six million of his own coreligionists at the hands of people who called themselves Christians and who prayed to him. I believed, and I still believe, that Jesus cried, and he continues to cry to this day. I also believe that God cries every day.

The Nazi state that launched a total and relentless genocide campaign against the Jewish people did not do it in the name of Jesus or Christianity but in the name of German national socialism and what it saw as the superior Aryan race, harkening back to the Barbarian gods of the Germanic people. As Hitler once said, "The world calls us Barbarians, and indeed we are." The regrettable part is that many good Germans and other Christians, particularly Pope Pius XII, did not confront this ultimate evil. The theological consequences of this greatest crime in all of history will be with us for generations to come.

My own religion teaches me to forgive but never to forget. There is no chance I or my descendants will ever forget, because those martyrs were our own flesh and blood. There is a lesson here we all must heed. While the stories and teachings of Jesus of Nazareth continue to bring comfort and spiritual strength to countless people around the globe, and while Christianity in all its different forms is the most dominant religion on the planet, we are still a long way away from the day when the teachings of the man from Galilee become truly assimilated by his adherents who are yet to practice such noble concepts as turning the other cheek or giving someone the shirt off one's back.

Even as a Jew, I have been greatly enriched by reading the Gospels. There are object lessons in the stories about the life of Jesus that have profound human meaning, and which I have not found elsewhere. At one point in my life, when I felt abandoned by all my friends, the story of Jesus telling Peter at the Last Supper, "Before the rooster crows today, you will disown me three times" (Luke 22:61), came to my mind. At the time I was on a mission, and I counted on my friends to support me, but they decided to bail out. I needed a scriptural reference to help me carry on—and for this I usually turn to my Hebrew Bible—but this time the Gospel according to Luke seemed to be the most effective.

In our search for the meaning of prophecy, I wouldn't be surprised if the majority of my non-Jewish readers will feel now they have found the answer, namely, Jesus. I remember a conversation I once had with the pastor of a very large Evangelical church in Denver, Colorado, whom I had befriended. We discussed the coming of the messiah, which to us Jews is the first coming and to Christians the second coming. I said to him, "Bill, you may be right or I may be right. But the important thing is that a messianic age does come, and when it does we will find out which one it is."

I still feel this way, because I believe that a messianic age is universal rather than sectarian. If it should come, it will be for everyone, not for Jews or Christians or Buddhists. All the religions seem to believe that at that stage labels will have little meaning. What will matter will be universal values like love and peace and the absence of any self-interest.

In modern and contemporary times, the greatest efforts for social reform, democracy, and world peace have come from Christian persons and groups that no doubt have been informed and inspired by the teachings of Jesus as well as the other great teachers of humanity. Everywhere we look in today's world, people are struggling to establish free and prosperous societies modeled after the Christian West. This is not to say that Christianity is going to replace all the other religions in the world. They all seem to have validity for their own followers. There are great shifts within the Christian world, especially in Latin America where many Catholics are embracing Protestant forms of Christianity. There is also a tendency in the Far East to embrace various forms of Christian faith. But the main thrust in the world today is to copy the progressive political and social institutions of the West, which afford equal opportunity to all citizens, equality for women, education for all children, social services, and so on. The best example is the current sudden outburst of social revolution in the Arab world from Morocco to Bahrain, which has already begun to change the face of the Arab world.

Christianity in our time has come a long way in the way it views the world and in the way it treats members of other faiths, particularly Jews. There are good reasons to believe that Christianity has learned the lessons of the Holocaust and of the rebirth of the State of Israel and has begun to apply them. This speaks well for Christianity, which, as a religious ideology, continues to show many signs of strength as it experiences a comeback throughout Eastern Europe in the countries of the former Soviet bloc, and in many other parts of the world. It is not the Christianity of the pre–World War II world, the Christianity of Franco and Mussolini and many other prewar tyrants, or the Christianity of religious demagogues of which the world saw more than a few in the twentieth century. It is, for the most part, a Christianity that pursues social activism and supports social causes.

Christian faith and Christian civilization continue to evolve. But at the center of it all is the simple story of a humble man of faith who personalized God to the world when he spoke about his "Heavenly Father," a Jewish way of understanding God that finds its most moving expression in the life and teachings of the prophet Jeremiah, who, as I pointed out in my book on this prophet, was Jesus's spiritual mentor. The great Rabbi Akiba said, "How fortunate you are, O Israel, for before whom do you purify yourselves, and who purifies you, but your Heavenly Father." To me, Jesus ranks among the great rabbis in history, alongside Hillel and Akiba.

MUHAMMAD—ISLAM

Islam is the world's second-largest religion. It is the youngest of the three monotheistic religions (it started in the seventh century AD), but it considers itself the culmination of its predecessors. As such, it has shown respect from the very beginning for both Judaism and Christianity, and for their scriptures. Unlike Christianity, which incorporated the Hebrew Bible in its own Bible (hence the Old and New Testaments), Islam has kept its own holy book, the Qur'an, separate from the other two. Muslims believe that the Holy Qur'an is the final and infallible word of God, while the other two have their errors. They are particularly uneasy with the Christian belief of the trinity, which they consider polytheistic, and with the divinity of Christ, which to them negates the oneness of God. They reject the concept of God as a divine father, which is central to both Judaism and Christianity. They look upon Jesus (as well as several biblical personalities such as Adam, Abraham, and Moses) as prophets who received the word of God, and upon Muhammad as both God's messenger who received the text of the Qur'an from God and the ultimate prophet.

Islam teaches the deepest reverence for God and for the Prophet, who is considered the greatest man in history. The word "Islam" suggests surrender to God, and therein lies the essence of this religion. Islam is perhaps the most monotheistic of the three religions. While

Judaism routinely refers to God as "our God" or the "God of Israel," Islam simply states that "there is no god but God," thus providing the most universal view of God possible. As a native of the Middle East, I have on many occasions observed Muslims at prayer, and I have always been struck by the depth of their faith and piety. I have no doubt in my mind that they are true people of faith, and that their faith affords them a great deal of comfort and peace of mind. I do believe that Islam is a distillation of earlier monotheistic traditions that include Judaism and Christianity, and that it provides its believers a very solid belief and ethics system. The Qur'an to a large extent is a retelling of the Hebrew Bible from an Arab perspective. Thus, for example, it focuses on Abraham's son, Ishmael, who is the progenitor of the Arab people, rather than on the second son, Isaac, who is the progenitor of the Jewish people. As a Jew, I find very little in Islam that is contrary to my own beliefs. Islam's practice of polygamy, for example, is derived from the ancient Hebrew practice. While this practice has long been abolished among Jews, it is still practiced in some parts of the Muslim world. A study of the Qur'an shows that all the Ten Commandments of the Hebrew Bible appear throughout Islam's holy book in a somewhat modified way. The Jewish prohibition against doing any work on the Sabbath, for example, is not included in the observance of the Muslim's holy day, namely, Friday, because Islam maintains that since God is never tired, it is not true that God rested on the seventh day following creation.

Unfortunately, many in the West have the wrong perception of Islam. They see it as a backward, intolerant, and repressive religion. This may be due to several factors, both historical and contemporary. First, there is the long-standing rift between the Christian and the Muslim worlds, dating back to the days when Islam first spread through the Middle East and North Africa and reached Europe in the early Middle Ages. At that time, the young civilization born in the Arabian Peninsula reached new heights in science, technology, and philosophy that eclipsed Europe's Christian civilization. This time is known as the Golden Age of Islam, a time which, in Muslim Spain, also produced a golden age for the Jews living under Islam, giving rise to such luminaries as Maimonides, Judah Halevi, and many others. Muslims to this day recall that time of glory, but they also recall the Crusades that lasted from the tenth to the fifteenth century, during which time Christian Europe began a centuries-long cycle of armed conflicts that reversed the fortunes of Muslim civilization. Subsequently, the Golden Age of Islam was replaced by the Christian Renaissance in Europe, and as the modern age began, Christian Europe became the dominant force around the world, while the world of Islam went into a decline that has continued to this day. In mosques throughout the Muslim world, religious teachers and preachers to this day keep reminding their followers of Islam's past glory, and keep praying for the day when it will once again become a reality.

This brings us to a second and more-immediate reason for the West's view of Islam, which is the spread of radical Islam in the twenty-first century, particularly since September 11, 2001, a watershed date in the present history of this centuries-long conflict. This and many other terrorist attacks committed by radical Muslims seeking to bring down the West have eclipsed in the minds of many in the West all that is positive and commendable in Islam. One of the great challenges of our time is to bring about a better understanding of Islam in the West.

As these lines are being written, what seems to be the greatest social and political upheaval in the history of the Muslim world is taking place, redefining Muslim history. While the results of this revolution that started in Tunisia and has now spread to all corners of the Muslim world are far from clear, not to take cognizance of these remarkable events-in-the-making is to render our discussion of Islam invalid. Suddenly, out of the blue, the common man in the Arab street who for many years has lived passively under repressive and corrupt regimes, and who has let autocrats and radical militants dictate his behavior and beliefs, has banded together with countless others, put his life on the line, and begun bringing down long-ruling tyrants. The political outcome of these events is not clear. What the experts believe is that it can go on for a long time, but no one knows how it will all play out in the end. But what is also not clear is how it will affect the future face of Islam. Will it help bring the gentler and kinder aspects of Islam to the fore, or will it be coopted by the radicals who distort the true teachings of Islam and swell their ranks? This question, which at this time is not the main focus of the world's attention, may be the most critical. If the answer is the former rather than the latter, then indeed Islam can become a great force for good not only for its followers but for the rest of the world.

BAHA'U'LLAH—BAHA'I

The Baha'i faith is a nineteenth-century offspring of Islam, and it is perhaps the most enlightened of all of the world's religions. Its world center happens to be next door to the house where I grew up in Haifa, Israel. This is not because it has a large following in Haifa or in Israel, but because of historical circumstances that caused its prophetic leader, Baha'u'llah, to be imprisoned by the Turks in nearby Acre, where he ended his days. To this day, the Shrine of the Bab, a marble palace with a gold dome, dominates the view of the port city of Haifa from the heights of Mount Carmel. It is surrounded by breathtaking Persian gardens where I often strolled as a youth and was captivated by the mystery of this place. Growing up, I did not know any Baha'i people, but I was once given a brochure that explained the Baha'i faith. I was struck by the fact that while I often experienced prejudice and distrust in my home town between Jews and Muslims and Christians, the Baha'i accepted all three faiths as legitimate and aspired toward a united humanity and world peace. I concluded that this was a highly idealistic faith that had little chance of ever seeing its ideals become a reality.

Now, in my search for the meaning of prophecy, and as I explore the utopian school of Hebrew prophets like Micah and Isaiah and Jeremiah who envisioned an end of days and world peace, I realize that Baha'u'llah might have been on the right track. Perhaps he is the one who has the answers for all of us. Perhaps he is the one who represents the fulfillment of the vision of the biblical prophets. Here is some of what he has to say.

> We desire but the good of the world and happiness of the nations . . .
> That all nations should become one in faith and all men as brothers;
> that the bonds of affection and unity between the sons of men should
> be strengthened; that diversity of religion should cease, and differ-
> ences of race be annulled . . . Yet so it shall be; these fruitless
> conflicts, these ruinous wars shall pass away, and the "Greatest
> Peace" shall come . . . These conflicts and this bloodshed and discord
> must cease, and all men must be as one kindred and one family . . .
> Let not a man glory in this, that he loves his country; let him rather
> glory in this, that he loves his kind. (Baha'u'llah, 1890)

In his book on the Baha'i faith, Anthony A. Lee offers the following principles as a summary of that faith.

1. The oneness of mankind.
2. Independent investigation of truth.
3. The common foundation of all religion.
4. The essential harmony of science and religion.
5. Equality of men and women.
6. Elimination of prejudice of all kinds.
7. Universal compulsory education.
8. A spiritual solution of the economic problem.
9. A universal auxiliary language.
10. Universal peace upheld by a world government. (*The Baha'i Faith in Africa*, 8)

Considering how lofty the Baha'i ideals are, it is no surprise that this faith has only some five million adherents worldwide. Nor is it any surprise that, as a breakaway from Islam, it has been severely persecuted by the Ayatollahs in Iran, its land of origin, or that close to half of the Baha'i believers live in India, a land of great religious diversity and tolerance. Now that I have had contact with some people of the Baha'i persuasion, I find them to be gentle and considerate, and they remind me in a way of Jehovah's Witnesses.

Some may argue that the Baha'i reach too high. For example, they do not allow for the fact that the human race is diverse, and that religious diversity and other kinds of diversity are inevitable. When the Baha'u'llah says, "Let not a man glory in this, that he loves his country; let him rather glory in this, that he loves his kind," he is overlooking the attachment people have to their own country, which does not necessarily preclude other kinds of attachments and commitments.

In a way, I see the Baha'i faith not as yet another religion, but as a meta-religious system that looks to create structures that unify the diversity of the human race. It is no wonder that the Baha'i are active in the various agencies of the United Nations. But it is certainly quite remarkable that such an idealistic movement sprang not from the bosom of Judaism or Christianity, but rather from Iranian Islam.

Our discussion of the Baha'i faith is a good place to conclude our survey of great prophetic figures of the world. We have not covered all of them, which does not in any way detract from any of the others. They are all great teachers whom vast portions of the human race consider to be prophets. They have created or given rise to belief systems that continue to inform and inspire humanity, and they may help us understand the universal elements of all faith systems. Whichever we happen to or choose to follow, it is incumbent upon us to show all of them respect and to approach them with humility. If all their millions of followers truly followed their teachings, this world would surely become near-utopian.

9

PROPHETIC PERSONALITIES

Certain visionary personalities in the modern world have been driven by moral compulsion and have had a profoundly positive impact on the human race. The following examples do not represent a value judgment and do not in any way seek to exclude other equally deserving personalities. It would be easy to be critical of any one of them, but personal bias cannot change the fact that they had a prophetic dimension, and their impact on human history cannot be denied. In our search for the meaning of prophecy, I believe they may help us sharpen our understanding and come closer to understanding the meaning of prophecy because their prophetic impulse bridges the centuries separating us from the Hebrew prophets of old and makes the teachings of the biblical prophets a living reality as these lines are being written. If history does produce prophetic personalities like these, who change the world for the better, then it is to be expected that more will come along in the future and help bring about a better world which, far off as it may seem, may be closer than any of us can imagine. The Hebrew prophets, even under the most dire circumstances, always believed in a better future. Those to whom we refer here as prophetic personalities have all shared this belief.

MARTIN LUTHER

According to the great twentieth-century theologian and philosopher Paul Tillich, Martin Luther "transformed the surface of the earth." He is "one of the few great prophets of the Christian church." Tillich makes these remarks in the following assessment of Luther:

> Now the turning point of the Reformation and of Church history as a whole is the experience of an Augustinian monk in his monastic cell—Martin Luther. Martin Luther didn't teach other doctrines— that, he also did; but this was not important, there were many others also who did; But none of those who protested against the Roman system were able to break through it. The only man who really broke through and whose breakthrough has transformed the surface of the earth was Martin Luther. That is his greatness. Don't measure his greatness by comparing him with Lutheranism; that's something quite different, and is something which has gone through the period of Lutheran Orthodoxy and many other things—political movements, Prussian conservatism, and what not. But Luther is something different. Luther is one of the few great prophets of the Christian Church, and even if his greatness was limited by some characteristics he had, and by his later development, his greatness is overwhelming. He is responsible—and he alone—for the fact that a purified Christianity, a Christianity of the Reformation, was able to establish itself on equal terms with the Roman tradition. And from this point of view we must look at him. Therefore when I speak of Luther, I don't speak of the theologian who has produced Lutheranism—there are many others who have done this, and Melanchthon much more than Luther—but I speak of the man in whom the breakthrough occurred, the break through the Roman system; and that is he, and nobody else. (Lecture 31: The Reformation, Luther and Catholicism)

In this lucid and concise statement, Tillich provides an honest and comprehensive summary of the seminal achievement of someone who is perhaps one of the most perplexing personalities in history. It would be interesting to know what the prophet of the Baha'i faith, Baha'u'llah, would have to say about Martin Luther. The Baha'i believe that unity among the religions is a good thing, yet Tillich praises Luther for breaking away from the Catholic Church. This raises a philosophical question as to whether Christianity and the world would have been better off had there been no Luther and the profound change that he brought about in the Christian faith by giving rise to what we generally refer to today as Protestantism. This is a purely speculative question because we will never know the answer. To further complicate matters, there is a third major division in the Christian world, namely, the Orthodox churches— Greek, Russian, and others. In other words, would it be better if the entire Christian world spoke with one voice rather than so many different voices? Are the divisions within the Christian world a hindrance to world understanding and world peace?

One only needs to recall the endless wars Christian nations have fought against one another, often in the name of the same savior. A recent example is the war in the Falklands between Great Britain and Argentina in 1982, when the Archbishop of Canterbury, breaking with tradition, refused to bless the British troops in the name of Christ as they were about to depart for the Falklands to fight another Christian nation. But what is clear is that such wars are fought along national rather than religious lines, and even if all Christians had been united under one religious tradition, they would still have fought each other.

A good case can be made for the historical benefits of the diversity within Christianity. The history of Latin America and North America is a good case in point. Latin America is almost monolithically Catholic, and the religious monopoly of the Catholic Church on that continent has not allowed for great social and economic progress. North America, on the other hand, particularly the United States, has given rise to a large number of Christian denominations, and the socioeconomic progress of this continent has been phenomenal. Protestantism has been the greatest force for socioeconomic progress in the twentieth century, and the Protestant Reformation of the sixteenth century was due primarily to the German priest Martin Luther.

Luther started out in life as a German Catholic priest, and from the very beginning of his ecclesiastical career he was a troubled soul. As he grew older, deteriorating health only made him more troubled, and despite the fact that he turned against what he perceived as a corrupt and autocratic church, he himself became a harsh and intolerant reformer who, as we shall see, let his zeal blind his better judgment. Luther's original intent was never to leave the church but to change the church from within. What sparked his outrage against the pope was the

Vatican's sale of indulgences, or forgiveness of sins, to people in his hometown in Germany, as a fund-raiser for building St. Peter's Basilica in Rome. He issued his ninety-five arguments against the church, hoping to reform the church from within, but before he had a chance to do it he was excommunicated by the pope. Things could have gone very badly for the rebellious priest, but he did find his protectors in high places in Germany, and his writings became extremely popular. As Tillich puts it, Luther in effect started a new Christian religion. This new religion, which evolved into the many forms of Protestantism, replaced the absolute authority of Rome with a direct relationship between the believer and the savior, and the word of scripture became accessible to the individual believer rather than controlled by the pope. Some of Luther's major contributions to this new Christian religion were his translation of the Old and New Testaments into German and his introduction of prayers and hymns. He also broke with the Catholic vow of celibacy, took a wife, and raised children, pointing the way for a new kind of Christian clergy.

I have no trouble understanding Luther's actions up to this point. Where I begin to have difficulties with the story of his career is his changing attitudes in midlife toward other religions, particularly Judaism and also Islam. Luther started out in life as one who understood and respected non-Christians and granted them the ability to live a righteous life. The change in his attitude seemed to occur when he began to spread his teachings of a Christian savior unfettered by the hierarchy in Rome and seemed to fervently hope that the Jews would finally see the light and join his ranks. When he began to realize that this was not happening, something must have snapped, and he seemed to take leave of his better nature. Consequently, he wrote the book *On the Jews and Their Lies*, in which he paints a picture of the Jewish people worthy of the worst examples of hate literature in human annals. In it he calls for persecuting and attacking the Jews and removing them from Christian lands. While he did not write a similar treatise against Muslims, he did have many negative things to say about them as well. Muslims to sixteenth-century Europe meant primarily the Muslim Turkish Empire that was at war with Christian Europe.

To this day, scholars continue to debate Luther's contribution to European and particularly German anti-Semitism in modern times, and especially the possibility that when Nazi Germany in the 1930s made anti-Semitism its official state policy, it found justification in doing so by pointing to Luther's writings. The great German philosopher of that time, Karl Jaspers, wrote, "There you already have the whole Nazi program." According to the American Jewish historian Lucy Dawidowicz in her book *The War against the Jews, 1933 – 1945*, both Luther and Hitler were obsessed by a "demonologized universe" inhabited by Jews, with Hitler asserting that the later Luther, the author of *On the Jews and Their Lies*, was the real Luther (23).

In his book *The Rise and Fall of the Third Reich*, William L. Shirer writes,

> It is difficult to understand the behavior of most German Protestants in the first Nazi years unless one is aware of two things: their history and the influence of Martin Luther. The great founder of Protestantism was both a passionate anti-Semite and a ferocious believer in absolute obedience to political authority. He wanted Germany rid of the Jews. Luther's advice was literally followed four centuries later by Hitler, Goering and Himmler. (236)

Luther's anti-Semitism must have been a great source of embarrassment to many an enlightened and fair-minded Lutheran and to other Protestants, particularly after the Holocaust. In 1994 the following item appeared in the media regarding a statement by the Evangelical Lutheran Church in America:

> The Evangelical Lutheran Church in America recently issued a profound apology that officially disavows the disturbing anti-Semitic writings of Martin Luther, who rebelled against the Roman Catholic Church in the 1500s and inspired the branch of Protestantism that bears his name.

It seems, indeed, that there were two Martin Luthers living inside the same body. There was Martin Luther the idealistic reformer, whose impact on the human race has been enormous and, in my opinion, mostly positive. But there was also Martin Luther the zealot, who did not practice Christian love, and who may have contributed to what became the greatest catastrophe in Jewish history. This perhaps should not surprise us, because one of the things Luther believed in was that in every person and particularly in every Christian a saint and a sinner exist side by side. Ironically, in his own life Luther succeeded in playing out this existential human drama. As we pointed out before, even the biblical prophets were only human. Certainly those we present here as prophetic personalities were only human.

THEODOR HERZL

If there has been a Jewish prophetic personality in modern times, it is certainly the Viennese journalist Dr. Theodor Herzl, who lived in Europe at the end of the nineteenth century and died in 1904 at the age of forty-four. Herzl can be viewed as a latter-day Moses in that, like Moses before him, he liberated his fellow Jews from centuries of passivity and subjugation to foreign rulers, and showed them a way to the Promised Land that resulted in the birth and growth of what he called *Der Judenstaadt*, or the present-day State of Israel.

The story of the young Herzl is typical of the stories of other great European Jewish luminaries in nineteenth-century central Europe and particularly in Germany, such as Felix Mendelssohn, Heinrich Heine, and many others, who had to assimilate into the dominant Christian culture to make their mark on the world. Like Moses, who was raised in the Egyptian culture and only discovered his people and their plight after he grew up, Herzl received no Jewish education to speak of, and pursued German nationalism as a young man. He had deep disdain for religion in general and Judaism in particular, and he thought of himself as a man of the world. But in his school days he became exposed to European anti-Semitism, which eventually would have a profound effect on this dreamy and idealistic young man who possessed the soul of a poet. In Vienna, where his family moved from his native Hungary when he was eighteen, Herzl became a journalist for the celebrated Viennese newspaper *Neue Freie Presse*. He was sent by his paper in 1885 to cover the trial of Alfred Dreyfus in Paris. Dreyfus was a Jewish officer in the French army who was falsely accused of treason. Herzl witnessed the crowds in Paris following the trial yelling, "Death to the Jews." Like Martin Luther and the indulgences, this was Herzl's wake-up call. Three things became clear to him: a Jew is always a Jew; anti-Semitism is here to stay; and Jewish life in Europe was in grave danger. Like Luther, although for totally different reasons, he came to the conclusion that the Jews had to leave Europe and establish their own land.

Herzl was a visionary. Apparently, what is known as the *pintele Yid*, that little Jewish spark that exists deep in the Jewish soul, even among the most assimilated and self-denying of Jews, did gleam in his heart, and almost overnight he changed from a European man of letters to a Jewish political activist, at a time when Jews had neither a state nor politics.

Later that year Herzl began to write his book *Der Judenstaadt* [The Jewish State], in which he delineated the reasons for an independent state for the Jewish people. When the book came out in early 1886, its ideas quickly spread throughout the Jewish world and among non-Jews as well, eliciting both enthusiastic approval and sharp criticism. The lines were drawn among Jews between Zionists, who accepted the idea of a Jewish state, and non- or anti-Zionists, who either dismissed or rejected such an idea. While the idea of Zionism, or the return of the Jews to their ancestral land, had begun to flourish in some Jewish circles, particularly in Eastern Europe, even before the time of Herzl, he was the first who put it before the world as a real and urgent solution to what was known as the "Jewish Question," namely, the ongoing persecution of Jews under various regimes in Europe and elsewhere, which required a lasting solution.

Herzl understood that it was only a question of time before Europe erupted and a great catastrophe befell European Jewry. He was not the only European visionary who understood it. The German philosopher Nietzsche, a contemporary of Herzl, wrote that a day would come when Germany would commit unprecedented atrocities in Europe. The Hebrew poet Uri Zvi Greenberg, one of the greatest Hebrew poets of the twentieth century, wrote a poem, years before the Holocaust, about Jews being brutalized and destroyed in concentration camps. But Herzl was not only a visionary. He was also a man of action, and he devoted the last eight years of his short life to organizing the Zionist movement and bringing its cause before the leading heads of state of Europe. By doing so he transformed the Jews' condition from the status of second-class citizens or residents in most parts of the world to a people beginning to redefine themselves and who eventually would succeed in establishing their own state, which today has taken its place in the forefront of human progress.

Zionism, which is still vilified in some quarters of the world as racist, is the liberation movement of the Jewish people. In the mid-twentieth century it inspired many other nations in Asia and Africa to overthrow colonialism and gain independence. It is my belief that the Jewish people have always been held by the world to a higher standard and that the world has always expected more from the Jews. This should not surprise us because, after all, the Jews gave the world the belief in one God, the Ten Commandments, and the great prophets, and the Jews have continued to this day to contribute to world civilization far beyond their small numbers. Jews and particularly Israeli Jews should also expect more of themselves, as the founder of the State of Israel, David Ben-Gurion, pointed out in his later years.

The most famous photograph of Dr. Herzl was taken in Basel, Switzerland, in 1897. This handsome, tall, prophetlike man with the long dark beard and the dreamy eyes is leaning over the parapet overlooking the river. He later wrote in his diary, "In Basel I founded the Jewish State. If I said this out loud today, I would be answered by universal laughter. Perhaps in five years, certainly in fifty, everyone will know it." Fifty years almost to the day, in 1947, the United Nations voted in favor of a partition plan establishing a Jewish and an Arab state in the land where the Hebrew prophets once walked and dreamed of a world at peace.

Two years before his death, Herzl published a utopian novel titled *Altneuland* [An Old-New Land]. It provides a blueprint for the Jewish national emancipation first enunciated in his book *The Jewish State*. Both ideological and utopian, it presents a model society that adopts a liberal and egalitarian social model, resembling a modern welfare state. Herzl called his model "Mutualism," and it is based on a mixed economy, with public ownership of the land and natural resources, agricultural cooperatives, and state welfare, with at the same time an encouragement of private entrepreneurship. This model was adopted by Labor Zionism in the early stages of the State of Israel. One of Labor Zionism's great achievements was the kibbutz model of agricultural settlements under common ownership, with state ownership of the land.

Herzl and the early Zionists have been accused of overlooking the Arab population of Palestine and not showing concern for their rights. This is not entirely true. While it is true that the main thrust of early Zionism was to establish a viable state in a land that for the most part was barren and infested with diseases like malaria, Herzl in his writings does make mention of the local Arabs, and shows concern for their welfare. Now that the Jewish State has been in existence for over sixty years, one could argue that it could have done more for its Arab citizens and by doing so would have diffused much of the animosity of the Palestinian Arabs. No objective observer would argue that the State of Israel is a utopia. But then again, the utopian dreams of European visionaries like Herzl at the end of the nineteenth century did not come true in the twentieth. The messiah did not come to Europe, but Hitler did. Israel, to a large extent, is a state of survivors. One can only hope that in time Arab and Jew will live there in harmony, as will all the other countries of the Middle East. That would be the day Herzl and his disciples dreamed about.

MAHATMA GANDHI

Mohandas Karamchand Gandhi, known to the world as Mahatma (the great soul) Gandhi, is honored in India, a nation of over 1.2 billion people, as the father of the nation. But his influence reaches to every corner of the world, and much of what he said and did is invaluable for healing and repairing our world. His life and teachings reflect the best in Buddhism and Hinduism as well as the three monotheistic religions of the West. He was indeed a prophetic personality who followed the words of the prophet Zechariah: "Not by might, nor by power, but by my spirit, says the God of hosts" (Zech. 4:6).

Few leaders or teachers in the history of the world accomplished so much without the use of power. Gandhi's secret weapon was people. He knew that people were the greatest force in the world. In his case it was hundreds of millions of Indians facing off against a colonial rule of much smaller numbers. No regime in history, no matter how strong or repressive, can ever resist the will of the people who rise up against it, especially if their cause is just.

Gandhi is India and India is Gandhi. He did not only free India from colonial rule and help it gain its independence, he captured the essence of this vast mega-nation of many religions, ethnic groups, and languages, and he defined its ethos. Today, as India has finally begun to take its place in the global economy as a major player, it can fully appreciate what that gaunt, ascetic, and bespectacled man has done for it, and it can bask in the glow of his growing stature around the world.

Gandhi was born and raised a Hindu, and he practiced Hinduism all his life. He often turned to the *Bhagavad Gita*, the Hindu scripture, for solace and inspiration. When asked if he was a Hindu, he replied, "Yes I am. I am also a Christian, a Muslim, a Buddhist and a Jew." This should not surprise us, because Hinduism is accepting of all religions. Regarding Buddhism, Gandhi said, "I know that Buddhism is to Hinduism what Protestantism is to Roman Catholicism, only in much stronger light, to a much greater degree." He said about Christianity, "I like your Christ. I do not like your Christians. Your Christians are so unlike your Christ." Regarding Islam, he commented, "The sayings of Muhammad are a treasure of wisdom, not only for Muslims but for all of mankind." Regarding religion, he said that God has no religion. But he reserved his greatest criticism for his own Hinduism. He rejected the caste system and worked to improve the lot of the untouchables in Hindu society.

Since Hinduism is not a monotheistic religion and does not believe in one personal God the way Judaism or the other two monotheistic religions do, Gandhi reached the conclusion that "God is truth." He later changed this statement to "Truth is God." He dedicated his life to the wider purpose of discovering truth, or *Satya*. He tried to achieve it by learning from his own mistakes and conducting experiments on himself. He called his autobiography *My Story of My Experiment with Truth*.

Gandhi's idea and practice of experimenting with the truth provides a key to understanding this great man's views, his achievements, and also his limitations, and it can be seen as an object lesson in our greater search for the meaning of prophecy. Few leaders in modern times have interfaced and interacted with a wider variety of humanity. While raised in India in the Indian cultures, the young Gandhi went to England to study law. He then moved to South Africa where he became a member of the Indian community, which was not treated as equal by the ruling white population. His social and political awakening took place when he was thrown off a train for refusing to move from first class to third class, even though he had a first-class ticket. He became a social activist and organized his fellow Indians in successful peaceful resistance to the discriminatory policies of the South African government.

When World War I broke out, Gandhi returned to India and became active in Indian issues. This was the beginning of his transformation from a returning expatriate to the author of Indian independence. Now he faced all the complexities and diversity of Indian society, which included almost every major religion and many lesser ones. India under British rule also included what later became Pakistan, and it had (and still does) a very large Muslim population. Muslims and Hindus had been at war for centuries, and they still are today in Kashmir. The task facing Gandhi was superhuman, and despite the great success of his policy of nonviolence and of bringing together many diverse people, he was not able to overcome the historical divide between Muslims and Hindus. Also, as early as World War I, he agreed to have Indians train as combat soldiers for the British war effort, eliciting criticism from close friends who considered it inconsistent with his unswerving rejection of the use of power.

Many Jews feel that Gandhi let them down at their hour of greatest need. In 1939, when Nazi Germany began its genocidal campaign against the Jews, Gandhi criticized the Zionist movement for its militant pursuit of a national home for the Jewish people in the Land of Israel. Gandhi argued that a Jewish homeland could only be achieved through the goodwill of the Arabs, and not by Western support. He also told the Jews of Germany to exercise peaceful resistance against the Nazi regime. While this second piece of advice sounded ludicrous, albeit in keeping with his own philosophy, he was far-sighted in understanding that Jews and Arabs must find a way to accommodate each other, which can also be said today of Muslims and Hindus in Kashmir, and of India and Pakistan, two countries that have developed nuclear weapons to protect themselves from a future attack of one side against the other.

As we have seen with other prophetic personalities of modern times, they all had their blind spots. Perhaps this is inevitable in a person who is totally dedicated to a cause. But what remains clear to me is that Gandhi, contrary to the accusations of his critics, was not an opportunist, and he was certainly not anti-Muslim or anti-Jewish. He was a man who undertook a seemingly impossible mission, and he prevailed. Better yet, he charted a course for other great leaders and social reformers of our times, the best known of which are Dr. Martin Luther King and Nelson Mandela, both of whom completely transformed the character of their societies and brought equality and hope to millions who were suffering from severe discrimination. As time goes on, Gandhi's stature will continue to grow.

MARTIN LUTHER KING

One can look upon the career of Dr. Martin Luther King Jr. as a turning point in American history. When I first arrived in the United States in 1959, I had occasion to visit New Orleans, and I remember seeing public toilets and water fountains with a sign "Whites Only" in a city where most people were black. I also recall overhearing two white truck drivers talking at a table next to mine in a small diner in Bogalusa, Louisiana, about Cain who killed his brother Abel and was punished by God by having his forehead marked. "Our preacher told us last Sunday that the mark meant that his skin turned black so people wouldn't mistake his identity," one of them told the other. The following year I saw a sign on a country club in Chicago that said "No Dogs or Jews allowed."

The 1960s were a time of great social upheaval in the United States. American society was beginning to transform itself, and social activism became the way to effect change. As a seminary student in Cincinnati, Ohio, studying to be a rabbi, I was caught up in the struggle for civil rights. My school, the Hebrew Union College, taught prophetic Judaism, and the teachings of the Hebrew prophets regarding social justice suddenly became real to us. As a result, a disproportionate number of us and of American Jews in general took an active part in spearheading the struggle for racial integration. As the 1960s unfolded, one person kept growing in stature and became the leading, iconic figure of the civil rights movement. He was a young preacher from Atlanta, Georgia, named Dr. Martin Luther King Jr. When he spoke, one could hear a Hebrew prophet speaking. Unlike the Hebrew prophets, though, he was not carried away by his moral compulsion to the point where, as happened to them, he became ineffectual and dismissed as a crackpot. Dr. King was both passionate and rational, a cool and composed visionary, a superb organizer, and a reconciler. When he gave his most famous speech, "I Have a Dream," on the steps of the Lincoln Memorial in Washington, DC, halfway through the speech he began to sense the mood of the huge crowd was beginning to change. He put aside his written text and began to speak extemporaneously, uttering words that clearly came from a higher place, words that Americans and the rest of the world will never forget.

> I have a dream that one day this nation will rise up and live out the true meaning of its creed: "We hold these truths to be self-evident, that all men are created equal."
> I have a dream that one day on the red hills of Georgia, the sons of former slaves and the sons of former slave owners will be able to sit down together at the table of brotherhood.
> I have a dream that one day even the state of Mississippi, a state sweltering with the heat of injustice, sweltering with the heat of oppression, will be transformed into an oasis of freedom and justice.
> I have a dream that my four little children will one day live in a nation where they will not be judged by the color of their skin but by the content of their character.
> I have a dream today!

King visited Gandhi's birthplace in India in 1959. The trip to India affected King in a profound way, deepening his understanding of nonviolent resistance and his commitment to America's struggle for civil rights. In a radio address made during his final evening in India, King reflected,

> Since being in India, I am more convinced than ever before that the method of nonviolent resistance is the most potent weapon available to oppressed people in their struggle for justice and human dignity. In a real sense, Mahatma Gandhi embodied in his life certain universal principles that are inherent in the moral structure of the universe, and these principles are as inescapable as the law of gravitation. (*The Papers of Martin Luther King, Jr.*, 135–36)

King's method of protest resulted in nonviolent marches throughout the South that exposed Southern white brutality to the world and precipitated racial integration. Not every black activist, however, agreed with King's methods. Many young blacks continued to feel disenfranchised even after schools were integrated and young blacks gained access to higher education. Young blacks interviewed by the media complained that even after they became qualified for better jobs, such jobs were not open to them. James Baldwin, a prominent black writer of the time, argued that he could sooner trust a Southern bigot than a Northern liberal. By the late 1960s more radical black activists came to the fore, such as the Black Panthers, who believed they had to resort to the use of arms to defend themselves against white America. Perhaps most prominent among them was the black Muslim minister Malcolm X, who was assassinated in 1965. Malcolm X believed in black separatism rather than the integration pursued by Dr. King. He became a symbol of pride for many blacks. In 1968, like his mentor Mahatma Gandhi, the nonviolent King was felled by an assassin's bullet.

But death is not the end of greatness. With the passage of time, King's legacy continues to grow. While African Americans are still experiencing widespread poverty and are still struggling to have their fair share of the American Dream, enormous progress has been made. Could King have imagined back in 1963 when he gave his celebrated speech that less than half a century later the United States would elect its first African American president? Perhaps he did, visionary that he was, but certainly most Americans are still rubbing their eyes.

Moreover, not only African Americans have benefited from the prophetic vision of Dr. King. American society as a whole in the twenty-first century is light years ahead of the society I was first introduced to in 1959. Back then it was a society dominated by one kind of person, the only kind that could run for president until then. Today, anyone, regardless of race, religion, ethnic origin, or gender can run for president and win.

NELSON MANDELA

Mandela, one of the most admirable visionary leaders of the late twentieth century, was inspired by both Martin Luther King and Mahatma Gandhi. But perhaps more than either one of them, he completely transformed his country's character in a way the entire world needs to study and learn from.

From a young age I read and learned about Apartheid in South Africa. As a young teenager I read the novel *Cry, the Beloved Country* by Alan Paton, and I remember it made me cry. It seems to me that it took the world too long to rally against Apartheid, one of the most horrific systems of discrimination and repression of modern times. We are fortunate today to be able to talk about it in the past tense.

A year ago I finally had the opportunity to visit South Africa. I visited Robben Island, a solitary place in the ocean near Cape Town, where Mandela spent eighteen of his twenty-seven years in prison. The first thought that crossed my mind when I saw the penal colony was Nazi concentration camps. I later found out that indeed those infamous camps had inspired the builders of this facility, who sought to protect the "superior" white race of South Africa against the "inferior" blacks who were so presumptuous as to aspire to equal rights (the Nazis referred to their concentration camps as "protective camps" for Jews and other dangerous elements who needed to be protected from those they had victimized [see Heinrich Himmler's manual for building concentration camps]). A former black political prisoner and a comrade of Mandela served as our guide. He told us how Mandela, instead of succumbing to despair, turned the prison into a university, where he studied for and received a law degree from the University of London, and where black activists educated themselves with a view to their future leadership roles in a free South Africa. Mandela never doubted that someday Apartheid would end and he would be called upon to lead his people. He knew South Africa better than his white oppressors. He understood the complexities of its human composition, its wide range of African tribes and their cultures, and the possibilities of racial peaceful coexistence, something that eluded the country's white supremacists. He survived long enough to become the first president of a free South Africa.

From Cape Town I traveled to Johannesburg, where I attended the hearing of a case brought before white and black judges, who continued the process begun in 1995 with the establishment of the Truth and Reconciliation Commission after the abolition of Apartheid. This process brought together victims and victimizers, mostly blacks who had lost family members and white police, jailers, and others who severely persecuted their victims. The victims or their relatives gave graphic and heart-rending testimonies, and the victimizers confessed to their acts, which were committed as part of a political program to suppress any dissent against the regime.

This process was based on the classical African concept of *Ubuntu*, defined by Archbishop Desmond Tutu, who led the process, as follows:

> A person with Ubuntu is open and available to others, affirming of others, does not feel threatened that others are able and good, for he or she has a proper self-assurance that comes from knowing that he or she belongs in a greater whole and is diminished when others are humiliated or diminished, when others are tortured or oppressed. (*No Future without Forgiveness*)

The Truth and Reconciliation process reflected the spirit of Nelson Mandela, and the way he brought together a seemingly irreconcilable society. It stands in sharp contrast to Western justice, which is generally based on such forms of punishment as incarceration and even executions. Not everyone in South Africa accepted this form of justice as fair. But my general impression from my visit was that on the whole both blacks and whites accepted it, and it reflected mutual efforts in the new society to promote a mature democracy with equal opportunities for all.

This is not to say that South Africa has solved all of its problems. When I was there, people, both black and white, were quite unhappy with the president of the country, Jacob Zuma, whom they considered a very disappointing successor to Mandela. There is still widespread poverty, and many suffer from HIV and pneumonia. South Africa still has a long way to go, but compared to some of its neighbors, like Zimbabwe, for example, which I also visited, it is practically a paradise.

Countries like India, the United States, and South Africa are fortunate when one of their best sons, like the prophets of old, is overcome by moral compulsion and decides to dedicate his life to right the wrongs of the society, and to bring freedom and hope to those members of society who for generations have been kept down on the social ladder without a chance to better themselves. Unfortunately, there are still many societies in today's world where this has not happened. The more fortunate societies need to help the less fortunate ones. Men of the stature of a Gandhi, a Martin Luther King, and a Nelson Mandela are rare, even as the biblical prophets and the founders of the great religions were rare.

But history has shown that such prophetic giants do appear, especially during a time of great need. It is to be expected that more will appear in the years ahead as the world today is in the midst of a major struggle to move beyond many of the repressive regimes that are still clinging to power around the globe. It is quite clear that there is much work still to be done.

10

MISGUIDED PROPHETS

MISGUIDED PROPHETS

History is full of false or misguided or even evil prophets. Some have brought great harm to the world. Some seemed to be true believers while others were cynical charlatans. It is not always possible to tell the difference between the two. One could wonder whether Stalin actually believed in communism, or was only using it as a weapon for wielding absolute power. Was Hitler a German patriot? There is evidence to the contrary. What we do know for a fact is that the likes of a Stalin or a Hitler brought upon their own people and upon the rest of the world great human catastrophes in the name of high-sounding causes. On the other hand, not all false prophets are human monsters. Some were very well-intentioned people, for example the sixteenth-century French philosopher Jean Bodin, who sought to define the most effective political system, and introduced the idea of the divine right of kings. Nor are all misguided prophets wrong on every score. Thus, the great German philosopher Friedrich Nietzsche was a remarkable thinker, but I believe that his ideas about the death of God and the superior morality of the so-called Superman make him and such disciples of his as Ayn Rand misguided prophets. Finally, those religious leaders who have turned their faith into an instrument of hate and destruction are false prophets. I picked the Ayatollah Homeini as an example.

In a way, the misguided prophets can be more insidious than the false ones. They are often thinkers of great intellect whose theories and arguments can hold great sway over many people for a long time, including some who also possess a great intellect, as was the case with a Karl Marx and a Friedrich Nietzsche. They presented powerful ideas, which on the face of it made a great deal of sense and inspired people to take action. The test of time, however, has shown that while at first their pronouncements appeared to be prophetic and self-evident, in the long run they failed to accomplish their goals and resulted in great harm to great numbers of people. In considering them, we gain a deeper understanding of the timeless nature and validity of biblical prophecy, which posits that while people have God-given rights, there is more to life than human will and interest.

Evil prophets can also be very persuasive when they first appear on the stage of history. But as a general rule, their impact is usually short-lived. They carry within themselves the seeds of their own downfall. While they invoke higher powers and lofty goals, they have no consideration for the sanctity of human life, and by playing God they become what Leo Baeck referred to as "masters of blasphemy." They are an ever-present danger to humanity, perhaps more so in recent times than in the past. They are the ones the prophets have inveighed against, and they must not be overlooked in our search for the meaning of prophecy.

THE DIVINE RIGHT OF KINGS: JEAN BODIN

One of the most brilliant concepts of the founding fathers of the United States was the separation of church and state. Thomas Jefferson wrote in his letter to the Danbury Baptists Association in 1802, "I contemplate with sovereign reverence that act of the whole American people which declared that their legislature should 'make no law respecting an establishment of religion, or prohibiting the free exercise thereof,' thus building a wall of separation between Church & State." As a consequence, the United States has become the country of religious tolerance par excellence, and while some may argue that the United States is essentially a Christian country, or that the belief in God is an official aspect of the state, such belief is the private affair of each citizen, and is not invoked as a standard of political authority. Essentially, people like

Jefferson and the other founders of American democracy were reacting to the eighteenth-century European concept of the "divine right of kings," which posited that the monarch derived his or her authority directly from God and therefore was not accountable to any human authority.

The idea of the divine right of kings has had a long history in civilizations around the world. Earlier we discussed the divinity of such monarchs in antiquity as the pharaohs. When Moses challenged the authority of the pharaoh he was actually challenging the authority of the gods of Egypt. The prophet Samuel resisted crowning a king over Israel, but when he was forced by the will of the people to anoint a king, it was understood that the king derived his authority from God, who could choose to withdraw it at any time. The biblical prophets continued to act as the ones who interpreted God's will during the time of the monarchy as a way of protecting the rights of the people against the willfulness of the king, but more often than not the king had the upper hand. Later on, when Europe was ruled by Christian kings, the church used biblical precedent as a proof text that those kings ruled by the will of God. Thus, two authorities joined hands in Europe, that of the church and that of the monarchy, both of which ruled by the will of God.

By the seventeenth century much of Europe had come under the rule of absolute monarchs, the best example of which was the French king Louis XIV, who proclaimed *"L'Etat ce moi"* [I am the State]. Monarchs like Louis XIV, known as the "Sun King," set a very high standard for their successors, not unlike some kings in antiquity such as King David. As could be expected, their successors failed to live up to such a standard, while they continued to wield absolute power. The result was the eventual fall of the monarchy and the replacement of the divine right of kings by the will of the people. To this day, however, the phenomenon of absolute rulers continues to sprout around the world. Such rulers wielded enormous power before World War II. Rulers like Stalin, Hitler, Mussolini, Franco, and an assortment of lesser dictators in Latin America and elsewhere come to mind. Recently dictators fell in Eastern Europe after the collapse of the Soviet Union, and at this moment they are falling in the Arab world. In Africa, the second largest continent, some, like Mugabe of Zimbabwe, still thrive. The day of the absolute ruler is far from over.

The man who first formulated the doctrine of the divine right of kings as a philosophical concept was the sixteenth-century French jurist and political philosopher Jean Bodin (1530–1596). Ironically, Bodin, whose name is not nearly as known to the world as Voltaire or Rousseau, was a man of vast knowledge and deep insights in political and economic theory, as well as religious pluralism. He wrote his *Colloquium*, an examination of truth, in the form of a conversation among seven educated men, each with a distinct religious or philosophical orientation—a natural philosopher, a Calvinist, a Muslim, a Roman Catholic, a Lutheran, a Jew, and a skeptic. Because of this work, Bodin is often identified as one of the first proponents of religious tolerance in the Western world. On the other hand, he wrote a history of the persecution of witchcraft, in which he advocates torture even in cases of the disabled and children to try to confirm the guilt of the accused.

Bodin, seen from the perspective of our time, was full of contradictions. But we have to keep in mind that he was very much a product of his own time. He lived in France during a time of religious conflict between the Calvinist Huguenots and the state-supported Catholic Church. He pursued a political career at the service of Francis, Duke of Alençon. In his political philosophy, he sought to define the best possible political system. His great fear was civil and religious strife undermining the state. He came to the conclusion that the best solution was an absolute monarchy. This prompted him to state, "The sovereign Prince is only accountable to God." Bodin's idea became popular among many of the monarchs of Europe, and provided philosophical legitimacy to tyrannical French monarchs, Russian czars, and other despots. While Bodin might be seen as well intentioned when he wrote those words, he turned out to be a misguided prophet.

Fortunately, in the years following Bodin's time, Europe produced some great and far-sighted philosophers who put to rest Bodin's idea. The first was the English philosopher John Locke (1632–1704), who argued that there was no legitimate government under the concept of the divine right of kings. Voltaire, Montesquieu, and the French Encyclopedists found in Locke the philosophical, political, educational, and moral basis that enabled them to prepare and advance the ideas that resulted in the French Revolution. In America, Locke's influence on Jonathan Edwards, Hamilton, and Jefferson was decisive (Paul Edwards, *The Encyclopedia of Philosophy*, 4:502).

The second was the French philosopher Charles Montesquieu (1689–1755). Montesquieu wrote that the main purpose of government is to maintain law and order, political liberty, and the property of the individual. Montesquieu, who lived during the long reign of Louis XIV, opposed the absolute monarchy of his home country and favored the English system as the best model of government. He concluded that the best form of government was one in which the legislative, executive, and judicial powers were separate and kept each other in check to prevent any branch from becoming too powerful. He believed that uniting these powers, as in the monarchy of Louis XIV, led to despotism. According to John R. Vile, "the most quoted European political writer during the American Founding era was France's Baron de Montesquieu" (*The Constitutional Convention of 1787*, 495).

THE DICTATORSHIP OF THE PROLETARIAT: KARL MARX

Not since the birth of Christianity has a Jew or any other person for that matter had a greater impact on the human race than the nineteenth-century German philosopher of Jewish descent, Karl Marx. By 1947 his philosophy, known as Marxism, held sway over the Soviet Union, China, and Eastern Europe and was spreading around the world. Many still remember the famous words of the leader of the Soviet Union in the late 1950s and early 1960s, Nikita Khrushchev, in reference to capitalism, "We will bury you." In the 1990s, after the demise of the Soviet Union, I ran into Professor Sergei Khrushchev, the son of the Soviet leader, on a cruise of the Greek Isles. I asked him whether his father actually believed that communism would bury capitalism, or was he only grandstanding. The professor replied that his father did believe in those days that Marxism was on its way to taking over the world, and that the days of capitalism were numbered.

Marxism in a sense has been a messianic movement. It was compared by the psychologist and social thinker Erich Fromm in his book *Psychoanalysis and Religion* to a form of religion. It sought to replace organized religion with a new social and ethical code based on reason and science rather than theistic faith. It focused on the plight of the working person, and made it its goal to do away with the upper classes and turn control of the state to the "masses." Marx referred to this process as the "dictatorship of the proletariat." This was to be a transitional phase after the defeat of capitalism, followed by a just social order in which all would live in peace and harmony. One may wonder whether Marx, the descendant of rabbis on both sides of his family, might have been influenced by Isaiah's vision of the end of days.

Marx believed that his theory would first take root in England. He lived in London during the time of the Industrial Revolution and saw the plight of the working class. From England, the Marxist revolution was to spread to the rest of the world.

This was the first unfulfilled prediction of this latter-day prophet, who was later deified by Marxist regimes as someone who was infallible. His gospel first took root in Russia at the end of World War I. This vast country was still ruled by the czars when the war broke out, one of the last holdouts of absolute monarchy in Europe. Russia did not have the advanced political institutions England had, which could deal with social and economic issues in an evolutionary and peaceful way. Absolutism in Russia had to be rooted out absolutely, and it was replaced after the war by a new absolutism, namely, the so-called dictatorship of the proletariat. It was, in reality, the dictatorship of the Bolshevik Communist Party, and eventually it became the dictatorship of a single man, the so-called Sun of the Nations, a former Georgian Orthodox seminarian named Joseph Djugashvili Stalin. Seldom in history has one man wielded so much power over so many people. Ironically, he wielded it in the name of social justice and brotherhood among the nations. But as the writer Arthur Koestler points out in his book *Darkness at Noon*, a single human life under Stalin was considered to be worth only one millionth of one million. His modus operandi was "the end justifies the means," and in the name of the greater good of the people he terrorized millions during his long reign, to which Koestler referred to as "darkness at noon." It is estimated that the communist regime in the Soviet Union, during the nearly seventy years of its existence (1922–1991), caused the unnatural death of over 100,000,000 people.

The anthem of the communist party, the *Internationale*, promised a united human race and an end to war.

> So comrades, come rally
> And the last fight let us face,
> The Internationale unites the human race.
> So comrades, come rally

And the last fight let us face,
The Internationale unites the human race.

This, alas, did not happen. The Soviet Union is gone. Communist China is now communist in name only. Economically—and Marxism is all about economics—China is no different from any other capitalistic country, only more so. It exploits Third World countries in total contradiction of Marxist ideology, and the benefits of its economic policies are yet to reach the Chinese masses. The few "true believers" in Marxism still left in the world, namely the rulers of North Korea and Cuba, are political dinosaurs.

On the other hand, in my recent travels to China and Vietnam I led a discussion on a cruise ship with a group of some twenty-five travelers, all of them professionals from Western countries, about the communist regimes in those countries. We came to the conclusion that Marxism does seem to serve a useful though temporary function in large societies that require fundamental social and economic change, such as China and Vietnam. It provides the revolutionary drive to overthrow repressive and backward regimes, and it presents the opportunity for the society to transform itself into a non-Marxist, open economic system that is able to compete in the global economy. In short, Marxism is not a long-term solution to the world's problems, but it has its value as a catalyst.

THE DEATH OF GOD AND THE SUPERMAN: FRIEDRICH NIETZSCHE

What can we say about that delirious German genius, Friedrich Nietzsche? His philosophy is intoxicating. He wrote like a poet and a prophet, except he was neither. His poetry is banal. His prophecies are the ravings of a feverish mind. He was a sickly man who glorified power. His theories about the "Superman" and the "death of God" gave comfort to people across the political spectrum, from Marxists to Nazis. Can he be taken seriously?

After World War I, the great expectations of the *fin de siècle* in Europe were dashed against the rocks of reality. Christian civilization, instead of bringing the millennium, saw a Europe lying in ruins. The world was waiting for a new gospel. In Russia, it was provided by Marxism. In Germany during the war, copies of Nietzsche's book *Thus Spoke Zarathustra* were distributed to the soldiers. Later on, the Nazi party embraced his teachings. Even though Nietzsche opposed German nationalism and militarism, his sister Elisabeth, who ran his archives after his death, became an ardent supporter of the Nazi party and provided Hitler with her brother's writings, which she sanitized to suit the Führer's purposes.

But Nietzsche's influence reached far beyond extreme German nationalism. He became one of the most popular philosophers of the twentieth century, influencing many great minds from Sigmund Freud and Paul Tillich to George Bernard Shaw and H. L. Mencken. Let us take a look at his masterpiece, *Thus Spoke Zarathustra*, and try to understand what it was Nietzsche sought to accomplish, and why I propose that he was a misguided prophet.

In the preface to his book *Ecce Homo*, Nietzsche writes about his masterpiece,

> With [*Thus Spoke Zarathustra*] I have given mankind the greatest present that has ever been made to it so far. This book, with a voice bridging centuries, is not only the highest book there is, the book that is truly characterized by the air of the heights—the whole fact of man lies *beneath* it at a tremendous distance—it is also the *deepest*, born out of the innermost wealth of truth, an inexhaustible well to which no pail descends without coming up again filled with gold and goodness.

Nietzsche, quite clearly, attempted to write a new bible. He even imitated the style of the Old and New Testaments. The title of his book imitates the common expression of the Hebrew prophets "Thus says Adonai." He chose the Persian prophet Zoroaster, also known as Zarathustra, as his hero who replaces the prophets of the Judeo-Christian God, since "God is dead." God is dead because the traditional values of Christianity have lost their power in the life of the individual. Christian morality is a "slave morality." The new prophet announces the emergence of the Superman (*Übermensch*), who is to replace God.

The first quote attributed to Zarathustra is

> *I teach you the Superman.* Man is something that should be overcome. What have you done to overcome him?

All creatures hitherto have created something beyond themselves: and do you want to be the ebb of the great tide, and return to the animals rather than overcome man?

What is the ape to men? A laughing stock or a painful embarrassment. And just so shall man be to the Superman: a laughing stock or a painful embarrassment.

In his previous works, Nietzsche indicates how one is to reach the rank of a superman. He maintains that all human behavior is motivated by the will to power. In its positive sense, the will to power is not simply power over others, but the power over oneself that is necessary for creativity. Supermen are those who have overcome man, or the individual self, and channeled the will to power into a momentous creativity. Supermen are creators of a "master morality" that reflects the strength and independence of one who is liberated from all values except those that he deems valid. Such power is manifested in independence, creativity, and originality.

There are two problems with Nietzsche's philosophy of the Superman. First, the premise that God is dead goes against the very nature of monotheism. Unlike pagan gods such as the Greek god Dionysus who is born and dies only to be born again, the God whom Nietzsche pronounced dead was never born and has nothing to do with the human experience of death. It would be different if Nietzsche were to say that for him God no longer existed. But to announce categorically that God, whose existence no one can either prove or disprove, has reached a ripe old age and died, is pretending to have knowledge one does not possess.

Second, while the idea of a Superman is quite intriguing and challenging, it is quite clear that only the lucky few can reach such heights. Perhaps Nietzsche thought of himself as a Superman. But how many people can reach the breadth of his knowledge and the depth of his thought? The Jewish and Christian scriptures provide a moral code for all people, while Nietzsche's "bible" is written for the few; the common man, on whom Nietzsche looked down, can hardly make any sense of this book. It is no wonder that great creative minds have been attracted to his writings, while most people never read him.

For these and other reasons I find Nietzsche to be a misguided prophet. I have always been fascinated by his writings, and I will continue to be. He certainly reached very high, and for this he deserves our attention. But as recent history has shown, his teachings were wide open to misinterpretation, and perhaps unintentionally they have caused more harm than good.

A recent example of a Nietzsche disciple is the enormously popular American writer Ayn Rand (1905–1982). Born Alisa Zinov'yevna Rosenbaum in Saint Petersburg, Russia, her novels *The Fountainhead* and *Atlas Shrugged* have enthralled several generations of readers around the world, and still do. Like Nietzsche, whom she read avidly as a university student in Russia, Rand rejected the common morality of civilization and glorified the creative genius who lives by his own rules. Rand developed her own philosophical system, which she called "Objectivism." It emphasizes personal happiness as the greatest good, and rejects all social systems and all religions. It argues for rational egoism or rational self-interest as the only proper guiding moral principle. The individual should "exist for his own sake," she once wrote, "neither sacrificing himself to others nor sacrificing others to himself." I remember once seeing her on television in a lively exchange with Erich Fromm, where she wore an oversized dollar-sign pin on her lapel.

Rand still exerts an influence on American life. Many readers are still enthralled by her novels and by her ideas. But as a philosopher who is only interested in the chosen few while looking down on the rest of society, she remains a misguided prophet.

II

PROPHETS OF EVIL

The twentieth century has seen human evil unlike anything we have seen in previous centuries. In fact, it has been a century of genocides. It began with the genocide committed against the Herero people in Namibia by the Germans in 1904 and the genocide committed by the Turks against the Armenians in 1915. It culminated in the genocide committed again by the Germans against the Jews of Europe during World War II, known as the Holocaust. It ended with genocides in Rwanda, Bosnia, Cambodia, and other places.

None of those genocides surpasses what was done to the Jews of Europe. What is remarkable is the fact that Adolf Hitler referred to himself in his speeches and writings as a prophet sent to redeem his people and to rid the world of its greatest enemy, namely, the Jews. Among the many sins he attributed to the Jews was their role in giving rise to what Nietzsche called the "slave religion," namely, Christianity. Espousing the principle of "Might is right," Hitler launched World War II in the hope of making Germany the leading world power and establishing a world order of master races and inferior ones. If ultimate evil ever had a prophet, it was certainly the failed artist from Austria who became the absolute ruler of Germany from 1933 to 1945.

Another major political phenomenon of the twentieth century has been communism, which promised the world a utopia that never became a reality. In the name of human solidarity and social justice, communist regimes across the world turned their backs on the teachings of their respective religions, which they called evil, or dismissed as an "opiate of the masses," and committed atrocities on an unprecedented scale. One of the starkest examples of such atrocities was the genocide committed by the Khmer Rouge under Pol Pot in Cambodia against their own people. Here again a pseudo-messianic movement, in an attempt to transform an entire society into one vast agrarian commune, resorted to Nazi-style methods of mass murder and snuffed out some two million lives in what has become known as the killing fields of Cambodia. Pot Pol has also acquired the dubious distinction of a prophet of evil.

A different kind of prophet of evil was the Ayatollah Khomeini, the founder of the present regime in Iran. Considered a holy man or a prophet by his followers, he did not shy away from using violence against other Muslims, even though he advocated Muslim unity, and he consistently preached hatred against those who dared to disagree with him. His disciple, Iran's president Mahmoud Ahmadinejad, has been calling for the destruction of Israel, and has sponsored terrorist attacks. Here we have an example of religion being used as a lethal weapon not only on others but also on its own people.

THE PROPHET OF ULTIMATE EVIL: ADOLF HITLER

To Hitler, Germans were superior beings, and Germany was a substitute for God. Born a Catholic, Hitler was not a churchgoer. He was a great admirer of Martin Luther, but he did not practice Lutheranism. Hitler thought of himself as a prophet who was going to save his people and rid the world of its mortal enemies. On January 30, 1939, the sixth anniversary of his rise to power, Hitler told the Reichstag,

> I have often been a prophet in my life and was generally laughed at. During my struggle for power, the Jews primarily received with laughter my prophecies that I would someday assume the leadership of the state and thereby of the entire nation and then, among many other things, achieve a solution of the Jewish problem. I suppose that meanwhile the laughter of Jewry in Germany that resounded then is probably already choking in their throats [loud applause].

Today I want to be a prophet again. If international finance Jewry within Europe and abroad should succeed once more in plunging the peoples into a world war, then the consequence will be not the Bolshevization of the world and hence a victory of Jewry, but on the contrary, the destruction of the Jewish race in Europe.

Hitler and his cronies were thugs who seized control of one of the most advanced nations in the world and held it in their clutches for twelve years, from 1933 to 1945. During those twelve years they managed to build the biggest war machine in the world and unleash the most brutal war in history, which caused the death of fifty million people. They invented an imaginary enemy of Germany, namely, the Jews. They believed that the Jews were involved in a world conspiracy, whereby Jews controlled the world. They further believed that by eliminating all the Jews of the world they would deliver the world from evil and enable the superior Aryan race, namely the Germans and perhaps also a few other northern European nations, to take control of the world, which was their birthright.

Whether they really believed all of this is hard to tell. In my opinion, they did not believe in anything. Like all thugs, they were cynical nihilists. When the young Hitler dictated his book *Mein Kampf* in 1925, he began to enunciate the theory of the Big Lie, which posited that if you can tell a big enough lie, people will buy it. He pursued this theory to the bitter end. A master of propaganda and a mesmerizing speaker, he and his close associates such as Goebbels and Himmler invented a new brand of German speak, known as *Nazi Deutsch*, which called the truth a lie and a lie the truth. Thus, for example, concentration camps became "protective camps," and victims became "victimizers." This technique is still used by present-day thug-leaders like several of the surviving dictators in the Middle East, Africa, and Latin America.

By the winter of 1942, failing to defeat the Soviet Union and beginning to lose the war, Hitler turned his attention to the Jews under his occupation with the objective of total annihilation. With fanatical German persistence, the Germans systematically murdered millions of Jews, mainly in highly efficient death camps. Even as they were losing the war in July 1944, they still managed to round up remote Jewish communities such as the one on the island of Rhodes south of Turkey and send them to Auschwitz, as if they had nothing better to do. I was a five-year-old child at the time living in nearby Palestine. If the British and the Australians hadn't stopped Rommel's panzers in the battle of Al-Alamein in North Africa, I would have ended up there myself. My relatives in Europe were not as fortunate.

There are not too many things these days historians agree on. But with the exception of some crackpots and Holocaust deniers, some of whom unfortunately teach at some major universities in the West, all historians agree that Nazism was evil, pure and simple. If we are on the subject of evil prophets, we need to revisit Nazi Germany, as a warning to all people that it can happen again, and indeed it is happening in the Middle East and other places as these lines are being written.

I will never understand how good German Lutherans and Catholics went along with Hitler. I will never understand how the great Swiss psychoanalyst Carl Jung could have said that "seventy million Germans couldn't be wrong," referring to the support Hitler received from the German public. There are many things I and many others like me will never understand. Here again I turn to Erich Fromm and his book *Escape from Freedom*. Fromm tried to understand why the Germans did what they did. He came up with the theory that sometimes people, in order to be protected against a great imaginary evil, lose their nerve and give up their freedom. Entire societies do. Germany after World War I was down on its knees. This great nation was humiliated by the Allies after World War I as the Allies imposed staggering war reparations on Germany and propelled it into a colossal economic crisis. The Germans needed someone to pin the blame on. That someone turned out to be the Jews, the eternal scapegoat. It was the Dreyfus trial all over again, multiplied by six million. In their mass gatherings the Nazis hung banners over the podium that read *Die Juden sind Unser Unglück* [The Jews Are Our Misfortune]. Apparently many Germans believed it at the time. The rest is history.

It appears that Hitler and his cronies had long-term plans not only for Germany but for the entire human race. They were out to reengineer the entire human species. They came up with the theory that the world was divided between superior and inferior races. Jews, blacks, Slavs, gays, gypsies, and an assortment of others were inferior. The Germans, Swedish, British, and a few others were superior. The inferior races had to be subjugated or eliminated altogether. The superior ones had to take their rightful place in the world, which was their birthright. This could only be accomplished through aggressive war. In his book *The Rise and Fall of the Third Reich*, William Shirer reveals secret Nazi plans to thin out the Slavic races by killing and castrating millions to create *lebensraum* [living space] for the German people in Eastern Europe. Hitler, after all, spoke of the "Thousand Year Reich," which could only endure if all its enemies were eliminated. Human engineering on this scale is unprecedented in history.

I am not a great believer in Satan. But if any human being has ever deserved this dubious distinction, Adolf Hitler is certainly the one. It is as though Satan appeared here on earth and showed us the limitless possibilities of evil. Have we, the human race, learned the lesson? In some parts of the world this lesson is yet to be learned. But major portions of our species have learned the lesson and continue to learn. The motto "Never again" has become part of the human moral vocabulary. When Hitler first started considering genocide, he cited the Turkish massacre of the Armenians in 1915, when the world looked the other way. He knew that in Europe of the 1930s he could massacre people, especially Jews, with impunity. This is no longer the case. The world today is fully aware of the ongoing threat of genocide, and action has been taken in places like the Balkans, the Sudan, and elsewhere. The world after Auschwitz is no longer the same world. The Hitlers of the world can no longer commit their nefarious acts under the cover of the Big Lie. Things have gotten much tougher for the prophets of evil.

SOCIAL REFORM THROUGH MURDER: POL POT

Thirty years after Hitler and his hordes murdered one-third of the Jewish people, another genocide took place in Southeast Asia, claiming the lives of some two million people and wrecking an entire society. This time it was Maoist-Marxist ideology inspired by the Chinese Cultural Revolution that prompted a Cambodian communist leader with the nom de guerre of Pot Pol to transform Cambodia, a country of eight million people at the time, into an "agrarian utopia." In an interview (which can be seen on YouTube) shortly before he died in 1998, Pol Pot admits to his interviewer that he was inexperienced and made mistakes that he regretted. He comes across as an unassuming person of few words. His biography reveals a man of average intelligence who was a poor student while growing up in Cambodia and later while studying in

Paris (Cambodia was under French rule for many years). When Pol Pot and his men took power in Cambodia in 1975, the country had been victimized by the Vietnam War and was in disarray. According to Elizabeth Becker,

> One of the most frightening aspects of the Khmer Rouge is the intent behind their madness. Much of the destruction of their revolution was done in the name of the future, or at least how the Khmer Rouge saw the future in counties calling themselves modern. In the name of efficiency and increased productivity, the Khmer Rouge abolished family life, individual life, the rhythms of agricultural life, and instituted a system of labor camp life throughout the entire country. The most frightening of futuristic fables was realized in this rural, third world country and not in the industrialized world. (*When the War Was Over*, xvi)

This experiment in social engineering was one of the most gruesome manifestations in our time of forcing an entire society to reinvent itself by combining elements of Nazi ethnic cleansing and Soviet purges in total disregard for human rights and human dignity. In this instance the rural population was romanticized while the urban population was demonized. Thousands of city-dwellers were forced out of their homes and either put into labor camps, where they were starved to death, or made to dig mass graves, Nazi-style, and buried alive in what became known as the "killing fields." This reign of terror lasted four years and claimed the lives of some two million Cambodians. To this day, Cambodia is in the process of recovering from this ghastly nightmare.

One of the casualties of the Khmer Rouge was the Buddhist religion practiced by the vast majority of Cambodians. Cambodian Buddhism is old and rich in cultural traditions. On my recent travels in Southeast Asia I met a British journalist named Denise Heywood who lived in Cambodia and was intimately familiar with the country and its traditions before and after the Pol Pot regime. She spoke about the young women who performed Buddhist ritual dances when the Khmer Rouge came to power and how they were persecuted during the social revolution. In recent years Heywood has returned to Cambodia and has been helping revive this ancient tradition.

RELIGIOUS ABSOLUTISM: AYATOLLAH KHOMEINI

The only country in the world today ruled by religion (unless one counts the Vatican, which is not exactly a country) is Iran. Iran is a major civilization with a long history, which includes one of the most enlightened emperors of antiquity, Cyrus the Great, whom the Second Isaiah called "God's anointed." It gave birth to a religion known as Zoroastrianism, which had a distinctive impact on monotheism. In the twentieth century it also gave birth to what may be the most enlightened religion in the world, namely, Baha'ism. But Iran today is a militant Muslim country. The majority of its people are Shiites, while the great majority of the world's Muslims are Sunni. The Shiites are by far the more militant branch of Islam. Ironically, the Iranians are not Arabs, yet they consider their branch of Islam superior to the Sunni, which is the one practiced by most Arabs. For centuries, Iran was a monarchy, but in 1979 the Shah of Iran was overthrown by a popular revolution inspired by an Iranian ayatollah, a high-ranking Shiite religious leader named Khomeini, better known as the Ayatollah, or Grand Ayatollah Khomeini. Khomeini came back from exile and became the absolute ruler of Iran, changing its political system from a monarchy to a theocracy.

Khomeini, who initially preached tolerance and equality, did not waste any time turning his regime into the most hated Muslim regime in the world. It started the same year he took power with the occupation of the U.S. Embassy in Teheran, holding the embassy staff hostage for well over a year, and it continued with such acts as issuing a fatwa to kill the British author Salman Rushdie for publishing a novel Khomeini did not like. At home, Khomeini began to persecute members of the Baha'i religion, a gentle and peaceful offshoot of Islam. It was quite clear that Khomeini was out to show the world he had no use for international law, international human rights, and most of all, for the "Great Satan," namely, the United States. He and his disciple, Ahmadinejad, later president of Iran, designated Israel the "Small Satan," which had to be eradicated. Khomeini's favorite expression in referring to his opponents was "I will kick in their teeth." And yet this hateful and violent man was considered a holy man by millions of Iranians. So much for the definition of the word "holy."

Unfortunately, even in today's world, Khomeini was in good company. He was an example of a false prophet who scorns all other faiths and considers his own to be the only true one. He even scorned other branches of his own faith, while at the same time he preached Muslim unity. He believed that all people were entitled to their own opinions, as long as they agreed with his. In other words, he represented religious absolutism in the form of an intolerant fundamentalist expression of Islam, which looks at the world as "they and we," in which "they" are evil and "we" are good.

Religious absolutists build a wall around themselves, not letting anyone else in except for their own kind. In today's world, they can be found in all the major religions of the world. Prior to the September 11, 2001, attack by radical Muslim terrorists on the Twin Towers in New York City and on the Pentagon, the most glaring example of a society taken over by religious absolutists was that of Afghanistan under the rule of the Taliban. This country reverted back to the dark ages, doing away with human rights and failing to treat women as human beings altogether. The country became a hotbed for future terrorists, notably Al-Qaida and its leader Osama bin Laden, who declared a holy war against the West. The resulting war against Islamist terrorists has been raging ever since, and there is no end in sight. In the great upheaval of today's Arab world, Al-Qaida and its kind are considered by many Arabs the enemy of progress in the Arab world as well.

Religious absolutism is usually at its worst when it acquires political power. In both Islam and Christianity, it has resulted in so-called holy wars. The concept of a holy war is ludicrous, going against all the tenets of religion. Nietzsche pointed out that life is a struggle, and in order to find meaning in life one has to embrace the struggle. This concept was sublimated by religions like Islam where jihad, or holy war, is also interpreted as an inner struggle to maintain faith. But all too often this concept is misused and serves as an excuse for committing violent acts against others. Such acts are committed by religious fanatics and absolute rulers who use religion as a deadly weapon, and by clandestine organizations that resort to terrorist acts to achieve their goals.

In all three monotheistic faiths, religious absolutism has to do with an autocratic religious authority that does not tolerate any dissenting opinions. The followers of such an authority are not encouraged to think independently, and instead they are told to follow a fixed set of

rules without any questioning. Such an authority often entertains a belief in a time when all the "heretics" and the "infidels" will finally see
the light and join it, and by doing so will become "true believers." It is
impossible for such an autocratic authority to accept the idea that there
may be more than one path to God.

All religions tend to give rise to sects and cults, the religious leaders
of which may either be sincere believers or charlatans. Sometimes it is
hard to tell the difference between the two. Was Jim Jones, the founder
of a sect in San Francisco who committed the mass murder of some
nine hundred members of his sect in 1978 in Jonestown, Guyana, a
believer or a charlatan? What about David Koresh, who proclaimed
himself a prophet and holed up in his compound outside Waco, Texas,
with scores of his followers, resulting in their death in a showdown with
the FBI? Such self-proclaimed spiritual leaders often engage in severe
child abuse and sexual acts that defy the teachings of the religion they
claim to uphold. They typically set a double standard for themselves
and for others, putting themselves above the law and above the precepts they expect others to follow.

Religion has always been a two-edged sword. It is quite easy to
distort religious teachings and in the name of love and justice to commit
acts of hate and cruelty. The biblical prophets knew this better than
anyone else. During the entire prophetic era, from the time of Samuel
to the time of Jeremiah and beyond, there were always plenty of false
prophets around. This has not changed throughout time. To this day,
we have many false prophets around us, some well intentioned and
some malicious. Some wield great power and bring great catastrophes
upon others and upon their own people. Others have limited power and
cause localized tragedies. And some, under the guise of great intellectual ability and literary skills, promote ideas that result in more harm than
good.

12

PROPHECY FOR OUR TIME

We have now looked at all aspects of prophecy from biblical times to our own time. We have seen how each religion and each school of thought has enshrined its own prophet or prophets, sometimes to the exclusion of others, and sometimes by including some of the others. I have tried to be as objective as possible, so as to address as wide an audience as possible and not exclude anyone. If I have erred, I ask the reader's forgiveness. It was not intentional. I have no interest in imposing my views on anyone, because I do not believe I or anyone else has access to absolute truth. If you believe in God, then God is the only one who has access to absolute truth. If you do not, then no one does. Unlike Nietzsche or Ayn Rand, I was not looking to bring down to mere mortals a new gospel. Instead, I invited the reader to join me in finding a common ground for all of us regardless of our faith or ideology upon which we can come together as one human race in peace and harmony.

One thing we all know for a fact: no prophet in all of human history, not even the one with the largest following, has been able to bring enduring peace and prosperity. I take this to mean that while great prophets and great leaders can do a world of good, it is an open question whether any one of them can redeem the world. A prophet can move and inspire his followers and change their lives for the better, but every prophet exists in relationship to his followers, and it is precisely the relationship that is critical, not the prophet per se.

As should be obvious from my assessment of the great teachers of some of the major faiths and ideologies of the world, my own life has been greatly enriched by the teachings of many of them. I regret that schools around the world do not put more emphasis on teaching those beliefs and ideas. Worse yet, in some societies and in some faith communities the "other" is portrayed as unworthy of serious consideration and is seen through the prism of prejudice rather than in the light of objectivity. This is most typical of totalitarian regimes and absolutist religions or sects within religions. Those tend to look at the world as "they" and "we," where "they" are always wrong and "we" are always right. Such an attitude can never make for an understanding among groups of differing views, and it can never bring about enduring peace.

We began with the question about hearing the voice. Now that we have taken a tour through the history of prophecy, let us revisit this voice.

WHO HEARS THE VOICE?

Did the Hebrew prophets and others actually hear the voice of God? Does God still speak to us today?

We have covered much ground leading up to this point, looking for answers to these questions. The time has come to offer some answers.

The Hebrew prophets, as we have pointed out, lived in very precarious times. Particularly an Amos, an Isaiah, and a Jeremiah lived with the reality of impending doom, and with the realization that despite the existential threat, their people, the small nation of Israel, represented the voice of God, and that voice could not be silenced. They never doubted the survival of their people despite all their adversaries and all the empires of the world. That realization created a tremendous sense of tension in Moses, Samuel, Elijah, and all the prophets of the word. Weighed down by the burden of their monumental mission, they heard a voice. They were stirred because of their excitable nature, their profound sense of justice, their moral compulsion, and their sense of mission that made them fearless. The voice they heard was the result of mental and emotional preparation, deep meditation, fervent prayer, and solitary communing with nature. Amos heard the lion roar, and then he heard the voice of God. There was no one way of hearing that voice. Each prophet heard it differently. It was a personalized voice. Yet it was all part of a tradition that was cultivated during a prophetic era that lasted for several centuries. But hearing voices in and of itself was not what made them prophets. A madman can also hear voices, but such voices may be inconsequential. What counts here is the nature of the message. If the prophets were warmongers, or if they had preached hatred and prejudice, they could not have possibly heard the voice of God. But justice, kindness, and compassion are the voice of God. An act of kindness is godly. When we perform such an act, we hear the voice of God.

In other words, God speaks to us all the time. To each and every one of us, who are all equal in the eyes of God. Every ray of sun, every blossom, every sound in nature is the voice of God. All we have to do is open our heart and listen. It is always there.

The great Hebrew writer S. J. Agnon was once asked by a young man, "Where is God?" God, Agnon said, is where you let Him in.

God does not walk around using a megaphone. The voice is usually a "still small voice," barely audible. An aching heart, a loving heart, a yearning heart is a heart that opens up to hear the voice. The prophets were not different from you and me. They were flesh and blood like the rest of us. They heard what we all hear. But perhaps they heard it better, and they knew how to put it into words. Their words are often sublime poetry.

And this brings me to one particular prophecy enunciated by a very minor prophet, one who, perhaps, was not so minor after all. I am referring to the prophet Joel, whose prophecies most people have never heard of. Joel said,

> Then afterwards I will pour out my spirit on all flesh;
> Your sons and your daughters shall prophesy,
> Your old men shall dream dreams,
> And your young men shall see visions.
> [29]Even on the male and female slaves,
> In those days, I will pour out my spirit. (Joel 3:1–2)

As was mentioned before, this passage is paraphrased in the New Testament.

> In the last days,
> God says,
> I will pour out My Spirit on all people.

Your sons and daughters will prophesy,
Your young men will see visions,
Your old men will dream dreams. (Acts 2:17)

It is precisely in this obscure prophecy, and not in the lofty words of an Isaiah or a Jeremiah, that I find the answer to our question.

I will pour out my spirit *on all flesh*.

These are the magic words! Here is the key to our question. Vox populi, vox dei—the voice of the people is the voice of God. If you want to hear the voice of God, then listen to what people have to say. But don't listen with a critical mind. Listen with your heart. If you analyze people, you may be disappointed. But if you hear what's behind their words, if you feel their joy, their pain, their hopes and fears, then you begin to hear the voice of God.

Joel is saying in effect that the time will come when everyone—all flesh—will be endowed with the spirit of prophecy. The word "flesh" in the Bible means "humankind," as in the following verse when God decides to bring about a flood to destroy life on earth because of people's evil: "And God saw that the earth was corrupt; for all flesh had corrupted its ways upon the earth" (Gen. 6:12). God did not destroy the human race entirely. Noah's family was spared, and humankind was given a second chance.

If we examine the history of the past three centuries, beginning with the American Revolution in 1776, we realize that there have been a few occasions when people became animated by the voice of God inside of them and brought about a profound change. In the Preamble to the Constitution of the United States of America we read,

> *We the People* of the United States, in Order to form a more perfect Union, establish Justice, insure domestic Tranquility, provide for the common defence, promote the general Welfare, and secure the Blessings of Liberty to ourselves and our Posterity, do ordain and establish this Constitution for the United States of America.

Many Americans and others believe that these are inspired words. They are certainly inspired by the teachings of the Hebrew prophets, who said, "Justice, justice you shall pursue" and "Proclaim liberty throughout the land." These are godly words. The framers of the Constitution knew their Bible. Their words faithfully reflect the teachings of the Hebrew prophets.

All of these things came together for me toward the end of my search for the meaning of prophecy. I began to think of my own life's events, and of the events of today's world, and I realized that there is where prophecy can be found. It can be found in all of us.

My earliest memories are the events leading up to the birth of my native country, Israel. I vividly remember the daily struggle of my parents' generation that led to this miraculous event. My parents and their friends were common workers with minimal formal education. But they had big hearts, high idealism, and great courage. They had good leaders, but no leader could have ever done it without those ordinary people, who in 1948 stopped seven invading Arab armies literally with their bare hands (with all due respect to the "new historians" who were born after those events, I was there, and I saw it with my own eyes). Then and there I learned the greatest lesson of my life: the will of the people is the will of God. When people become one in pursuing the right cause, no force in the world can stop them.

The same happened in India under Gandhi when millions of Indians joined his cause of nonviolent resistance; the same happened in the United States when blacks and whites joined forces, inspired by leaders like Dr. Martin Luther King, and put an end to segregation; the same happened in South Africa when people from across the spectrum of South African society, inspired by Nelson Mandela, rose up against Apartheid and put an end to one of the worst regimes of our time. We could mention the Solidarity movement in Poland, the fall of the Berlin Wall, and many other such events driven by the will of the people. And of course we must not forget the popular uprisings throughout the Arab world that have been taking place without any identifiable leadership, but rather as a spontaneous awakening of people from Gibraltar to the Gulf who could no longer put up with oppression and corruption. *Avanti popolo*! Forward, people!

One of the most moving events of my life was my visit to Vietnam a few years ago. I was very apprehensive when we arrived in the south of Vietnam. We were a group of American tourists visiting a country where the United States had unleashed a devastating war about thirty years earlier. Vietnam was still under communist rule, and the communists were mortal enemies of the United States. What kind of reception was awaiting us?

To my surprise, we were received with open arms by a group of lovely young Vietnamese who held up a banner welcoming us. It was explained to us that the Vietnamese people had decided to start a new era of openness to the West, and they were genuinely happy to see foreign tourists boosting their economy. For the next seven days of our visit from Ho Chi Minh City (Saigon) to Hanoi, we were treated like long-lost cousins, and we learned a great deal about this fascinating country. But what impressed me the most was the collective spirit of this ancient yet young nation (young because most people were under forty; the previous generation was nearly wiped out during the war). They made do with little, yet they worked hard, and they all seemed to have an indomitable sense of purpose. They were building a better future for themselves and for their children. (I have never seen a stronger sense of family anywhere else in the world. Ancestor worshipping is a central part of their spiritual heritage.) It reminded me of the formative years of Israel, during my youth, when everyone pitched in to make the dream a reality. Once again I witnessed the will of the people at work. It was a wondrous sight to behold.

HAS RELIGION DONE MORE HARM THAN GOOD?

Many in today's world, including some very astute intellectuals, see religion not only as a negative force, but also as the source of all the trouble in the world. In recent years I had an interesting exchange of e-mails with one of the world's leading intellectuals, Professor Noam Chomsky of MIT. Chomsky has established a reputation for himself as an avowed antireligionist. The son of a prominent Jewish educator, Chomsky refused to have his daughter celebrate her Bat Mitzvah. I had sent him something I wrote about the role of religion in establishing world peace. He wrote me back letting me know he disagreed with me, but then, as an afterthought, he added, "I very sincerely hope that I am wrong about this." It was most unusual for someone like Chomsky to make such an admission.

In the search for the meaning of prophecy I have put religion front and center, and it should be obvious to the reader that I believe religion, if practiced properly, can be a great force for good. This is why I did not mind investing so much time and energy in researching and writing this book. And yet I am keenly aware of all the evil that has been done and is still being done in the name of religion. In the Western world, Christianity became the dominant religion, and for centuries it controlled the lives of people along with the absolute rulers of Europe and later of the New World. Its prelates often enforced the faith by the sword and by severe torture. It preached love yet practiced fear. It fomented superstitions to keep its flock ignorant and submissive. It resorted to pseudo-beliefs such as witchcraft to dispose of those who challenged its absolute authority. And it kept giving its blessing to wars in which Christians slaughtered other Christians. No one has put it more brilliantly than the great Russian writer Fyodor Dostoevsky, who in his magnum opus *The Brothers Karamazov* offers the hypothetical scene of Jesus coming to Spain during the Spanish Inquisition, where the Grand Inquisitor decides to burn him at the stake so as to prevent him from making any trouble for the church.

As was mentioned before, when religion exercises political power, it is always a recipe for trouble. The Hebrew prophets always operated outside the political structure, and therefore they were able to work as a force for good, taking up the cause of the weak and the disadvantaged. Theirs was moral power, not political power. The same has been true in all the other religions, where prophetic and prophetlike personalities managed to live up to the ideals of the founders of those religions and make a difference for the better.

One may ask, Would the human race be better off without monotheism, without a belief in one God, without the Ten Commandments, and without established religions?

We may never know the answer to this question, but we may wonder. Certainly the world would not be better off if the ruthless empires of antiquity, from the Assyrian Empire to the Roman Empire—all those evil empires that vied for the title of world champion in human savagery—were still in power today. Or if conquerors like Attila the Hun or Genghis Kahn had taken over the world, or if godless leaders like Stalin or Hitler had taken over the world. Certainly attempts have been made in history outside of monotheism to humanize humanity. Plato believed that the ideal ruler would be a philosopher. He was invited to Syracuse in southern Italy to teach the young ruler how to rule, but failed to do so. A working alternative to religion that might establish peace and harmony in the world is yet to be found.

In the twentieth century, several nonreligious and antireligious ideologies sought to reshape the human race but all failed. The most outstanding example is Marxism. Karl Marx's *Das Kapital*, a treatise on political economy that provides a critical analysis of capitalism, sought to become the new Bible of the human race. It resulted in political regimes around the world, including Russia, China, and Vietnam, that attempted to bring about peace and brotherhood through the "dictatorship of the proletariat," in other words, by force. The Soviet Union is gone. China and Vietnam are communist in name only (I have mentioned my experience in Vietnam). And North Korea and Cuba are both police states that oppress their own people (I was in Cuba in recent years and I spoke to people on the street in their own language. I saw it for myself). In short, *Das Kapital* never really replaced the Bible, any more than *Thus Spoke Zarathustra* did.

The other glaring example is the ideology of Nazism, with its sidekick ideology of Fascism that was practiced by Mussolini in Italy, Franco in Spain, and by Latin American pseudo-socialists like Peron in Argentina. Here the state was elevated to the role of a divinity, and patriotism became the new secular religion. None of these regimes proved to be a force for good, and fortunately they are all gone.

As the twentieth century was coming to a close, it became clear that religion around the world, for better or for worse, rather than leave the stage of history, was experiencing a comeback. Islam has made enormous inroads in the Arab world in the past thirty years. When I once asked a former functionary of the Egyptian government why young people in Egypt were becoming more religious, he explained to me that it had more to do with politics than religion. Since Egypt had an autocratic regime where little dissent was tolerated, the only way of opposing the regime was through religion. Certainly in Iran religion managed to overthrow an unpopular regime, and the ideology used by extreme groups in the Arab world such as Al-Qaida is extreme Islam.

Another example is Israel in the 1950s, during the early years of the state, compared to Israel today. In my native town of Haifa in the 1950s we seldom saw a Jew wearing a skullcap, as religious Jews do. Today one can see skullcaps in Haifa everywhere. Religion in Israel today is a major political force. It is much more nationalistically militant than ever before, and as can be expected, in its extreme manifestations it has become a source of many problems for the society.

But perhaps the most remarkable religious comeback today is happening in the Christian world. Once the communist regimes began to disappear in the former Soviet Union and in its satellite countries in Eastern Europe, religion, such as Russian Orthodoxy in Russia and Catholicism in Poland, began coming back like the phoenix bird rising up from its ashes. During most of the twentieth century, religion was suppressed and persecuted by the communist regimes. But Marxism apparently never replaced the Christian faith. That faith was biding its time, and as soon as it was free to reemerge, it wasted no time in filling the ideological vacuum communism had left behind. I still remember visiting a Russian Orthodox church in Saint Petersburg in 2002. I was struck by the fervent singing of the worshippers who stood together and poured their hearts out in this city where millions died during World War II and where the survivors continued to suffer repression for a long time under the postwar communist regime.

Christianity is alive and well in North America, Latin America, and the rest of the world. Among American presidents in recent years, Jimmy Carter and George W. Bush were devout Christians who, at different ends of the political spectrum, were inspired by their faith.

On my trip to Southeast Asia a few years ago, I happened to visit Singapore, Thailand, Vietnam, and Hong Kong during the Chinese New Year. I visited Buddhist temples in all of those places, and I saw throngs of people in all of them. In the Vietnamese countryside I saw thousands of young families riding their motorcycles (often two adults and two children on the same two-seat bike) on their way to the cemeteries to honor their ancestors during the holiday. What I did not see was communist parades or crowds at the Ho Chi Minh Mausoleum in Hanoi. As an outsider, I got the impression Buddhism in Southeast Asia is alive and well.

Has religion done more harm than good?

One way of answering this question is to say this: Religion may not have lived up to man's highest expectations. To paraphrase Pope Benedict XVI, it may not have brought world peace, universal prosperity, or a better world. It has not solved all of our problems. But it did bring comfort and hope to many millions of people everywhere, and it still does. Religion is a universal human story that is still being written. It is a work in progress. It is being written by people everywhere. While religion can bring out the worst in people, it can also bring out the best. Religion is the expression of man's innermost feelings and yearnings. It is a bond with one's heritage; it defines one's values and beliefs. When it is a force for good, nothing can surpass it.

RELIGION AS A FORCE FOR PEACE

How can the religions of the world become a force for peace?

The key to this question is reconciliation between Islam, Christianity, and Judaism. The three monotheistic religions have been antagonistic to each other over the centuries. The time has come for all three to start a new chapter in their relationships. But before such action is taken, they must first make every effort to reach reconciliation among their own people. Each one of them is divided into many separate denominations, which in many instances have also been antagonistic to each other. Each one has recalcitrant groups and leaders who refuse to sit down with others and have a dialogue. Those may have to be bypassed at first. But there are many groups and leaders in all three who are willing and anxious to sit down and talk, and in recent years clergy and scholars of all three have been meeting to discuss reconciliation. I myself have reached out to Muslim and Christian clergy and scholars, and I know both the rewards and the frustrations of engaging in such an enterprise.

I am particularly disappointed in my own fellow Jews, who I believe can do a great deal more and have not been sufficiently forthcoming. I think too many of us are still busy licking our own wounds from the Holocaust and are so caught up in perceived existential threats against Israel by such deranged leaders as Ahmadinejad of Iran that we fail to see the greater picture. To me, the time has long passed for us Jews to behave like victims. The Hebrew prophets did not regard their people as a victim of the nations, but as a light to the nations. I propose that we begin to take the lead in the process of reconciliation with the Christian and the Muslim worlds.

How can this be done?

One possibility is going back to Isaiah's vision of the end of days, when the mountain of Adonai will be set at the top of the mountains. Let us not wait for the messiah to do this for us—it may be too late. Isaiah did not say anything about a messiah. He simply stated, "It shall come to pass at the end of days." I am sure he meant for us to take action, because throughout our long and difficult history we have always taken action. Besides, I believe the messiah is inside all of us. We can do a very simple thing. We can build a house, perhaps on the campus of the Hebrew University on Mount Scopus in Jerusalem, the city of peace, and call it the House of Spiritual Reconciliation, where scholars of all religions, including the Eastern religions, will come together and discuss ways for all religions to coexist peacefully. Surely, all the monotheistic religions will feel at home in Jerusalem, where Isaiah prophesied, where Jesus sat down with his disciples, and where Muhammad went up to heaven.

I hope I live to see that day.

THE ENDURING LEGACY OF THE HEBREW PROPHETS

The Hebrew prophets are revered by all the monotheistic religions and are respected by all people of goodwill. As I've noted, the vision of the prophet Isaiah proclaiming world peace at the end of time is engraved on the wall of the United Nations building in New York. To me as a Jew, the prophets are my teachers and my source of faith. But they also belong to the world. They were the first who spoke of a God who is not tribal or territorial, but rather the one and only God of the universe and of all living beings. Their teachings enabled a small, ancient people who should have long ago disappeared from the stage of history to survive and prosper despite centuries of persecution and dislocation. Whenever an evil is punished, the prophets' words ring true, and whenever an act of kindness is performed, it echoes their words. Whether we realize it or not, we are compelled to live by their words and by their precepts. To do otherwise is to let evil triumph.

Their words resonate in the teachings of all the great teachers of humanity. We have briefly discussed in this book some of those who tried to replace their teachings with new ideas, a new social gospel, but have failed. The Hebrew prophets remain the touchstone for what is good and right. Those who try to consign them to the dustbin of history are not able to replace their message with something better. Those who have incorporated their teachings into their own belief system have endured. When the prophets spoke of justice, they were uncompromising. We all know how difficult it is to practice justice. So did they, but they refused to compromise. They also knew the healing power of love, and they knew the destructive power of hatred. They were not afraid to speak truth to power, and they knew that the king was no better than the commoner. They knew that the strong had to help the weak, or else all would suffer.

Above all else, they knew that the world is not a free-for-all. There is a law in the universe, and there is a judge. There is an eye that sees and an ear that hears. They knew that man is here for a purpose. Man is not an accident of nature. And man is not mere flesh and blood. "Not by might nor by power but by My spirit," says the prophet Zechariah. The empires of the world will rise and fall, but the word of God endures forever. In other words, they knew the secret of eternity, and they bequeathed it to their people and to the rest of the world.

POSTSCRIPT

Our search for the meaning of prophecy, which began in biblical times and ends in the early years of the twenty-first century, has ended for me. Some readers may still be searching. But I have found my answer. It is all of us. Not Superman, not some revered personality, but "all flesh." We have seen it over and over again, and we will keep seeing it in the years ahead. The traditional Jewish affirmation is "I believe in perfect faith in the coming of the messiah." Such belief transcends human understanding, and I prefer to leave it for each of us to consider. I do believe, however, that the spirit of prophecy is shared by all people, and that despite all the man-made disasters of the past and the present, the good in the human heart is stronger than evil. The prophets' dream of a world at peace is not wishful thinking. It is doable, and it can only be accomplished by the will of people everywhere.

We have now reached a stage in the development of the human race where barriers are falling down everywhere. There is a process of globalization going on around the world that is irreversible. There are still some totalitarian regimes left on this planet, but their days are numbered. It is no longer possible to keep entire societies in the dark as to what is going on in the rest of the world. The digital age has reached the most remote corners of the earth, from the Amazon to the heart of Africa, and from Mongolia to the smallest islands in the Pacific. Even where literacy is lagging behind, everyone can listen to transmitted messages and see visual images that make the world transparent. The millennium may not be around the corner, but the dawn has begun, and the first rays of light can be seen. The prophets spoke of the day of Adonai. It is not a day in the ordinary sense of twenty-four hours. It is an age, or an era, and it has begun.

I am not a prophet or the son of a prophet. But it is quite possible that nature is giving us warning signals. We live on a small fragile planet. We are experiencing unprecedented population growth, and we have become globally interdependent for our well-being and even for our survival. There are still those in the world who think that some supernatural force will come to their rescue or will make them victorious over all of their perceived enemies. Such believers live in a fantasy world, and some of them have access to weapons of mass destruction. Most of the world today knows, to paraphrase the famous saying of Benjamin Franklin dating back to the American Revolution, that either we all hang together or assuredly we shall hang separately.

There is much more to be gained from respecting each other's rights and beliefs than from engaging in triumphalism. The prophets knew that when man begins to think of himself as all-powerful, he starts to court disaster. When man begins to think of himself as superior to others, he forgets that there is a higher authority in the world that negates such presumption. Now is as good a time as ever to revisit the words of the biblical prophets, which are reflected in all the major religious philosophies of the world. All of them have aspired to the same goal: "But to do justice, and love mercy, / And walk humbly. . . ." (Mic. 6:8).

I finished writing the first draft of this book on March 20, 2011, in Fort Lauderdale, Florida. My wife and I went out for a light supper. As we drove south on A1A along the ocean, the car ahead of us had a bumper sticker that said COEXIST. It consisted of the symbols of the three major monotheistic religions, as well as other symbols of world faiths and of peace and equality. I took it as a sign. There, in one word, on the back of that car, the essence of the prophetic message was defined.

REFERENCES

Ahad Ha'am. *Selected Essays*. Philadelphia: Jewish Publication Society, 1912.
Ames, Van Meter. *Zen and American Thought*. Whitefish, MT: Kessinger, 2006.
Baeck, Leo. *This People Israel*. Philadelphia: Jewish Publication Society, 1964.
Bahallah. *The Hidden Words*. Wilmette, IL: Baha'i Publishing, 2002.
Becker, Elizabeth. *When the War Was Over: Cambodia and the Khmer Rouge Revolution*. New York: PublicAffairs, 1998.
Benedict XVI (pope). *Jesus of Nazareth*. San Francisco: Ignatius Press, 2008.
Bodin, Jean. *Colloquium of the Seven Secrets of the Sublime*. University Park: Pennsylvania State University Press, 2008.
———. *On Sovereignty*. Cambridge: University of Cambridge Press, 1992.
Buber, Martin. *I and Thou*. New York: Scribner, 2000.
———. *Prophetic Faith*. New York: Collier Books, 1985.
———. *Two Types of Faith*. Syracuse, NY: Syracuse University Press, 2003.
Dawidowicz, Lucy. *The War against the Jews, 1933–1945*. Boston: Bantam, 1986.
Dostoevsky, Fyodor. *The Brothers Karamazov*. New York: Farrar, Straus, & Giroux, 2002.
Edwards, Paul. *The Encyclopedia of Philosophy*. New York: MacMillan, 1967.
Fromm, Erich. *Escape from Freedom*. New Haven, CT: Yale University Press, 1959.
———. *Psychoanalysis and Religion*. New York: Holt, 1994.
Gandhi, Mahatma. *Gandhi, An Autobiography: The Story of My Experiments with Truth*. Seattle, WA: Creativespace, 2011.
Halevi, Judah. *The Kuzari*. New York: Schocken, 1987.
Hawking, Stephen. *The Grand Design*. New York: Bantam, 2010.
Herzl, Theodor. *Der Judenstaadt* [The Jewish State]. Lawrence, KS: Digireads.com, 2011.
Heschel, Abraham Joshua. *The Prophets*. New York: Harper, 2001.
Heywood, Denise. *Cambodian Dance: Celebration of the Gods*. London: River Books Press, 2009.
Hitler, Adolf. *Mein Kampf*. Boston: Houghton Mifflin, 1998.
Jones, Ken. *The New Social Face of Buddhism*. Somerville, MA: Wisdom Publications, 2003.
Kaufmann, Yehezkel. *The Religion of Israel*. Chicago: University of Chicago Press, 1960.
Kierkegaard, Soren, *The Essential Kierkegaard*. Princeton, NJ: Princeton University Press, 2000.
King, Martin Luther Jr. *The Papers of Martin Luther King, Jr*. Berkeley: University of California Press, 1997.
Koestler, Arthur. *Darkness at Noon*. New York: Scribner, 2006.
Lee, Anthony A. *The Baha'i Faith in Africa*. Leiden: Brill, 2011.

Lemaire, Andre. *The Birth of Monotheism*. Washington, DC: Biblical Archaeology Society, 2007.

Lo, Ping-cheung. "Confucian Ethic of Death with Dignity." *Annual of the Society of Christian Ethics* 19 (1999): 313–33.

Locke, John. *Political Writings*. Indianapolis, IN: Hackett, 2003.

Luther, Martin. *The Jews and Their Lies*. Reedy, WV: Liberty Bell Publications, 2004.

Maimonides, Moses. *The Guide for the Perplexed*. Chicago: University of Chicago Press, 1974.

Marx, Karl. *Das Kapital*. Bel Air, CA: Synergy International, 2007.

Merton, Thomas. *The Seven Storey Mountain*. Boston: Mariner Books, 1999.

Montesquieu, Charles. *The Spirit of the Laws*. Cambridge: University of Cambridge Press, 1989.

Nietzsche, Friedrich, *Ecce Homo*. New York: Oxford University Press, 2007.

———. *Thus Spoke Zarathustra*. New York: Penguin, 1961.

Patton, Alan. *Cry, the Beloved Country*. New York: Scribner, 2003.

Rand, Ayn. *Atlas Shrugged*. New York: Plume, 1994.

———. *The Fountainhead*. New York: Plume, 1999.

———. *The Virtue of Selfishness*. New York: Signet, 1964.

Schreiber, Mordecai. *Light to the Nations: World Peace from Biblical Promise to Human Action*. Rockville, MD: Schreiber Publishing, 2005.

———. *The Man Who Knew God: Decoding Jeremiah*. Lanham, MD: Lexington Books, 2010.

Shirer, William L. *The Rise and Fall of the Third Reich*. New York: Simon & Schuster, 2011.

Silver, Abba Hillel. *A History of Messianic Speculation in Israel*. Boston: Beacon Press, 1927.

Tillich, Paul. Lecture 31: The Reformation, Luther and Catholicism. www.religion-online.org/showchapter.asp?title=2310&C=2336.

Toynbee, Arnold. *A Study of History*. New York: Oxford University Press, 1987.

Tutu, Desmond. *No Future without Forgiveness*. Colorado Springs, CO: Image, 2000.

Vile, John R. *The Constitutional Convention of 1787*. Santa Barbara, CA: ABC-CLIO, 2005.

Watts, Alan W. *The Way of Zen*. New York: Vintage, 1999.

INDEX

ABOUT THE AUTHOR

Mordecai Schreiber is author of over fifty books on linguistic and Judaic topics and two novels. He is an ordained rabbi and the founder of two companies, Schreiber Translations, and Schreiber Publishing. His books on biblical topics include *Ask the Bible* and *The Man Who Knew God: Decoding Jeremiah*. He is editor of the *Shengold Jewish Encyclopedia*, now in its eighteenth edition, and of *The Global Translator's Handbook*, now in its eighth edition. He is a native of Israel and the author of a memoir about his Israeli childhood, *Land of Dreams*, depicting the birth of the State of Israel.